The Grand Experiment

Mrs. Thatcher's Economy and How It Spread

Christopher Johnson

LONDON AND NEW YORK

First published 1991 by Westview Press

Published 2019 by Routledge
52 Vanderbilt Avenue, New York, NY 10017
2 Park Square, Milton Park, Abingdon, Oxon OX14 4RN

Routledge is an imprint of the Taylor & Francis Group, an informa business

Copyright © 1991 by Christopher Johnson

All rights reserved. No part of this book may be reprinted or reproduced or utilised in any form or by any electronic, mechanical, or other means, now known or hereafter invented, including photocopying and recording, or in any information storage or retrieval system, without permission in writing from the publishers.

Notice:
Product or corporate names may be trademarks or registered trademarks, and are used only for identification and explanation without intent to infringe

Library of Congress Cataloging-in-Publication Data
The grand experiment: Mrs. Thatcher's economy and how
  it spread / by Christopher Johnson
    p. cm.
  Originally published: London, England ; New York :
  Penguin Books, 1991.
  Includes bibliographical references and index.
  1. Great Britain—Economic Policy—1945–   I. Title.
HC256.6.J63   1993
338.941'009'048—dc20   93-9937
                                                              CIP

ISBN 13: 978-0-367-29263-8 (hbk)
ISBN 13: 978-0-367-30809-4 (pbk)

Contents

List of figures		vii
List of Tables		ix
Preface		1

1 *Economic growth: can one succeed without really trying?*   5
Oliver Twist asks for more · The decline arrested – for how long? · Services output outstrips manufacturing · The fall and rise of the profit share · Private-sector demand outruns supply · A failure of demand management

2 *Inflation: the monetarist experiment that was never tried*   27
New cures for inflation · The Howe Chancellorship – the sheep that roared · The Lawson Chancellorship – the 'teenage scribbler' comes of age · Flying blind into the storm · Fiscal success, monetary failure

3 *Public expenditure: the enemy country*   76
Pick it up, put it down and shake it all around · Real terms and what was really spent · How expenditure was controlled · The choice of priorities and objectives

4 *Taxation: piecemeal reform of the system*   107
A tax-cutting manifesto · Income tax comes down · Keeping up with the NICs · Tax allowances – his and

hers · Tinkering with tax on savings · Incentives a shaky foundation for tax cuts · The corporation tax that wished inflation away · Poll tax – the peasants' revolt · The changing structure of taxes

5 *Privatization: progress on some fronts*   144
Origins of a novel policy · Own sweet home · Mortgaging the future · Shrinkage of the rented sector · Moving on from the nationalized-industry battleground · How the monopolies were taken private · Private does not make perfect · Popular, but was it capitalism? · Selling the family silver

6 *Industrial performance: miracle or mirage?*   177
'General post' at the DTI · Subsidies – the sun also rises · Takeovers – dangers of the middle way · Price competition – the paper tiger · Deregulation – the U-turn · Company statistics over-extended · Miss Rosy Scenario brings financial headaches · The balancing act collapses

7 *Labour: the market that didn't work*   217
Conservatives divided on policy · Trade-union legislation – salami tactics · Fewer strikes but little effect on pay rises · Unemployment – first the solution, then the problem · Special job-creation measures · Working on the statistics

8 *Conclusions: the curate's egg*   250
Defects and qualities of Mrs Thatcher's style · Successes and failures

Appendix: Tables	265
References	319
Further reading	329
Index	331

Figures

1	GDP growth, 1970–89	12
2	Mortgage rates and bank base rates, 1979–90	71
3	RPI inflation, 1969–89	72
4	Planning totals, cash and real, 1974–88	90
5	General government expenditure and GDP, 1970–88	92
6	General government expenditure: transfers, and goods and services, 1970–88	97
7	Taxation changes, 1979–90	111
8	Main tax rates, 1978–90	112
9	Share ownership, 1988	170
10	Ministerial changes at economic departments, 1979–90	179
11	Rates of return: industrial and commercial companies, 1960–89	200
12	Current external balances as percentage of GDP, 1979–89	209
13	Non-oil trade volumes, percentage changes, 1980–89	210
14	Trade balances as percentage of GDP, 1979–89	211
15	Department of Employment activities, 1980–90	223

Tables

1	Economic growth trends, 1950–89	265
2	The UK and the Big Five: growth comparisons in the 1980s	266
3	Labour and capital contributions to economic growth	267
4	GDP growth by industry	268
5	GDP by type of income	269
6	GDP growth by type of expenditure	270
7	Money GDP, output and prices	272
8	Fiscal and monetary stance of budgets	273
9	The results of monetary targetry	274
10	The public-sector borrowing requirement, forecasts and outcomes	276
11	Money GDP: the split between prices and output	277
12	Taxation, public expenditure and borrowing	278
13	Monetary indicators	279
14	Inflation indicators	280
15	The UK and the Big Five: inflation comparisons	281
16	Public expenditure, 1970–89	282
17	Public expenditure, cash plans and outcomes	284
18	Public expenditure, 'real-terms' plans and outcomes	285
19	General government expenditure as percentage of GDP, plans and outcomes	286
20	Changing priorities in public expenditure	287
21	Social security expenditure by groups of beneficiaries	288
22	The volume of general government expenditure	289
23	Public-sector job cuts	290
24	Public-sector capital expenditure, 1989–90	291
25	Tax revenue as percentage of GDP: international comparisons, 1970–89	292
26	Tax allowance systems and costs	293
27	Gains from income-tax and NIC changes, 1978–79 to 1990–91	294
28	Tax burden by income range, 1987	295
29	UK taxes as percentage of total taxation	296
30	Public-sector housing sales to owner-occupiers	297

Tables

31	Changes in housing tenure	298
32	Privatization and the public finances	299
33	Main corporations privatized	300
34	Performance of public corporations	301
35	Personal-sector wealth	301
36	The public sector in the economy	302
37	Government expenditure on trade and industry	302
38	Takeovers and mergers, overseas investment and capital spending	303
39	UK acquisitions for over £500 million, 1985–90	304
40	Gross trading profits and other business income by sector	305
41	Contributions to increase in business income	306
42	Gross domestic fixed-capital formation by sector	307
43	Industrial and commercial companies 1989 account	308
44	Industrial and commercial companies: changes in assets, liabilities and ratios	309
45	The rise in the external deficit, 1984–89: forecast and actual	310
46	Export and import trends, 1980–89	311
47	Trade-union membership and stoppages	312
48	The rise in income inequality	313
49	International competitiveness comparisons	314
50	International unemployment comparisons	315
51	Employment creation	316
52	Changing employment patterns	318

Preface

This is not an economic history or an economic analysis, although it draws upon both disciplines. It is an attempt at political economy. It surveys the economic policies of the Thatcher Conservatives, from their intellectual origins in Opposition to their formulation in government papers and their implementation through three terms of office. It seeks to judge the appropriateness of the policies, the competence of their execution and the degree of their success in achieving the desired effects. Possible alternative policies are not discussed in detail, and we can now never know how they would have turned out. Appraisal of the Thatcher Government's policies, however, inevitably implies something about what the alternatives might have been, particularly those alternatives that members of the Government themselves seriously contemplated.

Although Mrs Thatcher herself was at all times the dominant figure in formulating and carrying out her Government's policies, she was the leader of a team with similar ideas, whose members held key posts. It is the actions and words of departmental ministers acting in her name, as much as her own words and actions, that therefore form the subject-matter of the book. Indeed, the source material for what the Prime Minister and her policy unit and key advisers were saying and thinking is scanty compared with the official papers and speeches of the main departments and their ministers. Some of Mrs Thatcher's remarks were in any case more by way of personal opposition to the line that she had resigned herself to allowing her Government to take.

It has not been possible to discuss the blow-by-blow details of policy implementation with the main participants, but some have already published valuable memoirs. A political history of this kind would have required a whole book to do justice to each chapter.

Rather than trying to cover the entire range of economic policies year by year, I have found it more illuminating to separate each main policy area and survey it over the decade, interrelating them by means of cross-references and in the conclusion. Inevitably, over half the book is devoted to policies for which the Treasury was responsible. Chapter 1 is about economic growth, for which no one in particular and everyone in general was responsible. Chapter 2 deals with the use of monetary and fiscal policy to control inflation. Chapters 3, 4 and 5 cover public expenditure, taxation and privatization, including home ownership. Chapter 6 is about industrial performance and the balance of payments and involves the Department(s) of Trade and Industry. Chapter 7 is about the closely connected topic of the labour market and involves the Department of Employment. Chapter 8 analyses the defects and qualities of Mrs Thatcher's style of government as it affected economic policy-making. It summarizes the findings of each chapter and tries to bring them together into a coherent verdict.

I make no apologies for drawing extensively on the reports of the Treasury and Civil Service Committee of the House of Commons, whose first decade of existence coincides with Mrs Thatcher's period in government. It was fortunate for the cause of open government that Mrs Thatcher allowed the select committees to be set up at the instigation of Norman St John-Stevas (now Lord St John of Fawsley), even though she may subsequently have regretted her decision. I apologize to the Select Committees on employment and on trade and industry, whose reports I have used much less, being relatively unfamiliar with their proceedings.

Preface xi

My work as a specialist adviser to the Treasury Committee, covering every Budget and Autumn Statement since late 1983, has given me a precious insight into the policy-making process. I here acknowledge the encouragement I have had from the two chairmen of the Committee, Sir Edward Du Cann (1979–83) and Terence Higgins (1983–), and the other members. The Committee's judgements, which seek to be tripartisan as far as possible, comment like a Greek chorus on the tragicomedy of the Government's economic policies. It may be assumed that when I quote the Committee's views I am in agreement with them; it would be tedious, if not improper, for me to specify which of them were the direct result of my advice.

I began writing this book in October 1990. Mrs Thatcher's resignation the following month made it all the more appropriate to attempt a summing-up of her three administrations, even if not all the statistics for 1990 are available as the book goes to print. Previous interim reports on Mrs Thatcher have inevitably had to contend with unexpected turns for the better – or the worse – after publication. Mrs Thatcher, OM, has quickly become part of history, even if it will require the history of the 1990s to be revealed before appraisals more definitive than the present work can be made. In view of the changes in ministers, and the substance as well as the style of policy, this book should be taken as a judgement not of John Major and his Government but of the legacy that they inherit.

I wish to acknowledge the opportunity that Lloyds Bank has given me to develop my ideas about economic policy in the *Lloyds Bank Economic Bulletin,* which began life in January 1979 and has thus covered the full span of three Thatcher terms. As well as inviting me to play the game of guessing in advance the contents of each Budget – a useful exercise in Treasury mind-reading – Lloyds Bank gave free rein to my comments on government economic policy. The bank – whatever that is – does not necessarily agree with the views expressed in this book, whose publication follows hard on the heels of my retirement from the post of the bank's Chief Economic Adviser.

In particular, I thank Patrick Foley, the Deputy Chief Economic Adviser, Teresa Fletcher, the Librarian, and her staff, Marcia Howard, my secretary, and David Thornhill, the chart artist, for their help with the book. I would also like to thank my publishers at Penguin: Andrew Franklin, who brought out *Measuring the Economy* in 1988 and encouraged me to write another book, and Ravi Mirchandani, who has given a welcoming reception to the idea of *The Economy Under Mrs Thatcher 1979–1990*. My wife, Anne, has supported me wonderfully, putting up with a husband who works all day at the office and all evening and all weekend at home.

A few notes on style for the reader are needed. I have deliberately not used footnotes because they disturb the narrative. Sources are either given in the text or should be easily identifiable from the references for each chapter at the end. The references should be taken not as a full survey of the voluminous literature on each topic but as lists of those sources referred to in the text or of particular significance in my own background reading. When a pair of years is given covering changes, it must be understood that the base year is the year before the first year of the pair. Thus the growth rate for 1980–89 is measured from base year 1979 to final year 1989, and 1980 is the first of the series of years in which the growth took place. Fractions are used to denote a number to the nearest one-quarter as opposed to decimals to one place, which denote it to the nearest 0.1.

Christopher Johnson
January 1991

Author's Preface to American Edition

The original edition of this book was completed just as Mrs Thatcher was ousted from the office of Prime Minister by her own Conservative Party in November 1990. The recession caused by her application of the brakes after a period of excessive inflationary growth was also the cause of her own downfall. The Party reckoned, probably correctly, that she would have lost the 1992 general election because the recession had shattered her popularity. Her successor, John Major, scraped home with a thin majority by softening the harsh edges of Thatcherism and, above all, by simply not being Mrs Thatcher.

The verdict of the book is that the recession was the price paid for the economic stop-go indulged in by Mrs Thatcher, who, like her predecessors, played politics with the economic cycle. When I reached my conclusions, neither I nor anyone else suspected how long the recession would last, and how high the price would be. Two and a half years later, at last, the recession seems to be over. The diehards' nostalgia for the return of Mrs Thatcher's magisterial style of government is more than counter-balanced by the bitterness of those who have not forgiven her or her political heirs for leading them up the primrose path of rising indebtedness and falling house prices. The passage of time has thus confirmed the judgment of instant history pronounced over the Iron Lady's political death-bed.

Some critics of the book failed to spot one original feature; it attempted to judge Mrs Thatcher not according to the art of the possible, but according to the more difficult aims she set herself in her election mainfestos, of transforming a backward Britain by the application of free market doctrines. Her defenders claimed, with some justice, that she brought about changes in the management of British business and that there were unavoidable external constraints on policy preventing her from doing more. She claimed to be able to do better than this, and by her own high standards, and those of her followers; she failed.

Technical progress has occurred under every post-war British government, and the constraints affecting Mrs Thatcher's were no worse than at any other time. Her excessive ambition made matters worse, and amplified the business cycle unnecessarily. Americans will recognize the similarity between the Reagan and the Thatcher regimes in the boasts to have transformed the supply side of the economy by means of tax cuts and deregulation, while neglecting until too late in the day longer-term improvements in the supply of the factors of production such as require higher public expenditure, notably education, training, and industrial technology.

In accepting membership of the House of Lords, Mrs Thatcher wisely excluded herself from making the kind of comeback to power that General de Gaulle made from Colombey–les–deux–Eglises in 1958. She and her supporters have nonetheless damaged John Major's government by taking up arms against European Monetary Union and the Treaty of Maastricht. The debate rages on about whether Britain was right to join the European exchange rate mechanism (ERM) in October 1990, right to leave it in September 1992, and right to hesitate before going back into it. It is one of the main themes of this book that Mrs Thatcher should have taken Chancellor Nigel Lawson's advice to join the ERM in October 1985; he has since then revealed in his own memoirs that he thought of resigning when it was refused, as I maintain that he should have done. I still believe that it was right to join, better late than never. Britain's chances of staying in would have been improved if she had joined at a lower exchange rate, but she will be able to rectify this mistake by re-entering at a lower rate when the monetary shock of German unification has subsided.

Mrs Thatcher's critics have never failed to remind her that she signed the Single European Act in 1985, which marked just as big a surrender of national sovereignty as the Maastricht Treaty, and that one of her last acts as Prime Minister was to join the ERM. History will judge her by what she did in office, not by what she wishes—from the back benches of the House of Lords—that she had left undone.

May 1993

I Economic growth: can one succeed without really trying?

> 'There always have been economic cycles, and there always will be economic cycles.'
> Nigel Lawson, MP, Hansard, 23 October 1990

Oliver Twist asks for more

All governments want economic growth. This does not mean that they want the maximum quantity of growth in the short term at any price. The quality, the stability, the durability and the composition of growth are important subsidiary objectives. While voters are interested mainly in jobs, personal incomes and consumer spending, these are correlated with the growth of the economy as a whole. In any case forms of expenditure other than personal consumption, such as current government spending on services and capital investment in new products, also contribute to consumers' welfare to some degree.

The Conservative Government at first appeared to be the exception to the rule of 'growthmanship' because it adopted a roundabout strategy for growth in view of what it condemned as the failure of previous, more direct, approaches by its predecessors. The stability of growth was stressed in 1977 in *The Right Approach to the Economy*, which called for 'the provision of a more stable economic climate with as few sudden changes as possible'. This was understandable in the light of the change from 7.4 per cent growth in 1973 to −1.5 per cent in 1974. The 1979 manifesto, not to beat about the bush, called simply for 'an expanding economy'.

In June 1979 Sir Geoffrey Howe, the new Chancellor of the Exchequer, always a somewhat underrated practitioner of what might be called philosophical economy, sounded an agnostic note in his first Budget speech: 'There is a definite limit to our capacity, as politicians, to influence these things for the better ... The notions of demand management, expanding public spending and "fine tuning" of the economy have now been tested almost to destruction.' He set out a four-point strategy 'to check Britain's economic decline'. He clearly meant relative, not absolute, decline. The aim was to raise the UK's growth rate again at least to the international average.

1. Incentives were to be strengthened by changes in the tax system, starting with the switch from income tax to VAT in that same Budget.
2. There was to be more freedom of individual choice and a reduction of the role of the state in the economy. There was thus to be a switch from public- to private-sector growth. This was argued for on the political grounds of greater market freedom and on the economic grounds of improved efficiency. It obviously precluded the use of the public sector to prime the pump for the growth of the economy as a whole, even in the good cause of offsetting the fluctuations of the private sector.
3. The burden of public-sector finance was to be reduced 'so as to leave room for commerce and industry to prosper'. The elimination of financial 'crowding out' aimed to lower interest rates for the private sector by reducing the public sector's call on the same financial markets.
4. It was necessary 'to ensure that those who take part in collective bargaining understand the consequences of their actions'.

This amounted to a switch of emphasis from demand-side to supply-side policies. It was only about halfway through its decade in office that the Government began to add education and training to the list of supply-side policies needed to improve the growth performance of the economy.

The Government's immediate preoccupation was to reduce rising inflation rather than to revive flagging growth. Its growth forecasts were extremely gloomy. 'After the recession forecast for 1980,' said Howe in his Budget speech in that year, 'the economy will grow by an average of only 1 per cent a year up to 1983-84.' Ministers made a virtue of necessity, arguing that lower inflation, far from being inimical to higher growth, was a precondition of it. The point was spelled out in the first version of the Medium-Term Financial Strategy (MTFS) in the March 1980 *Financial Statement and Budget Report* (Red Book), for which Nigel Lawson, then Financial Secretary to the Treasury, had a particular responsibility: 'The Government's objectives for the medium term are to bring down the rate of inflation and to create conditions for a sustainable growth of output and employment.' Clearly, growth had to be a medium-term and not a short-term objective. 'The process of reducing inflation almost inevitably entails some losses of output initially, though it promises a better growth of output in the longer term.'

In his 1981 Budget speech Howe made the same point, angled towards the growth of the private sector. His aim was to 'sustain the fight against inflation, and help redress the balance of the economy in favour of business and industry. It is only by giving priority to these objectives that we can strengthen the basis for sustained economic advance.'

The change in policy towards growth was sharpened into an intriguing paradox by Lawson in his Mais Lecture in June 1984, a year after he had taken over from Howe as Chancellor.

The conventional post-war wisdom was that unemployment was a consequence of inadequate economic growth, and economic growth was to be secured by macro-economic policy – the fiscal stimulus of a large Budget deficit . . . Inflation, by contrast, was increasingly seen as a matter to be dealt with by micro-economic policy – the panoply of controls and subsidies associated with the era of incomes policy ... There is indeed a proper distinction between the objectives of macro-economic and micro-economic policy ... But the proper role of each is precisely the opposite of that assigned to it by the conventional post-war wisdom ... It is the conquest of inflation, and not the pursuit of growth and employment, which is, or should be, the objective of macro-economic policy ... And it is the creation of conditions conducive to growth and employment, and not the suppression of price rises, which is, or should be, the objective of micro-economic policy ... This fundamentally important role reversal implies a major change in the nature of the macro and the micro policies themselves ... Instead of monetary policy simply accommodating increased budget deficits ... fiscal policy has to be in harmony with declining monetary growth ... And instead of micro-economic policy consisting of increasingly numerous forms of intervention and interference with market forces, its role is now seen as removing controls and allowing markets to work better.

The Government was already departing from Nigel Lawson's role reversal of policies before he had publicly proclaimed it as Chancellor. By late 1982 inflation had fallen, and economic growth was beginning to recover. In his 1983 Budget speech, in the run-up to the general election, Howe could not resist the temptation to declare victory in a battle in which he had previously declined combat: 'Domestic demand has been growing at almost 3 per cent a year in real terms. This is a stronger growth of demand than in most other industrial countries.' Lawson continued to make similar claims during his next four years as Chancellor, which culminated in the proud boast of the 1987 general election manifesto: 'We have moved from the bottom to the top of the growth league of major European countries.' (The league did not include the more rapidly growing USA, Japan and some minor European countries.)

Although demand was back in fashion, from 1984 onwards the Government's objectives were set in terms of nominal, monetary demand, which includes both real growth and inflation, thus conveniently linking two main policy goals. The policy as stated in the March 1984 Red Book was thus consistent with that adopted at the outset of the MTFS in 1980: 'Lower cost and price inflation within a given financial framework makes room for faster growth of output and employment.' In 1985 the Government began the annual publication, in the March Red Book, of four-year projections of money Gross Domestic Product (GDP), which were to take over from targets for the growth of money itself as the main guide to policy. In the 1987 Red Book Lawson was able to put money GDP into the framework of his Mais Lecture: 'Monetary and fiscal policy are designed to reduce the growth of money GDP, so bringing down inflation. They are complemented by policies to encourage enterprise, efficiency and flexibility. These policies improve the division of money GDP growth between output growth and inflation and help the creation of jobs.'

Money GDP was to be minimized, in contrast to real GDP, which was to be maximized. It was thus a fundamentally different kind of objective, based on a controversial proposition in economics. The Government, while not necessarily seeking to increase the rate of real growth once it had recovered to a sustainable medium-term figure of $2\frac{1}{2}$–3 per cent, did not wish the deceleration of money GDP to bring about a corresponding slow-down in real GDP. The conflict had to be resolved by bringing down inflation – measured in this case by the GDP deflator – which would both arithmetically allow real growth to be higher within a given increase in money GDP and actually cause growth to rise by a benign economic mechanism.

In the 1984 Red Book it was held that a lower saving ratio by consumers, due to the reduction in the inflation rate, would stimulate growth. This was a demand-side argument in the Keynesian tradition, which was to be offset a few years later by supply-side lamentations about the lack of savings to finance investment. It was also argued more consistently that, once inflation had come down, interest rates would fall and would thus stimulate growth in the economy. Over and above this, there would be a general improvement in business and consumer confidence as a consequence of lower inflation.

The Government began by erring on the side of pessimism about economic growth. As the recovery gathered pace, the growth assumptions became more optimistic, but it was assumed that, even when the current growth rate was higher, it would fall to about 2½ per cent after a year or two, allowing for a slow decline in North Sea oil output. It was thought better to aim low and be pleasantly surprised than to aim high and be disappointed. Lawson told the Treasury Committee, when appearing before it on the occasion of the 1987 Budget: 'Assuming that we do get 2½ per cent or more in 1987 . . . then we will for the first time since the war have had six successive years of 2½ per cent or more growth each year. [Not so – see table 1.] And so, while I do not rule out the possibility of the supply side of the economy becoming more effective so that a higher rate of growth is possible, I reckon that we should not act Oliver Twist on this occasion.' However, Lawson, though not obviously suffering from undernourishment, was not satisfied with the plain gruel of moderate economic growth. Like Oliver Twist, he asked for more; after tucking into a Gargantuan repast, he left the workhouse to seek his fortune elsewhere before the disapproving matron could expel him.

While hoping that its supply-side policies would raise Britain's medium-term growth potential, the Government did not take it for granted. Ministers never faced the dilemma thus created. If the medium-term growth potential had not improved, then growth in excess of about 3 per cent should have been taken as a danger signal calling for some restriction of demand. If the medium-term growth potential had improved, then a wide range of additional measures would have been called for to improve supply, requiring public-sector legislation or expenditure in such fields as training, infrastructure, housing and competition policy. Since public expenditure as well as GDP was being projected in cash terms and not in real terms, financial planning of the kind pioneered in the MTFS replaced any attempt to plan real magnitudes, which was regarded as a return to the bad old days.

The decline arrested – for how long?

For a Government that began by abjuring a specific growth objective, the Thatcher administration went to remarkable lengths to present the statistics of its record in the most favourable light. The six years from the beginning of the recovery in 1982, 1983–8, showed a growth rate of 3.7 per cent, considerably higher than the post-war average of 2.6 per cent. However, the economy grew at 3.4 per cent for the fifteen years 1959–73, including 3.7 per cent for the first seven years of that period, 1959–65. So 1983–8 were not the best years of the post-war period but only comparable with the best. The recovery was strong partly because the recession in 1980–82 had been so deep and there was such a margin of spare capacity to take up. As the severity of the recession was the product of the stringent monetary policy designed to pave the way for growth by reducing inflation, it is wrong to exclude it as being due only to high oil prices and the previous Government's misdeeds. The new Government's radical policies to stem relative decline by means of higher growth resulted at first not just in relative but in absolute decline.

The Thatcher Government did not measure growth from peak to peak, believing that the 1980–81 trough was a once-for-all purge; the 1990–91 recession indicates that a further substantial dose was required. Sir Alan Walters tried to justify excluding the recession in his American Enterprise Institute lecture: 'Mrs Thatcher suffered from a singular handicap; she came into office in 1979 at the top of the boom. The only way to go was down. It is therefore a little bit misleading to use the boom year as the basis for the discussion of achievements (or the lack of them).' Because Governments in power can choose election dates, most elections in the UK are held in boom years. What was unusual

The Economy Under Mrs Thatcher

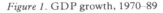

Figure 1. GDP growth, 1970–89

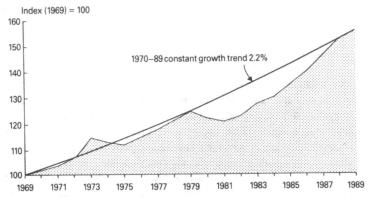

Source: Blue Book, 1990.

was the depth of the subsequent recession. We have used several different ways of measuring the Government's record, but some of them are bound to use 1979 as the base year. It is normal practice to measure economic growth from peak to peak of a cycle, and it is possible to do so for the Thatcher years, since there was clearly a peak in 1988.

As Mrs Thatcher was in power for ten years, a comparison of decades is appropriate. The growth rate in 1980–89 was 2.2 per cent (see table 1). This was exactly the same as the 2.2 per cent achieved in 1970–79, a fair comparison, since Mrs Thatcher dismissed both the Labour and the Conservative Governments that preceded hers with equal disdain (see figure 1, showing a loss of actual below potential output equal to nearly six months' GDP). Each decade also included a major oil price shock, followed by a subsequent fall in the price of oil. The 1980s were almost as good as the 1950s, which had a 2.5 per cent growth rate, but not as good as the 1960s, which had a 3.3 per cent growth rate.

If the cycle that began with the 1979 peak ended with the 1988 peak, then the 1980–88 growth rate was 2.3 per cent, almost the same as the figure covering the decade to 1989.

Economic Growth

However, there were two distinct cycles within the period, the first peaking in 1983. (Even without the depressing effect of the coal strike on GDP, growth would have been lower in 1984 than in 1983.) The 1980–83 cycle was the worst in the post-war period, with a growth rate of 0.6 per cent, but 1984–8 equalled the best, with 3.7 per cent. Comparisons are often made with the relatively low 1.4 per cent growth rate of the 1974–9 cycle. The Thatcher Government presided over one even worse cycle and one much better.

Economic growth can also be measured by the continuous tenure of office of political parties. Mrs Thatcher's 2.2 per cent average came between the 2.0 per cent of the five Wilson–Callaghan years and the 2.6 per cent of the four Heath years. The six Wilson years were only marginally better than the Heath years, with 2.7 per cent growth, but the thirteen Conservative years 1952–64 achieved a continuous growth rate of 3.0 per cent.

The stabilization of growth is an important subsidiary objective for any government. It keeps the economy close to the growth of productive potential, without alternating phases of unemployment and inflation, although business cycles can never be entirely eliminated. By this standard both the 1970s and the 1980s had unstable growth. The standard deviation of the growth rate was as high as the mean; in other words, the coefficient of variation has been close to one. In the two previous decades it averaged about a half. This was partly due to the two oil shocks of 1973 and 1979, which were followed by negative growth of the kind that had hardly occurred in the UK since the war. In the UK, because Governments can choose when to seek re-election, there is a clear political cycle of economic growth. Even the Thatcher Government managed demand to secure a growth peak sufficient to ensure its re-election in 1983 and in 1987. Its fundamental error was to mistake the short-term 1987 peak for a new high plateau of rapid growth.

The UK rate of growth in the 1980s was the same as the EC average. It was 0.2 per cent higher than Germany's, 0.1 per cent higher than France's and 0.3 per cent lower than

Italy's. However, it was 0.6 per cent lower than the Organization for Economic Co-operation and Development (OECD) average, which included the USA's 2.6 per cent and Japan's 4.2 per cent. Among major countries only the USA was similar to Britain in having two years of negative growth, and Germany had one such year. The convergence of growth rates with those of the EC was also due to the maintenance of successful anti-inflation policies in the exchange-rate-mechanism (ERM) countries, which slowed their growth rate down, and to their abandonment in the UK, which temporarily boosted its growth rate. The high variability of growth in the 1980s and the four-year political cycle were common to the UK and the USA, with a 0.9 coefficient of variation (see table 2). The average for EC or industrial countries was a half, the figure for France and Italy. It was three-quarters for Germany, but only a quarter for Japan.

In 1989 both GDP and GDP per head were remarkably close to each other in purchasing-power terms in the UK, France and Italy, which all had similar population sizes. GDP per head was 2 per cent higher in France than in the UK and 3 per cent lower in Italy. In Germany GDP per head was about 6 per cent higher.

Services output outstrips manufacturing

Economic growth is measured in three ways: output, income and expenditure. (The problem of reconciling the three has in recent years bedevilled UK statistics, but that is another story.) The UK record can be examined in terms of each of the three measures of GDP. In view of the Government's supply-side orientation, we begin with output, in the sense of output net of inputs, or value added. This can be analysed on the basis of a simplified production function, in which output is explained by two main factors of production, labour and capital. The contribution of each can be broken down into changes in the amounts of the factor used and changes in its productivity. These are then combined by means of averages weighted according to the income share

Economic Growth

of the two factors into total changes in the use of both factors and total factor productivity (TFP) (see table 3).

The use of employed labour fell sharply by 2 million or 9 per cent over the four years to 1983, then rose gradually by 1.7 million or 8 per cent over the following six years, giving an average annual fall of 0.2 per cent. Labour productivity rose most rapidly in 1981-3, when employment was still falling but output had started to recover. Its rise averaged 2.5 per cent for the whole economy in the 1980s, with a peak of 5.5 per cent in 1983, falling to -0.1 per cent in 1989 (due to a sharp fall in North Sea oil output). The position is considerably changed if we include the self-employed, who rose from 1.9 million to 3.4 million during the decade (see table 51). The 'workforce in employment', including them, rose by 0.8 per cent a year but its productivity by only 1.7 per cent a year.

The stock of capital rose by 2.2 per cent a year, moving up from 2 to 3 per cent during the period as companies reacted to accelerating output growth by investing more. There was virtually no change in the productivity of capital on average, but it fell sharply in the 1980-81 recession and rose later as the capacity utilization ratio increased. This was an improvement on earlier periods, when capital productivity had declined. About one-third of the UK's 2.2 per cent growth rate in the 1980s was due to greater use of factors, notably capital, and two-thirds to an annual increase of 1.6 per cent in TFP, accounted for entirely by rising labour productivity.

According to OECD's estimate, the increase in the capital stock may be lower than that shown by the official UK figures because the rate of scrapping old equipment could be higher than that which they assume. This would raise capital productivity, although at the cost of discarding equipment whose useful life might in other circumstances have been extended.

What was true of the whole economy was true of manufacturing in a more extreme form. Manufacturing employment fell by 29 per cent, or over 2 million, during the eight years to 1987 and rose only during the cyclical peak after that. Manufacturing output also fell by 14 per cent in the recession years 1980–81 but then recovered to peak at a rise of over 7 per cent in 1988. The rise in output averaged only 1.2 per cent over the decade, less than half the increase in GDP. There was still an impressive increase of 4.5 per cent a year in manufacturing labour productivity, due more to cutbacks in employment than to the recovery of output at a later stage, with peaks of 9.1 per cent in 1983 and 6.8 per cent in 1987 (see also table 49).

The capital stock in manufacturing rose quite steadily at 0.8 per cent a year, less than in the rest of the economy. Capital productivity, after a 16 per cent fall in the recession, rose quite rapidly in the recovery, going up by 11 per cent in the boom years 1987–8 taken together, but its average increase was only 0.4 per cent over the decade. TFP rose by 3.2 per cent a year, but combined-factor use fell by 1.8 per cent a year because the productivity of labour increased as its use was reduced in favour of more intensive employment of capital.

There was a more balanced development in the three-quarters of the economy in non-manufacturing, mainly private-sector, services. Employees increased by 1.0 per cent a year, or 1.6 million, and their productivity by 1.6 per cent. The capital stock rose by 2.6 per cent a year, but its productivity was static. The use of factors rose by 1.6 per cent a year, mainly due to capital, and TFP rose by 1 per cent a year, entirely because of labour productivity. Output rose by 2.6 per cent a year, faster than that of the whole economy, which was dragged back by the slow growth of manufacturing, especially in the early 1980s.

The productivity record of the 1980s was better than that of the 1970s, when the same economic growth rate was achieved but with higher increases in factor inputs. Labour use rose, instead of falling, by 0.2 per cent a year, so its productivity went up by 2 rather than 2.5 per cent a year. The capital stock grew by 3.3 per cent a year, so its productivity fell by 1.1 per cent a year instead of remaining static.

TFP thus rose by 0.9 per cent rather than 1.6 per cent a year. The contrast was even greater in manufacturing, where TFP went up by only 0.6 per cent a year and not 3.2 per cent; labour was reduced less rapidly, capital was increased faster, but output rose even more slowly than in the 1980s, at only 0.5 per cent.

The OECD has testified to the productivity improvement in the UK. In its 1987/88 *Economic Survey* of the UK, it wrote:

In Britain the fall in capital productivity decelerated sharply in the 1980s compared to the 1973–79 period. In fact, the relative improvement in capital productivity developments matched those of labour, so that recent efficiency gains are even more impressive when measured by TFP than by labour productivity alone. Apart from Britain, only Japan managed to reduce the trend decline in capital productivity in the 1980s ... In the other countries, overall efficiency either remained stable or declined.

There have been big differences in the rates of growth of the various sectors of the economy, and thus in their shares of total output (see table 4). In the first half of the 1980s the most rapidly growing sectors were North Sea oil and gas, and agriculture. The North Sea doubled its share of current-price GDP to 7 per cent, thanks to rising oil prices, while agriculture maintained its share at 2 per cent, reacting to falling prices, with production also rising at 7 per cent a year. Both primary sectors suffered falls in output and in prices in the second half of the 1980s, and each accounted for only 1.5–1.7 per cent of GDP by 1989. The stagnation of the 'other energy' sector was due to coal, where the 1984 strike depressed output and distorted the pattern of GDP as a whole, taking 1 per cent off its increase in 1984 and adding most of it back in later years. North Sea oil added about $\frac{1}{2}$ per cent a year to GDP growth in 1980–84. After 1985 it had a slight negative effect, apart from the interruptions to production in 1989, which took about 1 per cent off the rate of GDP growth.

The share of manufacturing in the economy fell from 28.4

per cent in 1979 to 22.2 per cent in 1989 in current-price terms but only from 27.1 per cent to 24.4 per cent in 1985 constant prices. The difference is due to the normal secular fall in the relative price of manufactured goods. The main fall in the share of manufactures was in the early 1980s. Much of it was matched statistically by the corresponding rise in the share of North Sea oil. There was also a causal link, in that the high exchange rate, due in part to oil, made manufactures less competitive. The position was reversed after the oil price fell in 1985, since the exchange rate then fell and manufacturing became more competitive for a time. However, the volume of manufacturing output passed its 1978–9 peak, and its higher 1974 peak, only in 1988. As Peter Jenkins put it: 'The first two years of [Mrs Thatcher's] first administration can be seen as a salutary short, sharp shock to a nation on the slide, or as the dogmatic vandalization of the manufacturing base.'

The construction industry did badly in the recession, only to become the fastest-growing industrial sector in the second half of the decade, with output rising at 4.8 per cent a year to reach 7 per cent of GDP in 1989. Much the fastest growth of the 1980s was in financial and business services, which had an average real growth of nearly 6 per cent in the first half of the 1980s and 9 per cent in the second half. Their more rapid rate of growth added $\frac{1}{2}$ per cent to the rate of growth of the whole economy, increasing it from $1\frac{3}{4}$ to $2\frac{1}{4}$ per cent. They accounted for over one-fifth of the whole economy in 1989, or one-seventh after adjusting for the fact that net interest is not counted as value added in UK statistics. Other private services, such as distribution, transport and telecommunications, expanded only slightly faster than the whole economy and saw little increase in their one-third share in GDP.

The public sector's growth was held back, as the Government intended. Health and education increased their output, measured mainly by staff numbers, by only 1.4 per cent a year, but their share of the economy rose to nearly 10 per cent. This was due to the relative price effect, consisting mainly of an increase in public-sector pay 1½ per cent a year higher than the rate of inflation (see table 22). The growth of administration and defence was virtually zero in view of the 20 per cent cut in Civil Service numbers.

The fall and rise of the profit share

The Government's aim of giving priority to profits can be judged by the changes in the shares of the factors of production in total domestic income (see table 5). It is necessary to put the energy sector – mainly North Sea oil and gas, and coal – into a separate category, since its up-and-down performance distorts the figures. The first result of the new Government's policies was to cut the national income share of non-energy gross trading profits from 14.1 per cent in 1979 to 8.4 per cent in 1981, from which they rose gradually to surpass their 1979 share only in the boom year 1988, then started falling again. The share of non-energy employment income has fluctuated less and has not been cut significantly. It has averaged 61.9 per cent, beginning and ending the decade very close to this figure. It actually rose to 63.6 per cent in the recession as that of profits fell, returning to a more normal level of 61.2 per cent in 1983.

Gross trading profits in the energy sector rose from 5.4 per cent of national income in 1979 to 8.5 per cent in 1983 and 1984, when they were 45 per cent of all gross trading profits. They then fell to only 3.2 per cent in 1989. The sector's employment income averaged 3 per cent in the first four years of the decade, then fell to 2 per cent as mining labour was reduced after the 1984 coal strike. The share of rent did not vary much from its average of 8 per cent, while that of self-employment income rose three percentage points to 11.9 per cent, in line with the increase in the number of self-employed.

There has been a rise in the non-energy profit share but only from the nadir due to the recession back to its 1979 level. This has been at the expense not of non-energy employment income but of the energy sector as a whole, both its profits and its employment incomes. In other words, from 1985 onwards the recovery of corporate profits was due to the fall in oil prices more than to any slow-down in the growth of labour costs. The oil price fall went into higher profit margins rather than lower prices (see page 192). There was also a marked rise in self-employment income, with an important shift in the structure of business from large manufacturing companies to smaller firms in the services sector. (If stock appreciation is deducted, the share of non-energy profits rose by 2.7 rather than 0.5 per cent over the decade, but this is a less relevant measure than that given here.)

Private-sector demand outruns supply

The Government's micro-economic policy for growth was directed towards the supply side and professed to be indifferent to the management of demand. While supply in the form of GDP eventually increased at a satisfactory rate after the recession, demand, both domestic and external, rose faster (see table 6). Private consumer demand, about three-fifths of domestic demand, was rising by 3.3 per cent, one percentage point faster than GDP, and averaged a peak real increase of 6.3 per cent in each of the three years straddling the 1987 election. This was due to the continuing rise in real earnings, combined with a fall in the personal-saving ratio from 11.9 per cent in 1979 to 6.7 per cent in 1989. In other words, personal borrowing rose faster than personal financial investment.

Fixed investment, mainly by the private sector, rose even faster, averaging 3.7 per cent a year. Being naturally cyclical, it changed by a multiple of total demand, according to the 'accelerator' effect. It fell 15 per cent in 1980–81 taken together, then gathered momentum to rise at a peak rate of 15 per cent in 1988, nearly twice the increase in domestic demand in the same year (see table 42 for details by sector). General government final consumption, current spending by central government and local authorities, rose by only 1.0 per cent a year owing to public expenditure restraints.

Stockbuilding changes, which accounted for the whole of the recession in 1980, were modest after that and made a nil contribution to demand over the whole period.

The Government's policy of restraining public-sector demand had still allowed private-sector demand to rise faster than the economy's capacity to supply it. Domestic demand rose by 2.9 per cent a year in real terms in 1980–89, peaking at 7.9 per cent in 1988. With GDP rising at 2.3 per cent, the average supply gap was 0.6 per cent of GDP, equal by definition to an adverse change in the balance of payments for goods and services. It was reversed only in the two recession years, then suddenly peaked at 3 per cent in 1988. Export demand rose in line with domestic demand, at a real annual rate of 2.9 per cent; this meant that total final expenditure, the aggregate of domestic demand and exports, also rose at the same rate. Imports had to rise at an average 5.1 per cent to fill the gap. They rose by a peak percentage of 12.8 in 1988, when exports were static in volume.

Excess demand thus totalled 6 per cent of GDP over the decade. Fortunately, the real national disposable income (RNDI), a version of GDP that allows for investment income from abroad and changes in the terms of trade, was rising by 2.5 per cent a year, 0.2 per cent more than GDP, so the gap in current-price terms was reduced by 0.2 per cent a year, or 2 per cent over the period. The remaining gap of 4 per cent of GDP was roughly equal to the swing into deficit of the balance of payments by 1988 from the equilibrium position of 1979. In cumulative terms, domestic demand rose by a third in real terms, and GDP only by quarter, in the 1980s. So, although exports also rose by a third, imports had to rise by two-thirds to close the supply gap.

The differential rates of change of the components of demand resulted in large shifts in its composition during the 1980s. The share of private consumption rose by three and a half percentage points, from $60\frac{1}{2}$ to 64 per cent, while that of public consumption by government was held at $19\frac{1}{2}$ per cent. The share of fixed investment rose by one point to $19\frac{1}{2}$

per cent. Unfortunately, this meant that domestic claims on resources rose by four points, from ½ per cent less than GDP in 1979 to 3½ per cent more in 1989. This gap, representing a shift from small surplus to massive deficit in the balance of payments, was mirrored by the fall of exports by three and a half points to 24 per cent of GDP, while imports remained at about 27½ per cent of GDP. (See page 206 for a further analysis of the balance-of-payments deficit.)

The opening of the gap between supply and demand can also be seen as an increasing divergence between domestic saving and domestic investment, which is equal by accounting definition to the difference between exports and imports of goods and services (see table 6). While investment in fixed capital and stocks rose slightly, from 19.7 to 20.2 per cent of GDP, saving fell from 20.0 per cent to 16.5 per cent. The positive gap of 0.3 per cent thus became a negative gap of 3.7 per cent, corresponding to the movement in the balance of payments.

The savings share in GDP of both the personal and the industrial and commercial company sector fell by nearly half; that of the financial companies and institutions and the public sector rose but not by enough to offset the fall in the two main sources of savings, whose share in the total fell from over 80 to 55 per cent. It is thus true only to a limited extent that, as the Government claimed, the balance-of-payments deficit was due to a healthy rise in investment. It was due rather to a deficiency in private-sector savings. The Government's deregulation of the financial services sector gave more incentives for borrowing than saving.

The Government underestimated the growth of real demand in 1987 and 1988 and even the rather lower growth of real GDP. This was due partly to deficiencies in the official statistical system and partly to a deterioration in the Treasury's previously impressive forecasting record. The statistics, which gave the latest present position used as a basis for the forecasts, were themselves in some measure to blame for the forecasts. The four-year projections for money GDP, the GDP deflator and real GDP are set out in table

7. In most Red Book projections the rise in money GDP was set to fall to 5½ per cent in the fourth year and the inflation rate, as measured by the GDP deflator, to 3 per cent. The increase in GDP, usually 3 per cent in the first year, was projected to fall to 2½ per cent the following year and to remain there. The objective of reducing money GDP growth was to cut inflation while leaving the growth rate virtually unchanged and giving it a higher proportion of the money GDP increase.

In almost every case the outcomes were higher than the projections, even those made at the beginning of the financial year projected. They were seriously higher only in the two crucial boom years of 1987–8 and 1988–9. In the five years 1985–9 the Government underestimated the growth of money GDP in the years immediately following by 8.0 percentage points. It underestimated the rise in the GDP deflator by 5.1 percentage points and that of real GDP growth by 2.7 percentage points. By 1989, however, it was still underestimating the rise in the GDP deflator by about 1½ per cent but overestimating the growth of real GDP, which was to halve to 1½ per cent compared with the previous year and was falling by the second half of 1990.

In the first two issues of its *Treasury Bulletin* the Treasury had exposed the defects in the official statistics and in the forecasts, which interact. For example, the April 1988 issue of *Economic Trends* reported that domestic demand had grown by 4.7 per cent in real terms in the year to the fourth quarter of 1987. Using this information, the Treasury then forecast in the March 1988 Red Book that domestic demand would rise by 4 per cent in 1988. The fourth-quarter 1987 statistic was gradually revised upwards to 7.1 per cent. Had this been known in March 1988, the Treasury might have forecast a bigger rise in domestic demand in 1988, which eventually turned out to be 8 per cent but only after some earlier lower estimates had been published. It takes time for the Treasury both to learn that the statistics are wrong and to discover how far out its forecast was – in this extreme case, by a margin of 100 per cent.

A failure of demand management

If it targets monetary demand, macro-economic policy cannot deal only with inflation but must, via the assumed inflation rate, also affect real demand. The Government's supply-side policies of tax-cutting and deregulation were not sufficient to stimulate the British economy to supply as much as they stimulated it to demand. The growth of demand, while it was originally claimed as a successful conclusion to the recession, eventually got out of hand because the Government both failed to measure it and did not believe in using fiscal policy to control it. 'No attempt is made to regulate demand in the short term,' said the Treasury's June 1988 *Economic Progress Report* in a year when real domestic demand was rising by 8 per cent.

Supply-side growth policies were more successful in improving productivity than in increasing output. They provided incentives for the more efficient use of capital, but only at a late stage did they reverse the rise in unemployment of labour. While the changes in corporation tax contributed to the higher rate of return on capital investment, the personal tax cuts of the second half of the decade were more successful in adding to consumer demand than to the supply of labour.

The attempt to control money GDP failed, but even if it had succeeded, it would not necessarily have controlled real demand or output. Looked at in one way, money GDP is the product of money and the velocity of money, measured by its turnover in relation to money GDP. Both these variables have in recent years been difficult to explain or predict. Looked at in another way, money GDP is the sum of real GDP and prices. These variables are each difficult to explain or predict separately but arguably easier than the combination of the two, which is money GDP. While economic growth and inflation do not increase in direct proportion to each other, as used to be thought, it is equally unlikely that their movements offset each other in inverse proportion within a given money GDP increase. Lower inflation may in some circumstances lead to higher growth, but there are many other independent factors influencing each of the two variables separately. Lawson's Mais Lecture recognized that different sets of policies must be used to maintain economic growth and to lower inflation. The Government attempted to control both economic growth and inflation by combining them into one money GDP objective but succeeded in controlling neither.

The Government's use of monetary rather than fiscal policy to control inflation interfered with supply while failing to curb demand. High interest rates were a check on the growth of the economy and nullified much of the incentive effect of supply-side policies on enterprise. According to the Bank of England, 'each one percentage point rise in interest rates reduces the level of GDP by just under 1 per cent after three years.' Tax relief on mortgage interest damped the effect of high interest rates on consumer demand, but they had a strong adverse effect on business investment.

The macro-economic monetary policy designed to check inflation could not help also restraining real economic growth until it was abandoned in the mid-1980s, when the Government became worried more by unemployment than by inflation. In the early 1980s monetary policy caused a traumatic drop in non-energy profits, of which part went into a rise in the share of labour incomes. Short-run antiinflation policy was thus working against the supply-side objective of improving the share of the national income going to industry and commerce. The deficiency of supply in the economy in the late 1980s can be traced back to the excessive severity of the 1980–81 recession. It took most of the Thatcher decade for the share of non-energy profits to climb back to where it had been in 1979. British industry was fitter, but it was also leaner.

In 1990–91 output was again falling, with profits more adversely affected than labour incomes. Money GDP was slowing down, but instead of lower inflation causing higher growth, higher inflation was causing not just lower but negative growth. The cost of the seven good years of the

Thatcher recovery was not only the stop–go of the early 1980s that preceded it but also the stop–go of the early 1990s that followed it. *Plus ça change...*

2 Inflation:
the monetarist experiment that was never tried

> 'We set as the overriding objective of macro-economic policy the conquest of inflation.'
>
> Nigel Lawson, Zurich speech, January 1981

New cures for inflation

All Governments are against inflation in principle. In practice they face a trade-off in which the conquest of inflation takes its place among other objectives, such as economic growth, market freedom, employment and public services. The price paid to reduce the rise in prices is some sacrifice of other objectives in the short run at least. The sacrifices Governments are prepared to impose on their electorates depend on how high the rate of inflation is, how low they aim to reduce it and how near the next election is. The Thatcher Government was no exception to these general rules, but there were important differences.

The Government persuaded itself that there was no conflict of objectives between low inflation and high growth and that one led to the other, with the help of supply-side measures to improve the functioning of the economy. It was unusually ambitious in aiming to reduce inflation from double figures to zero within a few years. It was convinced that it had a new and better kind of monetary and fiscal policy that would achieve its ambitions. The Thatcherites felt that it was the cardinal sin of the Heath Government to have departed from this kind of monetarist policy in a Keynesian U-turn designed to deal with unemployment in 1972.

'Our prime and overriding objective is to unwind the inflationary coils which have gripped our economy,' said *The Right Approach to the Economy* (*RAE*) in 1977. Since the Labour Government, under the terms of its agreement with the International Monetary Fund (IMF), was already pursuing a tight monetary and fiscal policy, with some initial success, there were elements of both 'me too' and 'better us than them' in the Conservative approach.

Monetary targets, openly proclaimed and explained [went on *RAE*], can have a crucial effect in reducing inflationary expectations. The extent of that influence will depend on increasing public awareness. The monetary authorities will often be subject, directly and indirectly, to political and industrial pressure to modify and relax their policies, frequently for reasons of short-term expediency. The danger of their yielding to such pressures will be reduced if monetary policy is the subject of regular and open public discussion, and if the authorities are expected as a matter of course to give an account of their conduct of policy and of their objectives for the future.

RAE then put forward a proposal for an independent Bank of England that was to disappear from view until Nigel Lawson revealed himself to be in support of it in his resignation speech twelve years later.

We favour a more independent role for the Bank of England ... We believe it would be helpful, as in other countries, to establish formal contacts between the Bank, Parliament and other bodies ... One possibility would be for the Bank to be represented at meetings of the National Economic Development Council. And as Parliament evolves a more effective structure of select committees ... there could be opportunities for regular and public contact between the Bank and an appropriate parliamentary committee.

The Governor of the Bank was indeed to appear regularly before the Treasury Select Committee after it was set up in

Inflation

1979 but only in the role of adviser and executant of Treasury policies.

The 1979 election manifesto made the most of the ineffectiveness of Labour monetarism in the face of determined trade unions. 'Inflation is now accelerating again. The pound today is worth less than half its 1974 value. On present form it would be halved in value yet again within eight years. Inflation on this scale has come near to destroying our political and social stability.' (Conservative performance improved on that of Labour. It took the Thatcher Government ten, not five, years to halve the value of the pound.)

The manifesto made the crucial link between monetary and fiscal policy. This was already part of the orthodoxy of 'pink' monetarism as practised by the Labour Chancellor of the Exchequer, Denis Healey, who was to differentiate the rival product as 'punk' monetarism and later as 'sado-monetarism'. 'To master inflation, proper monetary discipline is essential, with publicly stated targets for the growth of the money supply. At the same time, a gradual reduction in the size of the Government's borrowing requirement is also vital.' The long-term aim was at that stage not a balanced budget but a deficit sufficient to allow for a moderate public investment programme. As Sir Geoffrey Howe put it in his first Budget speech, 'the Budget deficit should be reduced to between 1 and 2 per cent of output.'

Prices and incomes policy, which had been used by the previous Conservative Government as well as by the Labour Government, was rejected by the manifesto: 'This Government's price controls have done nothing to prevent inflation ... All the controls have achieved is a loss of jobs and a reduction of consumer choice.' In fact, incomes policy had reduced the inflation rate from 24 per cent in 1975 to 8 per cent in 1978 and, even in the opinion of some monetarist economists, had done so in such a way as to minimize the loss of jobs, whatever its other defects. However, incomes policy had not effected a permanent reduction in inflation and was incompatible with the Conservatives' free-market principles.

The Price Commission, set up in 1972 by Edward Heath under Arthur Cockfield (one of Mrs Thatcher's advisers and later a member of her cabinet), was wound up as soon as the new Government took office in June 1979. The Government sought to influence incomes indirectly by trying to lower inflation expectations by means of monetary policy and by shifting the balance of bargaining power away from the unions (see page 217). It also intervened more directly by means of a 'crypto-incomes policy' holding down increases in public-sector pay (see page 85).

The objective was restated in Howe's first Budget speech in June 1979 as to 'squeeze inflation out of the system' and the method as to 're-establish sound money ... through firm monetary discipline and fiscal policies consistent with that'. In view of the pain inflicted by the squeeze, Howe recalled in his second Budget speech in March 1980 the reasons why inflation is bad, which are not always self-evident to everyone. 'As long as [inflation] persists, economic stability and prosperity will continue to elude us. And so too will social coherence. Nothing, in the long run, could contribute more to the disintegration of society, the destruction of any sense of national unity, than continuing inflation. For inflation sets worker against worker, employer against employee and sometimes even government against its own employees.' To make his point clear, he referred to the picket lines and the grave-diggers' strike of the 1978-9 'winter of discontent'. His critics later denounced high unemployment with arguments about social structure similar to those that he used against high inflation (see page 239).

The methods to be used were given in the first MTFS in the Budget Red Book (*Financial Statement and Budget Report*) for 1980-81 published with the 1980 Budget speech:

Control of the money supply will over a period reduce the rate of inflation ... Public expenditure plans and tax policies and interest rates will be adjusted as necessary in order to achieve the objective ... It is not the intention to achieve this reduction in monetary growth by excessive reliance on interest rates. The Government is therefore planning for a substantial reduction over the medium term in the public sector borrowing requirement (PSBR) as a percentage of GDP.

The 1983 election manifesto was able to claim that 'prices are rising more slowly than at any time since the 1960s. During the last year, inflation has come down faster in Britain than in any other major economy.' The anti-inflation objective was more strongly restated: 'In the next parliament, we shall endeavour to bring inflation lower still. Our ultimate goal should be a society with stable prices.'

There was no further progress in reducing inflation between 1983 and 1987. The election manifesto for the latter year restated the objective with some urgency:

Nothing erodes a country's competitive edge faster than inflation. Nothing so undermines personal thrift and independence as to see the value of a lifetime's savings eaten away in retirement through spiralling prices. And nothing threatens the social fabric of a nation more than the conflicts and divisiveness which inflation creates ... There is no better yardstick of a party's fitness to govern than its attitude to inflation. Nothing is so politically immoral as a party that ignores that yardstick ... The Conservative Government will continue to put the conquest of inflation as our first objective. We will not be content until we have stable prices, with inflation eradicated altogether.

The MTFS was updated each year from 1980 and published in the Budget Red Book. To gain credibility, it had to claim consistency. While the aim of defeating inflation did not alter, the methods used changed from year to year, to the point where they bore little resemblance in 1990 to what they had been in 1980. The MTFS celebrated its tenth anniversary with a return to its original message, which had become somewhat obscured, as the inflation rate had returned almost to where it had been when the Government came in.

The central objective of the MTFS is the defeat of inflation.

Inflation damages the economy by increasing uncertainty, discouraging investment and reducing profitability. It brings conflict into industrial relations and reduces confidence in the management of the economy, at home and abroad . . . Inflation redistributes wealth arbitrarily and capriciously. It erodes savings and is a disincentive to those who wish prudently to provide for their retirement. It bears most heavily on people least able to protect themselves.

The MTFS was plagued from the outset by disagreement about the choice of the various monetary instruments and about their effectiveness both in theory and in practice. Monetarism, like the Christian Church, was and still is split between fundamentalists and permissives, between rules and discretion. When disaster threatens people pay lip-service to the religion just in case it offers a ticket to salvation.

The Government's aim of reducing inflation had to be reconciled with its other main economic principle, that of the free market. Conservative policy-makers failed to spot the incompatibility of abolishing controls and restrictive practices in markets such as those for credit, foreign exchange, securities, housing and labour, yet seeking to retain strict official curbs in one key market – that for money. They were not prepared to accept that the equilibrium of demand and supply thrown up by the unfettered play of market forces in these other markets might cause an upwards adjustment in the price level, which could be spread over many years or even lead to continuously rising prices. (The post-communist countries of Eastern Europe have recently provided a melancholy reminder of this principle.)

Professor Alan Walters addressed the problem in 1971, in an influential monetarist pamphlet from the Institute of Economic Affairs, *Money in Boom and Slump*, ten years before becoming Mrs Thatcher's economic adviser. He argued in favour of market techniques of influencing the quantity of money rather than direct controls, but this was a change in the method rather than the principle of state intervention in the money market.

It seems quite absurd to attempt controls by ceilings on and discrimination in advances ... The authorities can exercise control over the quantity of money by open-market operations ... The financial institutions should then be free to innovate and develop new instruments for collecting and channelling credit into those activities where the rate of return is highest.

Lawson, who was then, as Financial Secretary to the Treasury, one of the architects of the MTFS, showed in his August 1980 Bow Group lecture 'The New Conservatism' that he also thought there was no incompatibility between monetary control and free financial markets.

The economic policy of the new Conservatism has two basic strands. At the macro-economic level, our approach is what has come to be known as monetarism ... At the micro-economic level, our emphasis is on the free market, in contradistinction to state intervention and central planning. While these two strands fit easily and harmoniously together, so much so that they are frequently confused, they are in fact distinct. It is quite possible to be a monetarist and a central planner.

In his 1984 Mais Lecture Lawson assigned macro-economic policy to the conquest of inflation and micro-economic policy to supply-side measures to stimulate economic growth (see page 7). It was the financial and business services sector that benefited most from supply-side decontrol, growing faster than any other (see table 4). It turned out to be impossible to control money while decontrolling credit. This was the lesson of Mrs Thatcher's first term. It then appeared that it might be possible to control inflation while decontrolling money. This was the lesson of Mrs Thatcher's second term. It later became apparent that inflation could not be controlled without controlling something – and that something could be the exchange rate. This was the lesson of Mrs Thatcher's third term.

The Howe Chancellorship – *the sheep that roared*

There were at least three schools of thought within the Government about monetary policy. First, there was the monetarist doctrine with which the politicians came into office. This was propounded by Lawson, who was a trained economist, and accepted on common-sense grounds by Mrs Thatcher and Howe, who were not. As Lawson put it in his Bow Group lecture: 'Monetarism is simply a new name for an old maxim, formerly known as the quantity theory of money ... It consists of two basic propositions. The first is that changes in the quantity of money determine, at the end of the day, changes in the general price level; the second is that government is able to determine the quantity of money.'

The second school of thought, represented by the Bank of England, was based not on the quantity theory, in which money determined prices, but on demand for money equations, in which money itself was determined by real output, prices and interest rates. Most of these equations had already been tested to destruction, but there were always one or two on the drawing board of the Bank's economics department that gave hope that the authorities, by setting interest rates, might be able to control at least one monetary aggregate. The direct control of real output and/or prices was excluded by the Government's free-market philosophy, so interest rates were all that was left.

The Bank came under pressure from the politicians and their advisers to adopt a version of the quantity theory called monetary base control, the subject of a Green Paper published by the Treasury in 1980. This would have meant tight control by the Bank of England of the monetary base, defined as notes and coins and the commercial banks' small working balances at the Bank. The result might have been more effective control of the money supply, but it would have left interest rates to fluctuate unpredictably. After a memorable debate with academics and City economists (including the present author) on 29 September 1980 at what one of them called 'the improbable venue of Church House in Westminster', Bank and Treasury officials joined in rejecting the plan as impractical, to Mrs Thatcher's disappointment. The Treasury Select Committee also concluded its

July 1980 report, *Monetary Control*, by saying it was 'unlikely that an automatic application of a single technique of control will be either appropriate, or acceptable to Parliament'.

The Treasury had always taken a broader view, which went back to the Radcliffe Report of 1960. Money was determined as part of a portfolio of different financial assets and liabilities. This was the only way that money entered into the Treasury's econometric model of the economy, which has always been Keynesian in structure and could not suddenly be retooled as a monetarist model incorporating the quantity theory. This view determined the choice of Sterling M3 (£M3), the broad monetary aggregate, for control purposes, since some, if not all, of its asset counterparts – bank lending, the PSBR and external flows – could to some extent be controlled by the authorities. However, the Treasury's view of the transmission mechanism from money to inflation was quite different from that of the quantity theory. A typical expression of it was given in a paper by Peter Middleton, then the Treasury Under-Secretary in charge of monetary policy, to the Institute for Fiscal Studies in March 1978. He said:

Under [a freely floating exchange rate] monetary policy has a rapid impact on the rest of the economy through its effects on the exchange rate and thence through the effects of changes in the exchange rate on prices, the current-account balance and the level of activity. The growth of M3 depends in large part on fiscal policy and the external position. Government can however exert a degree of control over the growth of the money supply by changes in the level and structure of interest rates or by quantitative restrictions on credit.

As it turned out, this was a good description of how the Treasury carried out a 'monetarist' policy in 1979–81, in spite of a number of measures of financial decontrol that made it more difficult.

When the Government came into office the pound was already going up. The oil price had been increased by the

Organization of Petroleum Exporting Countries (OPEC), and the rising price and output of North Sea oil was benefiting the UK balance of payments, even if it was pushing the British inflation rate into double figures, as the UK had to bear the higher oil costs like other countries, whether they were of domestic or foreign origin. The other countries of the European Monetary System (EMS) had in March 1979 started up their exchange-rate mechanism to control inflation by fixing their exchange rates to that of the D-mark. The Labour Government had joined the EMS but not the ERM. The new Conservative Government concurred in the decision. To join the ERM was incompatible with domestic monetarism, according to which the interest rate was used to determine the quantity of money and the exchange rate left to float – preferably up.

The main method chosen by the new Government to reduce the growth of £M3 was to cut the PSBR. This was in keeping with Howe's political aim of, as he put it in his first Budget speech, putting less restraint on the private sector and more on the public sector. Just as the PSBR had been the main source of money creation in the 1970s, it was to become the main instrument of monetary control in the 1980s. It was to be reduced from 5½ per cent of GDP in the previous year to 4½ per cent in 1979–80, while the £M3 target was cut from an increase of 8–12 per cent to one of 7–11 per cent.

The PSBR could not be reduced by more because the switch from income tax to VAT was accompanied by a slight relaxation in fiscal stance, (see table 8). The tax switch was also a setback to the reduction of the inflation rate and £M3 growth. By putting VAT up from 8 per cent (on some goods 12½) to 15 per cent, it raised the year-on-year increase in the Retail Prices Index (RPI) from 11.4 per cent in June 1979 to 15.6 per cent in July (see page 112) and undermined the credibility of the 7–11 per cent £M3 target. Contrary to the Government's intentions, therefore, Minimum Lending Rate (MLR) had to be raised by two percentage points to 14 per cent. Bank lending was still to be controlled by the 'corset' system of supplementary special deposits that penalized the banks by not paying interest on them.

In October 1979 the Government unexpectedly abolished all exchange controls, after taking some partial measures in July. This set back the pound's upward trend only temporarily. It was also successful, to the extent that it allowed the balance-of-payments surplus due to the North Sea to be invested overseas by the financial institutions for the highest return, while making British industry compete for funds by offering rates of return matching those available elsewhere. Yet it suddenly made the control of the sterling money supply both more difficult and less effective. Sterling interest rates became much more open to the influence of those in the USA and other countries, and British business was able to deposit and borrow freely in dollars and other currencies, thus circumventing restrictions on the creation of sterling money and credit.

The abolition of exchange controls led to the end of the banking 'corset' in July 1980 and the abolition of the 12½ per cent bank reserve–asset ratio, which had never actually been used as an instrument of monetary control. The abolition of the 'corset' caused a once-for-all rise of five percentage points in the growth of £M3, as funds that had become 'disintermediated' by bypassing the banking system became 'reintermediated' within it. Both the RPI and £M3 were running way over their expected levels soon after Howe presented the new MTFS with his second Budget in March 1980.

The MTFS's most striking innovation was its commitment to four-year descending target ranges for £M3, which was to come down from 7–11 per cent growth in 1980–81 to 4–8 per cent in 1983–4 (see table 9). This was to be achieved by reducing the PSBR from 3¾ per cent of GDP to 1½ per cent over the same period, starting with a sharp reduction from the estimated out-turn of 4¾ per cent in 1979–80 (see table 10). The object of this sharp fiscal contraction was to avoid any further pressure on interest rates, already at 17 per cent. Howe showed in his Budget speech that he had a less doctrinaire approach than Lawson to the new MTFS. 'Monetarism,' he told the House of Commons, 'means curbing the excessive expansion of money and credit ... It is a great pity that its practical, common-sense importance has been so confused by arid, theoretical disputes.'

The main effect of 17 per cent interest rates was not to curb the growth of £M3 but to drive up the exchange rate at a time when North Sea oil had already made it strong. It reached peaks of DM5 and $2.50 briefly in early 1981. This was effective in reducing inflation, halving the 20 per cent rise in average world import prices between 1979 and 1980 to only 10 per cent in UK sterling import prices, including oil, because of the 10 per cent rise in the effective exchange rate. At the same time it made many manufacturing exports unprofitable because of the high price of their goods in foreign currency and caused widespread industrial closures and unemployment. Mrs Thatcher's response to criticism on this score was summed up by the acronym TINA – There is No Alternative. Her speech-writers gave her the celebrated quip at the October 1980 Conservative Party conference: 'The lady's not for turning. You turn if you want to.' Mrs Thatcher's reputation in her dealings with the Soviet Union as the 'iron lady' was to be turned to advantage as the 'Thatcher factor' to establish the credibility of policy in financial markets. As Professor Patrick Minford, a Government supporter, commented: 'The inflation battle, like many battles in history, did not go according to plan, and the plan itself could have been improved. But it was won . . .'

During the Government's first two years £M3 was overshooting the upper end of its target ranges by about one-third. Howe recognized in his 1980 Budget speech that higher interest rates had actually increased borrowing in the short term: 'The recent pressure on companies has resulted in a strong demand for bank lending, which has contributed to the upward pressure on both money supply and interest rates.' This was followed by exhortation, which proved an inadequate substitute for 'corset' controls once they were removed: 'Banks and their customers would be well advised, in the difficult conditions foreseen for 1980–81, to be cautious about the scale of their lending and borrowing.'

The Bank of England, far from seeking to curb bank lending by the traditional system of nods and winks, eased its qualitative guidance, which told banks to go easy on lending for personal consumption, imports and property investment and to favour instead that destined for industrial investment and exports. The Governor, Sir Gordon Richardson, was unfairly blamed by Mrs Thatcher for the overshoot of the monetary targets. He was, in fact, implementing the 'free-market' thrust of the Government's own credit policy, which was welcomed on all sides in the City. Mrs Thatcher also expressed to the chairmen of the clearing banks her dismay at the continuing increase in lending, which was seen as a gaping breach in the walls of the monetarist citadel. She did not accept that the banks were in business not to bale out the Government's monetary policy but, with the encouragement of the Bank of England, to rescue their own customers from its worst effects. In fact, the banks were able to increase credit considerably faster than money because they were replacing gilt-edged with advances to the private sector and funding them with overseas deposits and increases in capital that were not within any of the UK monetary aggregates.

Professor Alan Walters, a strong internal critic with Mrs Thatcher's ear, had always argued that a narrow aggregate would be better behaved than a broad one such as £M3. He wrote: 'The MTFS and political reputations were based on the volatile credit base of £M3.' He pointed out that increases in loans and deposits on both sides of the banks' balance sheets did not necessarily lead to more spending, which might cause inflation. In fact, there was during this period a good deal of arbitrage, known as 'round-tripping', by companies borrowing in the bill market and making a profit by redepositing in banks at a slightly higher rate of interest. To this day controversy continues within the monetarist camp between the advocates of 'narrow money' and those of 'broad money', reminiscent of Swift's dispute between 'Little-Endians' and 'Big-Endians' about which end of a boiled egg should be cracked open.

Charles Goodhart, a Chief Adviser to the Bank of England, had in 1975 stated Goodhart's Law: 'Any observed statistical regularity will tend to collapse once pressure is placed on it for control purposes.' This appeared in 1980 to be particularly true with regard to £M3 and the inflation rate, since the former was rising while the latter was falling. His colleague Christopher Dow, then Economics Director of the Bank, pointed out in 1987 in the *Lloyds Bank Review*: 'If the growth of money is driven by bank lending, and if that tends to rise along with rising real incomes or rising prices, and if the authorities lack effective means to control bank lending, it follows that prices cause money, and not the other way round; and that control of money is not a way to control inflation.'

In the summer of 1980 the Treasury Select Committee, which had been in existence for only nine months, opened a major inquiry into monetary policy, of which the report was published in February 1981. The Committee concluded: 'There has been no true "monetarist experiment". The Government moderated upward pressure on interest rates and decided against trying to cut the PSBR to the level it stated was consistent with its monetary target. Despite this, monetary conditions have been tight.' Monetary conditions, in line with the pragmatic approach of both the Treasury and the Bank of England, included, as well as £M3, other monetary aggregates, the interest rate and the exchange rate.

We believe [the Committee said] that there are risks attached to a subordination of fiscal policy to monetary targets. In a recession caused by a fall in private domestic demand, built-in automatic stabilizers tend to raise the PSBR which in turn, with unchanged interest rates, may lead to a rise in monetary growth above the target. Meeting MTFS targets may then require either a rise in interest rates or a tightening of fiscal stance ... In these conditions, additional sacrifices of output may be made to meet anti-inflationary monetary targets.

Some of the expert witnesses went further than the Committee's report. Milton Friedman, the high priest of monetarism, said in his memorandum of evidence:

> The key role assigned to targets for the PSBR ... seems to me unwise ... There is no necessary relation between the PSBR and monetary growth.

Friedman referred to the Treasury in tones usually reserved for a first-year student who has not done his homework. Alluding to the Green Paper *Monetary Control,* he wrote:

> I could hardly believe my eyes when I read ... 'The principal means of controlling the growth of the money supply must be fiscal policy ... and interest rates.' Interpreted literally, this sentence is simply wrong. Only a Rip Van Winkle, who had not read any of the flood of literature during the past decade and more on the money supply process, could possibly have written that sentence. Direct control of the monetary base is an alternative to fiscal policy and interest rates as a means of controlling monetary growth.

The Committee cast doubt on the Government's main premise of a direct link between money and inflation.

> Although over the long term the money supply and the price level have moved together we have not been convinced by evidence of a direct causal link from growth in the money supply to inflation ... We discuss the view that monetary policy can work directly, through expectations, to reduce inflation without significantly affecting output. We conclude that in the light of experience this view is not valid ... It is unrealistic to suppose that negotiated wages and administered prices respond rapidly and automatically to announcements about monetary policy, however credible they may be. The influence of monetary policy on wage and price inflation does not therefore appear primarily through the setting of targets or through expectations, but rather in the short term through the lowering of economic activity and the appreciation of the exchange rate.

Far from heeding the Committee's advice, the Government proceeded to fight against the automatic stabilizers raising the PSBR in recession. In March 1981 Howe introduced the toughest Budget of the Thatcher decade. The 'dead sheep' of Healey's jibe roared, and Mrs Thatcher had to postpone her ambition to cut the burden of tax. The 1981 Budget marked a move from monetarism to fiscalism, with more emphasis on the PSBR than on £M3. The 1981 Red Book virtually disowned £M3.

Other indicators also suggest that financial conditions in 1980–81 were tight: the high exchange rate; high interest rates; the absence of any marked upwards movement in the price of houses or other real assets. Taken on its own, therefore, M3 has not been a good indicator of monetary conditions in the past year . . . it should not have the implications for future inflation which generally follow an increase in money supply.

The Government suffered the embarrassment of being confronted by its own monetarist supporters with high inflation forecasts based on the supposed link between money and prices. The Treasury's experts were adopting a compromise position summed up in a paper by Simon Wren-Lewis that attempted to test the quantity theory: 'Money appears to be important, but it is certainly not the only variable that may be significant in determining prices.' To most economists it seemed obvious that, whatever high interest rates did to money, they slowed down the economy, causing import prices to moderate through the exchange rate and also affecting domestic price increases through high unemployment, lower pay rises and slack demand.

In his Budget speech Howe blamed the overshoot in £M3 on the unexpected growth of bank lending. 'Public borrowing increases in a recession, but this is normally offset by private-sector borrowing . . . On this occasion bank lending did not fall away as quickly as might have been expected.' He had noted the insensitivity of bank lending to interest rates in the previous year; now it seemed that bank deposits were behaving in a similarly perverse way, since an increasing proportion of them were interest-bearing, and their rise outweighed the expected fall in non-interest-bearing deposits when interest rates went up. He commented: 'To the extent that it merely involves returning to a more normal level of financial assets it need not fuel inflation.'

Still searching for a well-behaved monetary aggregate, Howe announced that monetary base, or M0, statistics were to be published with a view to controlling a new M2 aggregate, defined as retail deposits, that would draw a line between spending money, which was potentially inflationary, and saving money, which was not. This idea came to grief with frequent changes in the definition of M2, which never caught on, as it became apparent that depositors could switch with ease from saving to spending accounts and, indeed, that some accounts could be used for either purpose.

The Treasury's economists had made two more important findings, published in a 1981 working paper by Joe Grice and Adam Bennett. First, 'in the long run the wider aggregates appear to be affected only by relative interest rates and not by the absolute level.' It followed that one way to control £M3 was to lower, not raise, short-term interest rates while increasing yields on gilt-edged bonds; this could lead to the perverse result that lower short-term rates would fuel inflationary demand, while higher gilt yields would create higher inflation expectations. Second, 'the influence of financial wealth on the demand for money cannot be ignored.' Since the liberalization of financial markets meant an increase in holdings of bonds and equities, the demand for money, as one portfolio asset among many, was bound to rise in the long run, even if relative interest rates could result in short-run switching out of money into other financial assets.

The scepticism of the experts was well expressed by John Fforde, an adviser to the Governor of the Bank of England, in a paper published in June 1983: 'As time went by it came to be realized that the strategy was more likely to be judged by its actual effect on the economy, and on the actual behaviour and expectations of the principal agents in it, than by the puzzling short-term behaviour of a particular monetary aggregate.'

The PSBR for 1980–81, instead of falling from 4¾ per cent of GDP in the previous year to 3¾ per cent, rose to 6 per cent because of the recession. On unchanged policies it would have remained close to that level in 1981–2 instead of falling to 3 per cent, as laid down in the MTFS. Howe compromised by setting it at 4¼ per cent. Even this required a massive fiscal tightening of 1¾ per cent of GDP, or over £4 billion. As well as the usual public expenditure cuts there were major tax increases: the non-indexation of income tax allowances, the raising of excise duties by more than the inflation rate, the usual contribution from the oil companies and a special tax on the banks' non-interest-bearing deposits – as if to punish them for having failed to restrain lending.

Walters, who had advised on the 1981 Budget, later wrote: 'In retrospect it seems that the Budget decisions of 1981 represented a clear and resolute decision to restore financial integrity and to restore the economy to the basic path of the MTFS.' In the same work, *Britain's Economic Renaissance*, he expounded a new theory, that 'the effect of a change in the deficit depends on the level of the deficit'. From this it could be inferred that if the deficit stood, as it had, at 6 per cent of GDP, a further rise would add to inflation but not output, while a fall would reduce inflation but not output. The theory was the opposite of the Keynesian conventional wisdom and was based on the effects of fiscal policy on financial-market confidence.

It was something of an *ad hoc* theory, but it appeared to be confirmed by the results of the Budget, which was followed by a fall in inflation and, over a year later, by the beginning of a recovery in output. However, Walters had also advised that, while fiscal policy was too loose, monetary policy was too tight. The fiscal tightening made it possible to ease monetary policy by cutting interest rates a full two percentage points, to 12 per cent, after the 1981 Budget, but they were back up to 16 per cent by the end of 1981. The Bank of England's MLR was withdrawn, although the Bank continued to set rates by means of the unpublished band of rates at which it dealt with the market. Index-linked gilt-edged securities were introduced, suggesting that the Government was not confident of its ability to sell debt to buyers fearful of high inflation in spite of one tough Budget.

In its report on the 1981 Budget the Treasury Committee queried an old theory that had been raised by Lawson, then Financial Secretary, as a reason why lower inflation might stimulate economic growth by creating a real increase in the money supply – known as the 'real balance' effect. 'The rate of growth of the money supply,' it argued, 'cannot surely be used in advance as an instrument to control both independent objectives of the rate of inflation and the real level of output. It is unclear why, in the Financial Secretary's view, money-supply growth above the rate of inflation should end up increasing output rather than prices.' It was an acute observation because, from that time on, fiscal policy became the main anti-inflation instrument and monetary policy the main instrument of real growth.

The 1981 Budget was attacked by a letter in *The Times* of 30 March from 364 academic economists, including four former Chief Economic Advisers to the Treasury, which stated:

(a) There is no basis in economic theory or supporting evidence for the government's belief that by deflating demand they will bring inflation permanently under control and thereby induce an automatic recovery in output and employment;
(b) Present policies will deepen the depression, erode the industrial base of our economy and threaten its social and political stability;
(c) There are alternative policies; and
(d) The time has come to reject monetarist policies and consider urgently which alternative offers the best hope of sustained economic recovery.

The Government paid little attention to such criticisms, although they reflected views widespread within the Conservative Party and the Government itself, as well as in the

Opposition. It was later to claim that events had disproved the 364, since inflation came down and output and employment recovered. However, there was still room for doubt about whether the Government had got inflation permanently under control, and the industrial base was eroded, even though it was later restored to some degree. The irony of the whole episode, however, was that the Government had already, by the time of the 1981 Budget, abandoned monetarism in the strict sense of the term and owed its success to a return to a more pragmatic approach to policy.

The 1981 Budget was the first to achieve its PSBR objective, and the 1982 Budget made very little change in the pre-set path of decline in borrowing. Even after a cut in the National Insurance Surcharge, it set and achieved a reduction from $4\frac{1}{4}$ to $3\frac{1}{2}$ per cent of GDP. Following the pattern of the 1981 Budget, there was a major relaxation of monetary policy. The target range for £M3 in the coming year was raised from 5–9 per cent to 8–12 per cent. £M3 had overshot because of what Howe called in his Budget speech 'structural changes in the market-place – such as the rising market share of the banks', which were competing with the building societies in the mortgage market, thus fulfilling the Government's wish to introduce competition into a key area that had suffered from self-imposed rationing by the lenders.

The same higher target ranges were applied to two new target aggregates, M1 and PSL2. M1, a kind of narrow money, was mainly non-interest-bearing, and the Treasury warned, correctly, that it might overshoot its targets when interest rates were falling. PSL2, a broad liquidity measure, included building society deposits (not then counted as money), so as not to put the banks at an unfair disadvantage by controlling their liabilities but not those of their competitors.

In July 1982, in a further significant measure of financial liberalization, the controls on hire-purchase agreements, which were no longer being used to restrict consumer borrowing, were abolished. Technically, it made little difference, but it was interpreted by the banks and their competitors in the finance houses as a green light to compete in and expand consumer credit.

By that time the Government was no longer inhibited from upping the monetary targets by the fear that they might adversely affect inflation expectations, since any direct link between money and prices appeared to have been discredited. 'It may be unduly optimistic,' Howe told the Treasury Committee in evidence on his 1982 Budget, 'to imagine that the [monetary target] was likely to be in the forefront of the minds of actual pay bargainers . . . It is the actuality of falling inflation, and the expectation of further falls in inflation, that transmits itself into the minds of pay bargainers.'

Helped by the raising of the target ranges, both £M3 and PSL2 fell within their target ranges in 1982–3. Monetary control was also being assisted by the practice of 'overfunding'. As public borrowing shrank, the continuing demand for gilt-edged, now including indexed bonds, by the financial institutions appeared to justify the issue of more than were needed just to finance the PSBR. Holdings of short-term money were thus neutralized by being switched into long-term bonds, and credit to industry was unaffected, except that it was funded by commercial bills in the Bank of England's 'bill mountain' and not by bank deposits counted as part of the money supply.

The drawback of over-funding was that long-term interest rates were being kept up, and potential corporate borrowers continued to be 'crowded out' of the long-term bond market, resorting instead to short-term credit. However, since it was relative and not absolute interest rates that determined the demand for money, over-funding fitted in with the latest Treasury thinking about techniques of monetary control, even though the Chancellor seemed less inclined than the Governor of the Bank of England to acknowledge it as part of official policy, as the Treasury Committee remarked in its report on the 1982 Autumn Statement. It would have been more in line with the Government's philosophy if bank credit had simply been replaced by corporate bonds held by the institutions. Since over-funding was in effect nationalizing an increasing proportion of industrial credit by putting it into the Bank of England, and the effect on the monetary aggregates was purely cosmetic, the practice was terminated in 1985.

The success of fiscal rather than monetary policy was confirmed by Howe in his evidence to the Treasury Committee on the 1982 Autumn Statement. After admitting the difficulties of monetary control, he said: 'The thing that has been most consistently put in place has been the manifest determination to reduce the real burden of public borrowing.' The Treasury Committee was still critical of monetary policy in its report: 'The relationship between the monetary aggregates and prices has ... turned out not to be as simple as the Government thought ... It is unclear what the existing monetary targets imply for the future paths of either prices or real activity.'

Inflation fell from its May 1980 peak of 22 per cent in 1980 to only 4 per cent in April 1983, just in time for the June election – and the MTFS appeared to be vindicated. The PSBR in 1982–3 fell even below its objective of $3\frac{1}{2}$ per cent of GDP to the figure set for 1983–4, $2\frac{3}{4}$ per cent. This figure was maintained as the objective for 1983–4, even after some over-indexation of personal allowances to make up for their non-indexation in 1981, as were the monetary targets of 7–11 per cent. Howe rejected a suggestion from the Treasury Committee that, as inflation had come down faster than expected, the monetary targets could have been notched down a point. It was a pre-election Budget, and he had achieved the rare combination of a boost to public capital spending combined with a fall in bank base rates to single figures soon after the election that was to last until the middle of 1984. The MTFS had abandoned any strict adherence to monetarism, but it had engineered a fall in interest rates and inflation sufficient to win another term. In February 1983 Mrs Thatcher, recalling that Keynes had held monetarist views, seemed to have squared the circle with her statement to Hugo Young: 'I am the true Keynesian.'

The Lawson Chancellorship – the 'teenage scribbler' comes of age

Lawson was in the rare position of a financial commentator given a chance to improve on the performance of those he had criticized. He had also been thoroughly prepared for his six-year reign as Chancellor by being both the architect and expositor of the MTFS and the Financial Secretary to the Treasury whose name actually appeared on the annual Budget Red Book. It was thus natural that he should wish to persevere with the framework of the MTFS, even though there was little left of its original content. Since inflation no longer appeared to be the main problem, Lawson switched to supply-side measures to promote economic growth within the framework and thus to reduce unemployment, which was to continue rising until 1986. His Chancellorship was notable more for its taxation changes (see chapter 4) than for its handling of monetary policy, which was characterized by frequent changes of tack and disagreements with Mrs Thatcher that ended in disaster.

Lawson was consistent, however, in carrying on the policy of reducing the PSBR. In view of the accompanying reductions in taxation and the acceleration in the expansion of credit, this was more effective in restraining public expenditure than in controlling any of the many and various monetary aggregates. Lawson showed his colours when, soon after the election in July 1983, he made much publicized public-expenditure cuts of £500 million. In his first Budget in March 1984, for the only time in the history of the MTFS, illustrative ranges for the PSBR and the monetary aggregates were given for five years ahead, the full life of a Parliament.

Although the PSBR in 1983–4 had overshot by ½ per cent of GDP, Lawson planned to cut it by a full percentage point to 2¼ per cent in 1984–5 and then to reduce it to 1¾ per cent after another three years, something like the ultimate destination always intended. This was enough to justify the now routine cut of ½ per cent in bank base rates after the 1984 Budget. M1 and PSL2 were scrapped after only two years in use, since they had overshot their targets in 1983–4. £M3 was kept on sufferance, as it had stayed within its 7–11 per cent range, which now came down to 6–10 per cent, the figure set for 1984–5 two years before, and was targeted to fall to 2–6 per cent in 1988–9. A new narrow aggregate, MO, or wider monetary base, was added, with ranges starting at 4–8 per cent and falling over the five years to 0–4 per cent, hinting at the ultimate goal of zero inflation.

The Treasury had established that MO was sensitive to short-term interest rates and that it tended to rise, rather steadily, at a slower pace than money national income because money transmission was using fewer notes and coins, its main constituents. Lawson therefore took it as a signal to raise interest rates when MO was overshooting its targets. It also had the merit of being easy to control even in low target ranges, which might therefore lead to low inflation expectations. He clearly preferred it to £M3, of which he said in his Budget speech: 'A large proportion of this money is in reality a form of saving, invested for the interest it can earn.'

The Treasury Committee established in its evidence from Lawson that, in spite of the MO targets, he did not expect inflation to fall to zero until 1993–4. 'The presumption is,' he said, 'not that inflation will get down to zero within the next three years . . . It will take a little longer than that.' He justified a decline in the PSBR during an economic recovery as consistent with no decline in recession years; both were different cyclical phases in the gradual downwards trend.

Lawson was also attracted to a new monetary target, money GDP, which had been mentioned as an assumption in Red Books since 1982 and could be derived arithmetically from the Treasury's assumptions about the growth of real GDP and prices that were published in the Red Book from 1984 onwards. In October 1984 the Governor of the Bank

Inflation

of England, Robin Leigh-Pemberton, advised against the use of money GDP in a lecture published in its December *Quarterly Bulletin*:

The ulterior objective is framed in terms of nominal income, and the main difficulty of monetary targets has lain in the unpredictability of their relationship to nominal income. Why not then, it is suggested, target nominal income directly? I do not, however, think that this would work as an operational target. There would be disadvantages, for example, as a result of the distance between the operational instruments of policy and their impact on national income, and the unsuitable nature, for this particular purpose, of the national income statistics, since they are available only after a considerable delay and are subject to sizeable revision.

He went on:

Besides this first source of delay, in obtaining information, there is a second delay, even longer and therefore more troublesome, before the instruments of policy are able to affect and correct the course of the target ... It would be misguided to relate policy to what has happened, when what is needed is to adjust policy so as to prevent future developments going off track.

This turned out to be a prescient comment on what was to go wrong in 1988, when inadequate statistics played a major role.

In October 1984 the Governor was pressing British membership of the EMS ERM as preferable to any of the domestic monetary targets. Having given the thumbs down to money GDP, he said:

A second alternative, in place of a domestic monetary target, has been the adoption of an exchange-rate objective, through a pegged relationship with a foreign currency, or in earlier times with gold. For the UK, with its close political and economic ties with our European neighbours, there could be a number of attractions in taking a full part in the exchange-rate mechanism of the EMS.

By 1984 it was clear that, in the five years of the ERM's

existence, member countries had succeeded in both stabilizing their exchange rates and reducing their inflation rates, perhaps not as rapidly as the UK but with less sacrifice of output and employment. The rise in the sterling exchange rate in 1979–81, which was generally thought to be due more to high interest rates than to North Sea oil, would have been considerably reduced even if an upwards realignment of the pound might have been required because of oil. The severity of the impact of monetary policy on the economy would thus have been mitigated.

Lawson chose to ride both horses, and in the 1985 Budget he announced the first four-year set of objectives for money GDP, starting at $8\frac{1}{2}$ per cent and falling to 5 per cent by 1988–9 (see table 7). The last four years of the previous five-year ranges for MO and £M3 were carried over unchanged from the previous year; the former was inside, the latter outside, its range for 1984–5. 'All the measures of broad money,' said the MTFS, 'have been affected to some extent by financial liberalization and intensified competition between banks and building societies.'

The new money GDP target, at a time when unemployment was still high, had a Keynesian flavour. It promised pay bargainers a one-for-one trade-off between lower pay and higher real income. 'Moderate pay settlements will lead to more jobs and lower unemployment; adherence to the MTFS guarantees that this moderation will not result in a reduction in overall demand,' said the 1985 MTFS. In his evidence on the Budget to the Treasury Committee Lawson sought to distinguish his new policy of managing monetary demand, which had been put forward by Professor James Meade as 'new Keynesianism' in the 1970s and by Samuel Brittan in a 1982 Institute of Economic Affairs pamphlet, from the discredited 'old Keynesian' policy of managing a real demand. 'We are no more interested in having inadequate monetary demand in the economy than we are in having excessive monetary demand in the economy,' he told the Committee. 'What you can do is to influence money demand. But in addition you need, by supply-side measures, to assist in getting the best possible breakdown of that money demand between real demand and inflation.'

In 1984–5 the PSBR overshot its objective, 2¼ per cent of GDP, by one full percentage point, mainly because of the coal strike. Lawson stuck to the previous year's strict policy of two years of 2 per cent followed by two of 1¾ per cent PSBR as a percentage of GDP. As he put it in the Budget speech: 'A substantial reduction in the PSBR must take precedence over our objective for reducing the burden of tax,' although there were some concessions in the form of over-indexation of personal allowances and reform of national insurance contributions (see page 116).

Lawson was also thought in 1985 to be 'shadowing' the D-mark, keeping the pound close to it in spite of being outside the ERM. He had been drawn into the heady atmosphere of international meetings of the major powers to deal with exchange-rate fluctuations, from which the UK suffered more than most. The achievements in the battle against inflation were put at risk when the pound fell almost to a dollar in January 1985, pushing the inflation rate up briefly to 7 per cent in mid-year. This was due less to the pound's weakness than to the dollar's strength, which also affected the D-mark and the EMS currencies. The Plaza Agreement of September 1985 gave the dollar a push after it had already started moving down from its February peak, and the Louvre Agreement in February 1987 attempted to stabilize the dollar close to its new, lower, levels. Here, and at the annual IMF meetings, Lawson was in his element as he sketched out grand designs for world currency reform.

For Britain to join the ERM seemed to Lawson to fit well into this wider picture. His proposal came to cabinet in October 1985 and was vetoed by Mrs Thatcher, acting on the advice of Walters, in spite of widespread support from other ministers and the Bank of England. It was a crucial moment at which to seek to stabilize the exchange rate because the sharp fall in oil prices that had just begun was to pull the 'petro-pound' down. After the decision not to join the ERM the pound fell by 18 per cent in effective-rate terms between the third quarter of 1985 and the fourth quarter of 1986, which reversed much of the benefit of lower oil prices to inflation, even though it made UK manufactured exports more competitive.

Lawson, who was Energy Secretary from September 1981 to June 1983, had been thinking about the 're-entry' problem for the UK as oil production declined, although neither he nor anyone else could have foreseen how rapidly the oil price would fall, creating similar difficulties. He told a Cambridge energy conference in April 1984:

> Once oil production is past its peak, it is reasonable to expect that there will be some return to the traditional trade pattern of a surplus in manufacturing and invisibles offsetting deficits in food, basic materials and, eventually, fuel. This will probably require a real exchange rate lower than it is today. But this does not necessarily mean that the nominal exchange rate has to fall. The real exchange rate can also adjust by better productivity performance and greater restraint on pay. Policy will need to be conducted to make it more likely that the adjustment will occur in that way.

The RPI increase fell to only 2.4 per cent in August 1986. It was understated by nearly one percentage point by the inclusion of mortgage interest at a time of falling interest rates, and it then rose by two percentage points over the next year. Consumer prices in other major countries such as West Germany and Japan were static or falling, and the UK missed its chance to lock into the ERM at a low and stable inflation rate. Although the GDP deflator rose by only 2.7 per cent in 1986, this was due mainly to the fall in the price of North Sea oil. The deflator for non-oil GDP rose by about 6 per cent. Manufacturers took advantage of the fall in energy costs to notch up profit margins sharply (see page 192). The fall in unemployment, which began in mid-1986, would have been slower with a higher exchange rate but, like the fall in inflation, more lasting.

Little did the Treasury Committee know how ironic its comment on the 1985 Autumn Statement must have sounded to the Chancellor. It said: 'A policy which centred upon holding the money supply to some specified target rate of growth seems to have shifted towards concentrating upon the exchange rate.' What was true of the Chancellor's inclinations was less so of the Prime Minister's decisions. The £M3 target was suspended in October. The 'cosmetic' solution of over-funding in the gilts market to curb the growth of £M3 was abandoned because of the distortions caused to the financial system, so it was increasing by nearly twice the top end of its 5–9 per cent target range. There was to be no exchange-rate target to replace it. M0 ('little M0') and money GDP proved inadequate substitutes.

In March 1986 £M3 was dragged out of its coffin for a last death-ride. Unlike El Cid, riding dead in the saddle at the head of his troops to his final victory, it impressed nobody. In the 1986 MTFS it was given a range of 11–15 per cent for the coming year, but 'illustrative ranges for future years are not given, because the uncertainties surrounding its velocity trend are too great'. Lawson tried to explain away the high figures in his Budget speech by remarking: 'Throughout the 1980s broad money has grown far faster than money GDP – experience has demonstrated that this has not posed a threat to inflation.'

Lawson told the Treasury Committee that the target set for £M3 the year before had been too low. The Committee's report commented: 'Scepticism at the continued use of £M3 as a target aggregate stems in part from the fact that the authorities now seem to have virtually no control over it. A very high £M3 target was set so that the authorities could be assured of achieving growth within the target range.' In the end even the 11–15 per cent range was not high enough, and the last £M3 target was overshot by over 3 per cent (see table 9). After that £M3 went out of favour, to the point where, in July 1989, the Bank of England announced that it would no longer publish £M3 statistics. The last straw in financial innovation was the Abbey National's change in status from building society to bank, which overnight would have increased £M3 by over 10 per cent because it covered bank but not building society deposits. M4 and M5, which included both bank and building society deposits, had become more appropriate measures of broad money, but they were not used as targets. No more hostages were given to fortune.

Leigh-Pemberton demonstrated in a lecture in October 1986, published in the Bank's December *Quarterly Bulletin*, that the overshoots in £M3 had been due mainly to cash holdings by the financial institutions, which had little to do with inflation in the economy. Speaking in the last year of the £M3 target, he commented: 'It is ... perfectly fair to ask whether in these circumstances a broad money target continues to serve a useful purpose.' He concluded on a cautious note: 'It would be just as unwise to pay insufficient regard to the behaviour of broad money ... as it would be to lay too much or too precise emphasis upon it.'

In the 1986 Budget Lawson was able to announce success in meeting the objective of 2 per cent of GDP for the PSBR for the year just ending. The targets for the next four years were notched down by ¼ per cent, allowing a cut of 1 per cent in interest rates, even after a cut in the basic rate of income tax from 30 to 29 per cent – the first since the 1979 budget. The main focus was the new money GDP objectives.

'Economic policy,' it was stated in the 1986 MTFS, 'is set in a nominal framework in which public expenditure is controlled in cash terms and money GDP growth is gradually reduced by monetary and fiscal policy. As the growth of money GDP declines, inflation is squeezed out, and the division of money GDP between output growth and inflation is improved.' Lawson noted in his Budget speech that the rate of growth of money GDP had been halved in the previous six years and that the increase of 8½ per cent set for 1985–6 had been overshot by under 1 per cent. The Treasury Committee commented: 'The Government seems to have an inflation objective rather than a pure money GDP aim or objective ... Monetary policy as originally propounded is in abeyance. Implicitly it has been replaced by an exchange-rate and interest-rate policy.'

The Committee was reacting to a passage in Lawson's

Mansion House speech in October 1985, when the £M3 target was suspended. 'The acid test of monetary policy,' he said, 'is its record in reducing inflation. Those who wish to join in the debate about the intricacies of different measures of money and the implications they may have for the future are welcome to do so. But at the end of the day the position is clear and unambiguous. The inflation rate is judge and jury.'

The Government clearly wished to minimize inflation and to maximize real growth within the money GDP framework, with medium-term objectives of 3 per cent for the former and 2½ per cent for the latter (see page 23). It was not clear to what extent the authorities intended to act on either objective independently by means of other policies so as to keep to the figure set. In particular, there was no clear policy for either interest rates or exchange rates except that, here again, there sometimes appeared to be a trade-off within the framework called 'monetary conditions'. In this case a one-point movement of the interest rate in one direction was roughly equivalent to a four-point movement of the effective exchange rate in the other. Unfortunately, like growth and inflation, the exchange rate and the interest rate often moved in the same direction and not in contrary motion.

In its Autumn Statement report in 1986 the Treasury Committee, quoted in a *Financial Times* leading article, summed it up: 'Monetary policy is uncertain because the Government wishes both to prevent interest rates from rising and the exchange rate from falling ... The danger is that the Government, by not committing itself firmly to either objective, may weaken market confidence to such a point that neither is achieved.' The Committee had been impressed by the Governor of the Bank of England's comparison of the build-up of liquidity with an 'overhanging glacier' that might melt into a flood of demand if high interest rates did not keep it frozen as savings deposits.

By the 1987 Budget it had become evident that, if inflation rather than monetary aggregates was the target of monetary policy, short-term interest rates and not fiscal policy was the chosen instrument on the grounds that they could be 'varied more frequently'. Fiscal policy was assigned to the medium-term tasks of holding public expenditure down, cutting taxes and at the same time reducing the PSBR, thanks to the buoyancy of the revenue induced by an acceleration of economic growth. Yet Meade, in advocating money GDP targets, had proposed flexible taxes or National Insurance contributions as the instrument by which to achieve them. The PSBR was simply set at 1 per cent of GDP for five years, having come in well below its 1¾ per cent objective in 1986–7. In the Budget speech Lawson congratulated himself on facing out his critics: 'Had I or my predecessor at any time heeded the advice of our so-called expansionist critics, the British economy would never have been in the unprecedentedly favourable position it is in today.'

The Treasury Committee was worried because inflation was rising, but Lawson dismissed it in his evidence as 'a slight blip upwards', which at that stage is all that it was. He reaffirmed, 'Over the medium and longer term the Government's objective is zero inflation.' The Committee commented, 'There seems to be considerable uncertainty about the extent to which bank lending and the demand for credit generally respond to changes in short-term interest rates,' even though Lawson had reassured it that the excessive growth of credit was relatively harmless because it had gone mainly in mortgages. Lawson was riding high. He said that a PSBR at 1 per cent of GDP 'will ensure that public debt does not rise as a share of GDP. This is the modern equivalent of the balanced-budget doctrine.' RPI inflation had risen to only 4.2 per cent in April, and the rosy picture of the economy played a big part in the election victory of June 1987.

Flying blind into the storm

A severe test of monetary policy came with the October 1987 stock-market crash. The Treasury reacted by cutting bank base rates by one and a half percentage points to 8½ per cent before letting them rise again. When Nicholas Budgen, MP, asked Lawson to explain during his Autumn Statement appearance before the Treasury Committee, the reply was: 'Obviously interest rates are something which I watch carefully all the time and when I think they ought to go up they go up, and when I think they should come down they come down.'

Budgen: 'I thought they were decided by markets.'

Lawson: 'No, that would be an abandonment of monetary policy and that I am not prepared to do.'

The Treasury, unable to reconcile monetary targets and the free market in money, jettisoned them both in favour of politically administered interest rates.

It was in early 1987 that Lawson began to 'shadow' the D-mark exchange rate but without being able to admit it openly because of the Prime Minister's opposition. He did, however, tell the Treasury Committee, 'Keeping the pound in line with the D-mark is likely to be over the medium term a pretty good anti-inflation discipline.' When Giles Radice, MP, quoted the Prime Minister as saying, 'There is no specific range – we are always free,' Lawson suggested that he should ask the Prime Minister to appear before the Committee if he wanted further elucidation.

'Shadowing' the D-mark, far from allowing Lawson the autocratic power over interest rates to which he professed, caused him to bring them down by stages, from 11 per cent at the beginning of 1987 to 9 per cent by March 1988, in order to prevent the pound from rising above the DM3.00 barrier. Even though the impact of interest rates on the demand for credit was uncertain, as Robin Leigh-Pemberton pointed out in his Mais Lecture in May 1987, it seemed more certain that lower interest rates would stimulate the demand for credit than that higher interest rates would damp it down.

The authorities were also intervening massively in the foreign exchange market, although it was not clear whether they were acting under the Louvre Agreement to support the dollar or as country members of the ERM. The $22 billion addition, which doubled the reserves, was arguably a useful war-chest for the future, and their impact on monetary growth was almost entirely sterilized by the issue of gilt-edged at a time when fewer such issues were needed to fund the shrinking PSBR.

It was unfortunate that during this period Lawson was engaging in massive income-tax cuts as the grand pay-off for the patience of the people who had been promised low taxes for so long. Tax revenue continued to exceed even the most optimistic forecasts, so there was for a short time a Fortunato's purse effect, allowing taxes to be cut without the tax burden falling and easing the fiscal stance. However, what ERM rules would have required to offset easier monetary policy was not just static but tighter fiscal policy. By the 1988 Budget to cut another two percentage points off income tax to get it to the magic figure of 25p seemed not only risky from the point of view of domestic demand but also politically redundant, since the Conservatives had already won the June 1987 election on the strength of the 2p off income tax in the 1987 Budget.

Mrs Thatcher intervened a few days before the 1988 Budget and forced Lawson to uncap the pound, with the words 'You can't buck the market,' although that was what he had been doing with some success for a whole year. The pound floated upwards, and Lawson unwisely continued to cut interest rates, which reached a floor of $7\frac{1}{2}$ per cent briefly in May, in an attempt to brake its rise. Since he took the correct view that the rise was unlikely to be sustainable, he could have let it go even higher for a short period in the knowledge that the pound would fall again, as it did. Mrs Thatcher was later repeatedly and inaccurately to blame the full cut in interest rates on 'shadowing' the D-mark, when in fact she had brought that policy to an end two months before rates were cut to $7\frac{1}{2}$ per cent. Once again policy was suffering from an interest rate and an exchange rate both floating aimlessly.

In his 1988 Budget speech Lawson defiantly proclaimed

that 'exchange rates play a central role in domestic monetary decisions as well as in international policy co-operation'. The buoyancy of the revenue and the overshoot in public spending restraint had, for the first time since Roy Jenkins's Chancellorship in 1969–70, put the Budget into a surplus of ¾ per cent of GDP in 1987–8 against the objective of a 1 per cent PSBR. The surplus, called the public-sector debt repayment (PSDR), was targeted to continue for another year, then return to balance. Lawson threw over his previous notice of a 1 per cent PSBR as a 'modern version' of a balanced budget and proclaimed: 'A balanced budget is a valuable discipline for the medium term. Having achieved it, I intend to stick to it. In other words, henceforth a zero PSBR will be the norm.' Or, as he put it in the Red Book: 'The strength of the economy coupled with fiscal prudence has enabled the Government to achieve a balanced budget on a sustainable basis.'

The MTFS in the Red Book acknowledged that the main monetary objective, money GDP, which had overshot slightly during its first two years in operation, was well over the top in 1987–8, with an estimate of a 9¾ per cent increase, compared with the set figure of 7½ per cent (it later turned out to be 10¾ per cent after the statistical revisions). This was justified on the grounds that the GDP deflator (the rate of inflation) at 5 per cent was only half a percentage point over the objective, while real growth, at 4½ per cent, was 1½ percentage points over. It was a better division of money GDP, with supply improvements boosting growth more than inflation.

The Treasury Committee was unimpressed by this argument. 'The 1987 out-turn for the GDP deflator,' it reported, 'is the same as the out-turn for the 1983 figure.' In other words, inflation had remained stuck at 5 per cent during Mrs Thatcher's second term. The Committee showed that the MTFS for reducing inflation was three years behind schedule and published a table showing that, for four years running, a 3 per cent inflation rate had been shown as occurring in not less than three years' time (see table 7).

Lawson brushed aside such comments by telling the Committee: 'The more buoyant the economy is, the stronger the inflation forces tend to be, therefore it is not surprising if the progress that the anti-inflationary policy makes is a little slower.' Leigh-Pemberton was more concerned: 'We have ... in this country an indifference towards inflation at the 4 or 5 per cent figure, which does not prevail in Germany or Japan.'

The Committee was worried not just that inflation had not come down but that it might go up because of overheating due to excess demand and uncontrolled credit. 'We questioned Treasury officials, the Governor of the Bank of England and the Chancellor on the problems of overheating after the Budget measures. None of them saw it as a significant danger. Nevertheless, we consider that the Government's Budget strategy contains an element of risk.' The author's evidence as a specialist adviser, published with the Committee's report, read: 'The case for expanding the economy by means of a fiscal boost now seems weak in view of the private-sector credit boom and the twin dangers of inflation and external deficit.'

It was clear that the Treasury was 'flying blind', because the official statistics were so inadequate. Revisions to the figures for domestic demand were always in the upwards direction but did not come in in time to prevent the forecast for the coming year, on which policy was based, from being biased downwards by the unrevised statistics for the most recent period. The Treasury responded to the Committee's criticisms by setting up an inquiry into official statistics headed by an assistant secretary, Stephen Pickford. This resulted in numerous improvements to the collection and departmental organization of official statistics. It came too late to reveal the overheating of domestic demand that all the Committee's official witnesses had failed to spot.

The Committee was also unimpressed by Lawson's balanced Budget. 'The simplicity of the balanced Budget concept may have certain attractions,' it reported. 'It appears to us, however, to have been fastened upon almost accidentally as the latest in a series of "appropriate destinations" for the PSBR.' The report then returned to the point about the lack of any close connection between the PSBR and money creation that had been revealed in the Committee's 1981 report *Monetary Policy*. 'Although the government now has a fully funded public sector which neutralizes money creation from public-sector transactions, the private sector continues to borrow voraciously.'

The Treasury had discovered that, in the unfamiliar situation of a Budget surplus, which tended to take money out of the economy, the repayment of public-sector debt was putting the money back into the private sector. It was not exactly creating money, but it was neutralizing the withdrawal of money that would otherwise have occurred. As in the early 1980s, over-funding came to the rescue, but in this case it meant not redeeming gilts to the full extent of the surplus or replacing them with Treasury bills. This helped to maintain gilt yields and curbed monetary growth, while leaving credit unaffected.

During the early 1980s there seemed to be a trade-off between the reduction of public-sector borrowing and the increase in private-sector borrowing, so that together the two came to a constant total. Borrowing was being privatized in accordance with the Government's wish to switch economic activity away from the public into the private sector. By the late 1980s it had become evident that the growth of private-sector borrowing – 12 per cent of GDP in 1987–9 – was far in excess of any conceivable contraction of public-sector borrowing or increase in public-sector debt repayment. The idea of a changing mix of monetary and fiscal policy still giving a constant anti-inflationary pressure had to be abandoned. Interest rates, instead of being lowered as a result of the contraction of public borrowing, had to be raised in order to cause a contraction of private borrowing.

It would have been possible to pursue a tighter fiscal policy, but the unprecedented imbalances – surplus in the public finances, huge deficit in the private sector – would have made it difficult for the Thatcher Government. It would have meant the postponement or reversal of tax cuts – which went against supply-side principles – and the repayment, within the foreseeable future, of the national debt, an idea that rather appealed to Mrs Thatcher, if to few of her supporters in the City who lived by trading it. It would have meant a return to the fiscal austerity of the 1981 Budget – and possibly also to its successful outcome against the odds. As it was, the 1988 Budget put exactly the same into the economy through tax cuts – £4.3 billion – as the 1981 Budget had taken out of it in tax increases.

In his appearance before the Treasury Committee after the 1988 Autumn Statement Lawson defended himself against the charge that had been made by Edward Heath that he was a 'one-club golfer' because short-term interest rates were his only policy instrument. Tax changes, he said, were 'extremely inflexible ... very slow acting ... and the reversal of them is extremely complicated'. However, it was evident that high interest rates were having a severe impact on relatively small sectors of the economy – recent house-buyers, construction and property companies and capital goods industries – while tax increases would have had a much less severe impact on a much wider range of people and were thus preferable in terms of fair sharing of the burden of adjustment.

Lawson admitted to a 'demand problem' but was still trying to pursue simultaneously both the objectives contained in money GDP. 'Curbing inflation has been at the heart of our policy ... But that has not been inconsistent with a good growth performance.' Ever confident, he told the Committee: 'The slowing down of the growth of demand is a relatively simple and straightforward task.' With some justice, he blamed the inclusion of mortgage interest in the RPI for his difficulties, calling it 'extremely perverse and inimical to policy': 'It is a little bit absurd that a tightening in monetary policy leads to an apparent increase in inflation.' He said that the RPI advisory committee, which had reported in 1986, had rejected his views for inadequate reasons, but it was never clear why he did not impose them. It would have been easier to do so in 1986, when the RPI was lower than the index excluding mortgage interest, than when it was higher, as it was in the second half of 1988.

The Committee was scathing about the MTFS. Of the GDP deflator it said: 'The out-turn for 1988 at 6¼ per cent is more than double the projection made in 1985 ... Tactics now appear to change so frequently that it is difficult to discern the underlying policy ... The money GDP objectives have been repeatedly modified and exceeded.' This was borne out in the 1989 MTFS, when it turned out that the money GDP objective for 1988–9 had again been exceeded by over 3 per cent, but this time the overshoot was nearly all in terms of extra inflation rather than extra growth, with the GDP deflator rising by nearly 7½ rather than 4½ per cent.

As always, the good news came from the fiscal rather than the monetary side. The PSDR for 1988–9 had come to 3 per cent of GDP, far more than the ¾ per cent budgeted for. However, this did not represent the same degree of fiscal tightening, since some of the overshoot came from unexpectedly high sales of public assets. For future years the PSDR was to move back towards balance, so the programme was for fiscal loosening. Lawson explained in his Budget speech: 'To go further than this, and seek to achieve the maximum possible repayment of public debt ... would mean deferring for a long time the benefits of a reduction in the burden of taxation.' Some of his critics thought, however, that this was exactly what the situation demanded.

If Lawson was unrepentant on fiscal policy, he was apologetic on monetary policy before the Treasury Committee after the 1989 Budget. 'We started 1988 with too low a level of interest rates and a monetary policy that was with the benefit of hindsight too loose.' However, he justified his decision in March 1988 to extend to August of that year the deadline for the termination of double tax relief for mortgages for two-person unmarried households, on the grounds that to do otherwise would have been unfair and that the surge in mortgage demand was only temporary.

Lawson resigned in October 1989 because of Mrs Thatcher's refusal to sack her economic adviser, Sir Alan Walters, whose views on the EMS she clearly preferred to his. He revealed in his post-resignation speech in the House of Commons that he had advocated ERM entry since 1985 and that he was in favour of an independent Bank of England – the policy advocated in 1977 in the pre-manifesto pamphlet *The Right Approach to the Economy* (see page 28). He told the House of Commons on 31 October 1990: 'There is, I believe, one other way in which anti-inflationary credibility might be enhanced in the eyes of the market and that is why, a year ago, I proposed to my Right Hon. friend the Prime Minister a fully worked-out scheme for the independence of the Bank of England.' It would, he explained, be a buttress to, rather than a substitute for, ERM membership. He was followed as Chancellor by John Major, who was moved from the Foreign Secretaryship after a tenure of only a few months.

Major abandoned the monetarist doctrine on his first appearance before the Treasury Committee following the 1989 Autumn Statement. Referring to the quantity theory that control of the money supply will reduce the rate of inflation, he said: 'That used to be the theory ... the Government may have followed some time ago. It certainly has not been the theory that the Government have followed during any period I have been in the Treasury.' He then admitted, with remarkable frankness, some of his predecessor's mistakes.

'It is, I think, clear in retrospect,' he said, 'though it was less clear at the time, that demand probably grew at a faster pace than was desirable right the way through 1987 and 1988.' He dealt with the aftermath of the October 1987 Stock Exchange crash. 'Because we did not wish to disturb the growth pattern, and at the time of the Stock Exchange crash believing that there would be a very substantial slowdown ... we relaxed monetary policy ... In retrospect it is clear that we relaxed monetary policy perhaps at precisely the moment that we should have made it a little more severe.' He concluded by referring to the end of multiple mortgage relief. 'We were concerned about the social impact of the ending of multiple mortgage relief without any period of warning ... It was ... a policy misjudgement that added to the growth of the housing market on the back of which there was considerable borrowing for other purposes.'

Major's first Budget differed from those of his predecessor in being slightly restrictive in its tax impact – more than slightly, if the increase in the new poll tax over the previous year's domestic rates was included. Owing to the slow-down in the economy, the PSDR for the year then ending had come to 1¼ rather than the planned 2¾ per cent of GDP and was set to remain there in 1990–91, then relaxing the fiscal stance to move to balance by 1993–4. This Major presented as maintaining a 'tight fiscal policy', but there was no significant further tightening, and he restated Lawson's objections to using fiscal rather than monetary policy changes for short-term economic management. He examined, but rejected, the case for a return to direct controls on money and credit or to a broad money target.

The MTFS, on its tenth anniversary, appeared to pay lip-service to the principles of monetarism with which it set out in March 1980. 'Inflation occurs when monetary growth is excessive: "too much money chasing too few goods" is a traditional characterization. That is why the rate at which money is growing is an essential concern of economic policy.' Yet, a few sentences later, monetarism was rejected again: 'Growth in the money stock need not be inflationary.'

The Treasury Committee, on the contrary, celebrated the tenth anniversary of the MTFS with a criticism: 'The objective of zero inflation remains as elusive as ever, as does a low and constant inflation rate.' It was also critical of the Chancellor's reliance on short-term interest rates. 'The time which it has taken for successive increases in interest rates to restrain demand calls into question the effectiveness of interest-rates policy on its own.' In discussing entry into the ERM, it commented: 'In future the Chancellor will have to rely more on fiscal policy.'

The OECD, in its 1989/90 *UK Economic Survey*, offered equally far-reaching censure of the MTFS.

Although the Government's strategy has resulted in rates of inflation significantly lower than in the 1970s, in recent years major policy objectives have been missed by a wide margin ... The output/inflation split has deteriorated sharply. As the MTFS was drawn up to enhance the Government's credibility and to act as a disciplining device for inflation expectations, the failure to come to grips with the inflation problem would threaten to undermine the framework's usefulness. Another problem is that, especially since the abandonment of broad money targets, the strategy lacks a sufficiently credible anchor for monetary policy. This has stimulated the public debate on possible gains from joining the ERM of the EMS.

The outcome of the money GDP objectives can also be judged by means of the split of the money GDP change between output and prices (see table 11). Part of the Conservatives' objection to the Labour Government was that too much of the increase in demand was monetary, not real. The split in the 1970s averaged 18 per cent output and 82 per cent prices. In the first two full years of the Thatcher Government it regressed to the 1974 position of −13 per cent output and 113 per cent prices. It then improved to 52 per cent output and 48 per cent prices in 1986 (3.9 per cent growth, 3.6 per cent inflation). This was the year following the sharp cut in oil prices. After that the split deteriorated again by 1989 to 23 per cent growth, 77 per cent inflation, the worst result since 1982. However, the average for 1980–89 was 27 per cent output, 73 per cent prices, five percentage points better than that for 1970–79. The rate of output growth was virtually the same at 2.3 per cent, but the inflation rate in the 1970s, 12.9 per cent, was 70 per cent higher than the 7.6 per cent of the 1980s.

Major, like Lawson, had for some time been a supporter of ERM entry. Although Mrs Thatcher agreed to the principle of entry at the June 1989 Madrid summit, for some time afterwards it was not clear when she would agree that the time was ripe; it was the doctrine of unripe time that had kept the UK out ever since Lawson put the proposal to the cabinet in October 1985. Mrs Thatcher, in an act of political death-bed repentance, finally allowed Major to take the UK into the ERM on 8 October 1990 with the unwise condition – aimed at the following week's Conservative Party conference – that base rates were cut at the same time to 14 per cent from the 15 per cent level where they had been for the previous year. Although the MTFS presented ERM entry as complementing rather than replacing existing monetary policy, it was the end of an era that had lasted over ten years. The ERM was to provide a totally new framework for monetary policy, in which a fixed exchange rate became the main anti-inflation instrument and domestic interest rates became subordinated to it.

Fiscal success, monetary failure

Much of the fall in inflation in the UK in the early 1980s was due to the fall in world commodity prices, as Wilfred Beckerman was among the first to point out. It was not until 1987 that a Treasury economist, Penelope Rowlatt, was allowed to publish a paper pointing this out. The decline in the price of oil and other commodities caused inflation to fall in all industrial countries and had nothing to do with British policy. The reason why inflation fell faster in the UK at first, and later rose in the UK while remaining low elsewhere, had everything to do with British policy. The effects of monetary policy on inflation were not those intended because it operated through high unemployment (see page 235).

The main success of the MTFS was the reduction of the PSBR by $6\frac{1}{4}$ per cent of GDP between 1979–80 and 1989–90 (see table 12). Although the PSBR rose because of the recession caused by monetary policy in 1980–81, the tough 1981 Budget and the subsequent recovery made it relatively easy to reduce it with the help of drastic cuts in public expenditure as a percentage of GDP. PSBR objectives were achieved more often than not and sometimes improved upon (see table 19). While in the first half of the 1980s PSBR objectives tended to be relaxed as the year to which they related approached, they were generally tightened in the second half. Thanks to the buoyancy of tax revenue, almost every Budget contained some cuts in taxation, with the important exception of the 1981 Budget (see table 8). The fiscal stance, judged by the reduction of the PSBR from the previous year's outcome, was restrictive in almost every year since 1986–7 but then became neutral or slightly looser.

The reduction in the PSBR was achieved by raising the tax burden as often as by lowering it, while reducing the public-expenditure burden. However, the addition of privatization proceeds slightly offset the reduction of general government expenditure and of the PSBR, adding about one percentage point to the PSBR in the second half of the decade, to give a somewhat larger true financial deficit. The change from a PSBR of 5 per cent of GDP in 1979–80 to $-1\frac{1}{4}$ per cent in 1989–90 was the result of a 1 per cent of GDP increase in government revenue and a $5\frac{1}{4}$ per cent of GDP fall in government expenditure.

The tightening of the fiscal stance in most Budgets from 1981 to 1988 permitted a loosening of monetary policy from its peak of tightness in 1981, with each Budget from 1981 right up to 1988 accompanied by a cut in interest rates (see table 8). However, there were sharp rises in interest rates between Budgets, and at the beginning, middle and end of the 1980s, due to external as well as domestic influences, (see figure 2). Interest rates had an uncertain effect on monetary aggregates, which in their turn had little apparent correlation with changes in inflation. In only two out of eight years were broad money targets hit in spite of increases in targets, changes in target aggregates, base drift and overfunding (see table 9). Financial liberalization was incompatible with monetary control and not sufficiently predictable to allow broad money targets to be formulated or achieved. The narrow money target, M0, was too easy to hit, but even that was overshot by the end of the decade.

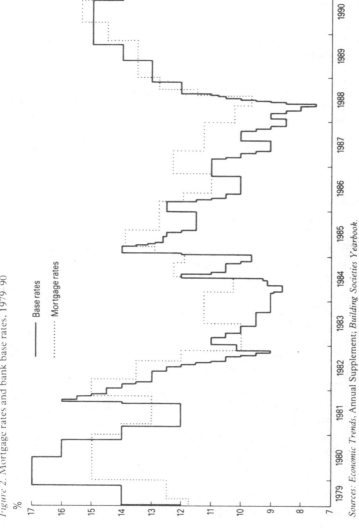

Figure 2. Mortgage rates and bank base rates, 1979–90

Sources: *Economic Trends*, Annual Supplement; *Building Societies Yearbook*.

Figure 3. RPI inflation, 1969–89

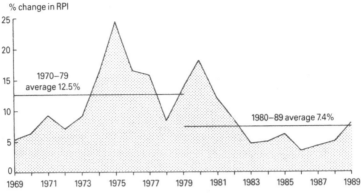

Source: *Economic Trends.*

Interest rates averaged 11.8 per cent during the decade and fell to single figures on average only in election years 1983 (continuing into 1984) and 1987 (see table 13). The Government managed monetary and fiscal policy so as to help secure its own re-election for a second and a third term. Real interest rates averaged 4.1 per cent, fluctuating widely between −2 per cent in 1980 and 8 per cent in 1986. The effective exchange rate ended the 1980s 13.5 per cent below its starting level. After rising over 10 per cent in 1980–81, it fell for most of the time until 1988. Monetary conditions, the combination of the exchange rate and the interest rate, tightened at the beginning, middle and end of the decade but were relaxed in 1981–4, 1986 and 1987. M0 (narrow money) rose by 5 per cent a year, M4 (broad money) by 15½ per cent, the former at two-thirds, the latter at double, the pace of inflation.

Inflation, as measured by the RPI, rose by 7.3 per cent a year, so that the price level doubled during the 1980s compared with 12.5 per cent during the 1970s, when the price level was multiplied by 3.3 (see figure 3 and table 14). The inclusion of mortgage interest both made the RPI more volatile and added an average of 0.5 per cent a year to it over the decade as the stock of housing debt rose. The RPI, without mortgage interest, rose at a pace similar to that of the consumers' expenditure deflator. UK import prices rose by 4.8 per cent in sterling terms, less than the domestic GDP deflator, which rose by 7.3 per cent a year. The anti-inflationary effect of commodity-price deceleration in every year except 1980 was offset by the depreciation of the pound for most of the time after 1981.

The GDP deflator rose at a similar pace to the RPI. Within it the rise in unit business income costs, at 8.1 per cent, was somewhat higher than that of unit labour costs, at 6.9 per cent. Business incomes accounted for 2.8 per cent, labour for 4.5 per cent of the 7.3 per cent average increase in the GDP deflator, compared with 2.6 per cent and 4.7 per cent had they both risen at the same rate. Average earnings rose by 9.9 per cent, however, 2.4 per cent faster than the RPI, and were notably high in real terms, not coming down in response to falls in inflation (see page 232). Their upwards effect on prices was offset by lower use of labour and higher productivity (see table 3). Since the influence of business income and labour costs on inflation is more clearly established than that of monetary growth, we shall examine government policy in these areas in chapters 6 and 7.

The UK, together with the USA, reduced inflation faster than France and Italy (see table 15) because monetary policy caused a more severe recession and unemployment had a dampening effect on pay and prices, at least when it was rising sharply. The ERM countries, relying on a stable exchange rate while the UK and the USA made more use of interest rates and exchange-rate appreciation, achieved a more permanent reduction in inflation than the UK. The UK's 7 per cent average inflation rate was very close to that of France and the EC average but higher than the OECD average of 5½ per cent, which was similar to the US figure. West Germany achieved the 2.9 per cent figure over a decade, which remained a distant ambition for the UK, while Japan did even better with 2.2 per cent.

While Mrs Thatcher's first term succeeded in getting inflation down to 4 per cent with Sir Geoffrey Howe as Chancellor, her second term, with Nigel Lawson as Chancellor, did no better than mark time. Her third term, with Nigel Lawson as Chancellor for the first three years, was marked by classic overheating of demand, which pushed inflation back into double figures, to the same level as when she took office. The UK returned to stop–go, although with a long stretch of go between two stops.

The MTFS was weakened by its shaky foundations in monetary theory. It was just as plausible to say that prices or money GDP caused money as that money caused prices or money GDP. Even if money could be controlled, it might have no effect on prices, and if inflation could be tackled by other means, monetary growth would slow down as a consequence. When things were going well the framework of the MTFS helped to augment confidence, but it became devoid of meaningful content at moments when it was most needed.

The MTFS was more successful in fiscal than in monetary policy. Public borrowing was reduced, but it was difficult to control money while private credit was being liberalized. After the failure of monetary targets in the first half of the 1980s, the wrong decision not to join the ERM was taken in 1985. The use of money GDP created further confusion and was ineffective in controlling either real growth or inflation. The right decision to join the ERM was made in 1990 but only after inflation had reached a level from which even the discipline of the fixed exchange rate will have difficulty in reducing it. The Government's decision in 1985 to target inflation directly rather than via monetary targets was correct, but short-term interest rates on their own were inadequate to achieve it and needed to be supplemented by fiscal and other types of policy within the framework of the ERM.

When Mrs Thatcher came to office in May 1979 the RPI inflation rate had just reached double figures at 10.3 per cent. After falling briefly to 2.4 per cent in August 1986, inflation again rose into double figures, to a peak of 10.9 per cent, in October 1990, the month before she left office. The battle against inflation was a Pyrrhic victory, won at an unacceptable cost in unemployment, followed by a self-inflicted defeat that could have been avoided by a more cautious management of demand.

Mrs Thatcher has claimed that there are other achievements to be set against this disappointing performance (see page 256). This means that, in effect, the Government departed from the top priority it originally gave to the conquest of inflation in order to pursue other objectives. The achievement of those other objectives too has been jeopardized by the failure to consolidate the progress originally made against inflation. Membership of the ERM will make it more difficult to depart from the battle against inflation in search of new, more popular, contests. By the same token, it will deprive British politicians of their freedom to juggle with priorities in the search for electoral advantage.

3 Public Expenditure: the enemy country

> 'Monetarism is not enough . . . unless there is also the essential reduction of the state sector and the essential encouragement of enterprise.'
> Sir Keith Joseph, 'Monetarism is not Enough',
> Stockton Lecture, 1976

Pick it up, put it down and shake it all around

The Thatcher Government's attitude to public expenditure always suffered from inner conflict after the formative Opposition period of the late 1970s. At the level of free-market ideology Mrs Thatcher, Sir Keith Joseph and some of their advisers saw the public sector as an enemy country to be conquered, deprived of much of its territory and put under the yoke of the Treasury. Nationalized industries, public-sector trade unions, Labour-controlled urban local authorities, autonomous bureaucratic structures in health and education and all kinds of 'quango' were to be dealt with in this manner. At the level of populist electoral appeal, however, most of the main public services were to be protected and developed in a new, more efficient, style. Social security, health, education, defence and law and order were all named as priorities. It followed that anti-public-expenditure ideology could be put into practice only by means of disproportionately radical cuts in non-priority areas such as housing, trade and industry and transport.

The public sector was seen as a territory where the writ of the free market or, in most cases, that of the price mechanism did not run. Even the nationalized industries, which were in the market sector of the economy, were generally both subsidized and supervised by Whitehall and were not subject to the disciplines of competition. Those public services that were not in the market sector were to be improved by free-market influences in two ways. First, a small but influential private sector in areas such as health and education was to be encouraged to expand and to set standards for the public sector to follow. Second, 'shadow' market forces were to be introduced into public services to make them more efficient, reducing input costs and raising the quality of output.

The desire to open the public sector to market forces did not fit easily with the aim of curbing its expenditure within strict Treasury limits. The idea of planning in the private sector had been discarded by both major political parties yet was being applied with a new rigour in a public sector that was supposed to behave more like the private sector. The solution to this dilemma was to encourage the public sector to become more efficient and thus to limit its spending by techniques borrowed from private-sector financial management.

The reason for tightening spending controls was that public expenditure had its part to play at a more technical level of economic policy, alongside the monetarist doctrine. When Sir Keith Joseph said, 'Monetarism is not enough,' the title of his lecture at the London Business School in January 1976, he meant not that spiritual values mattered too but that the growth of public expenditure as well as that of the money supply had to be curbed. 'Monetarism is not enough . . . unless there is also the essential reduction of the state sector and the essential encouragement of enterprise.'

Monetarism was a language with two dialects, the American and the British. In the American version tax cuts could be financed by a huge deficit covered by Treasury bond issues. The purist monetarist Milton Friedman told the Treasury Select Committee of the House of Commons in 1980 that public-sector borrowing had no bearing on monetary control because it could be financed in the bond market. In the English version of monetarism, however, the PSBR was an undesirable source of money creation, and tax cuts could be financed only by even larger public-expenditure reductions. While the Americans theorized about a balanced Budget and failed miserably when they belatedly legislated for it, the British set about achieving it.

The belief that public expenditure should be reduced overrode the Keynesian view, prevalent until the 1970s, that it should be used as an economic regulator, which had the disadvantage of causing disruption to important public services and capital investment programmes. This Keynesian view had in any case been modified by the discovery of 'automatic stabilizers', which cause public expenditure to rise faster in recessions and more slowly in recoveries without any need for the Government to intervene. Income support for the unemployed is an obvious example. The Thatcher Government was unusual in being prepared even to override the automatic stabilizers, cutting public expenditure in slump and increasing it in boom.

The Conservative view was influenced by the experience of the Labour Government in 1974–9 and by a seminal work by Robert Bacon and Walter Eltis published and serialized in 1976; *Britain's Economic Problem: Too Few Producers*. Bacon and Eltis argued that the 'non-marketed' share of output had become too great a burden on the 'marketed' sector of the economy because of excessive taxes and subsidies. In *The Right Approach to the Economy* Sir Geoffrey Howe, Sir Keith Joseph, James Prior and David Howell wrote about the Labour Government:

This share [of public expenditure in the national income] was allowed to rise by a staggering 11½ per cent in real terms. The Government's borrowing needs soared to the highest level in our peacetime history, while interest rates soared to record heights as a near-bankrupt Government struggled desperately to persuade people to buy its bonds and finance its deficit. And of course industrial recovery was completely inhibited. The consequences of that period are now before us in the shape of an inflation rate still twice as high as that of our competitors, personal taxes at some of the highest rates in the Western world ... That is why it is so important to reduce the share of the nation's wealth consumed by the state – by central and local government and those agencies and authorities which spend the taxpayer's money but produce nothing ... Our intention is to allow state spending and revenue a significantly smaller percentage slice of the nation's annual output and income each year ... This will be in contrast with Labour's recent panic cuts, which fell too heavily on capital rather than current spending and did great damage to the construction industry.

The incoming Government was also influenced by a well-timed Institute of Economic Affairs seminar held on 6 April 1979, contributions to which were published in September under the title *The Taming of Government*. Lionel Robbins introduced it with some of the classic critiques of the role of government, quoting not only Adam Smith but also Maynard Keynes. He summed up:

'Taming' government implies confining it to the functions only it can perform, notably devising the requisite framework of law ... Government has, in practice, far exceeded those functions and must now be restricted to functions which permit rather than impede the creative activities of the citizen.

One of the key speakers was the American professor Gordon Tullock, a representative of the 'public choice' theory explaining the growth of the public sector, who said:

Bureaucrats can gain from the general growth in government; they therefore use their powers over information, their relative security from dismissal, their ability to deflect instructions, their power as voters and employees to influence political decisions to expand government or obstruct its contraction. Bureaucrats can be disciplined by making them compete among themselves and with outside suppliers by varying their remuneration and limiting their voting powers.

The 1979 manifesto, however, suppressed all mention of

public expenditure, doubtless for fear of losing the votes of some of those bureaucrats to whom Tullock was referring. The main feature of the election campaign was the Conservatives' pledge to honour the findings of the Clegg Commission on public-sector pay set up by the outgoing Labour Government (see page 221).

The new Government's policy was soon made clear in the 1979 Budget speech by Howe, the Chancellor of the Exchequer:

In order to reduce the borrowing requirement and the burden of direct taxation, we must make savings in public spending and roll back the boundaries of the public sector. We are totally committed to improving standards in the public services. But that can be achieved only if the economy is strong in the first place. So that will be our first priority. Finance must determine expenditure, not expenditure finance. Substantial reductions in expenditure can and will be made in the remainder of this financial year.

The order of priorities was, first, to conquer inflation by reducing public expenditure and borrowing, then to stimulate economic growth in the private sector by tax cuts and lower interest rates and finally, to use the fruits of growth to finance selective increases in some public services. The public sector had been 'crowding out' private enterprise; it was now its turn to be crowded out and go to the end of the queue.

The Government's policy was set out in a 'one-off' public-expenditure White Paper (PEWP) in November 1979. 'Public expenditure is at the heart of Britain's economic difficulties,' it began. It called for 'a plan for spending which is not only compatible with the necessary objectives for taxation and borrowing, but is also based on a realistic assessment of the prospects for economic growth'. As the economy was slowing down, this was a statement of the new anti-Keynesian view that public expenditure should move with the economic cycle and not counter to it. If the economy was not going to grow much, if at all, then public expenditure could be prevented from rising as a share of it only by a freeze. 'The Government's economic strategy must be to stabilize public spending for the time being.'

By the time of the regular PEWP in March 1980 the more radical Thatcher tendency had hardened against the relative 'wetness' of Howe and the other ministers who had formulated the moderate 'declining-share' objective of *The Right Approach to the Economy*. 'The Government intend to reduce total public expenditure progressively in volume terms over the next four years, to a level in 1983–4 about 4 per cent lower than in 1979–80.' The priorities were set out: 'Expenditure on defence, law and order, health and social security rises over the survey period. The plans for the industry, energy, trade and employment programmes, housing, education and nationalized industry borrowing are substantially reduced over the survey period.'

Defence had to rise by 3 per cent a year in real terms, owing to a NATO commitment already entered into by the Labour Government. The growth of social security, though accepted as inevitable, was to be curbed by two crucial changes. 'The minimum uprating of long-term benefits will be based on price movements only, rather than the greater of earnings or prices.' The earnings-related supplement to unemployment benefit was also to be abolished. The cuts for industry and trade were an expression of opposition to subsidies. Unlike his departmental colleagues, Sir Keith Joseph, then Secretary of State for Industry, was willing, if not always able, to preside over the dismantling of his own programmes. The cuts in local-authority housing programmes were linked with council-house sales to tenants, the first manifestation of the privatization programme that was to gather momentum in other areas only after the 1983 election. The education cuts were based on the projections of falling school rolls. Hope was held out of further cuts if Mrs Thatcher succeeded in her aim of renegotiating Britain's contribution to the EC budget. The passion concerning the EC budget with which Mrs Thatcher 'handbagged' her European colleagues owed as much to her crusade against public expenditure, whether in Britain or in Brussels, as to her chauvinistic suspicions of European integration.

To implement the cuts a number of structural changes were made. The size of the Civil Service was reduced, although this did not include the much greater numbers in the National Health Service and the local authorities. Departments were encouraged to react to higher-than-planned pay awards by staff cuts, which were supposed to increase efficiency without impairing the level of service. Sir Derek Rayner, a Marks and Spencer executive, was put in charge of a series of scrutinies of Civil Service functions and their costs. New management systems – such as MINIS (Management Information System for Ministers), introduced by Michael Heseltine at the Department of the Environment, and FMI (Financial Management Initiative) – were introduced into Whitehall departments in an attempt to impart the ethos of private-sector corporations. Peter Hennessy coined the term 'Raynerism' for the new wave of cost-effectiveness that spread through Mrs Thatcher's Whitehall. The system of cash limits on blocks of expenditure, which had been introduced by the Labour Government in 1976, was to be extended to cover all future public-expenditure plans, even though many of them, being demand-determined like social security, could not be managed within cash limits as could discretionary expenditures.

By the March 1981 PEWP it was evident that the real cut planned in public expenditure for the year just ending had become a real increase. 'The totals in 1980–81 and future years are higher than previously expected and higher than the Government would wish. The recession and other factors have exerted upward pressure, for example on unemployment benefit and special employment measures.' However, the proposed real cuts of 4 per cent over the next three years were simply postponed by a year. The Treasury hoped to introduce better control by planning in cash terms and abandoning the old volume terms. By March 1982 all future plans were expressed only in cash and not volume terms.

Seemingly arcane distinctions between different accounting conventions had profound effects on the Government's objectives. The Prime Minister was personally involved in the decision to plan in cash. The old volume planning had become discredited because it had been used to justify inflationary increases in salary and other costs in order to meet volume targets. Volume planning was held to be an open-ended licence to spend and made it impossible to plan cash. Since tax revenue and borrowing were in cash, public expenditure had to come into line.

Volume planning was also open to more fundamental objections. Because most public-sector output is not marketed, it is impossible to measure it in the normal way by the prices and quantities at which it is sold, net of the external costs incurred, giving the value added accruing to labour incomes and profits. Public-sector accounts measure only inputs, not outputs. They record what the government buys from the economy rather than what the consumer gets from the government, as in theory they should. Some of the inputs are intermediate output, exchanged between government organizations and private-sector companies, of the kind normally netted out in calculating value added as part of GDP. Labour incomes paid to public employees are, in principle, part of value added, but there are no public-sector profit or rent incomes, except for a few relatively minor charges. Worst of all, there are for the most part no prices, sales figures or recognizable units of output by which public-sector GDP could be estimated. The numerous performance indicators introduced over the last decade to try to measure the efficiency of the public sector have yielded valuable information but few conclusive answers. The question is: if a given number of public-sector employees are increasing their output, or a given output is being produced by fewer public employees, is there an improvement in productivity and economic growth, or is there a fall in the quantity and quality of service provided? There is a similar measurement problem for some private-sector services.

Cash planning was, however, even less reliable as an indicator of public-sector activity than the old volume planning. A strict implementation of cash plans meant that unexpected or unavoidable inflation would cause real cutbacks in politically sensitive priority programmes. 'Cost-terms' (later renamed 'real-terms') planning was the compromise, reluctantly revealed in public by the Treasury only in March 1984. Cash plans had formerly been inflation-adjusted by the 'survey price', or specific deflator, for each type of expenditure so as to give an accurate indication of volumes. Instead the Treasury adjusted all cash plans for inflation by one and the same general index of inflation, the GDP deflator. Unlike the RPI, this is a general measure of home costs and is not influenced by import prices or mortgage interest. It is intended to be an indication of what a programme is costing the Treasury to finance in real terms, by a general yardstick, rather than what level of real service output the programme is giving. The Treasury was reluctant to publish 'cost-terms' plans until 1984 because that would have meant also publishing assumptions about the future course of the GDP deflator (i.e. the inflation rate).

The difference between the general GDP deflator and the deflator specific to each type of expenditure is called the 'relative price effect' (RPE). Although the Treasury published RPEs for public expenditure in general in the PEWP in March 1981, they are now published only by some departments. They have been banished from public-expenditure plans. For most current expenditure programmes RPEs are positive most of the time because pay, which averages half the total cost, tends to rise faster than general inflation, as measured by the GDP deflator (or the RPI). Therefore if the Government publishes RPEs that are positive, it is approving pay claims in excess of inflation in advance and returning part of the way to one objectionable feature of volume planning.

In 1981 the Government actually set about planning for negative RPEs to try to reverse the positive RPEs due to higher-than-inflation public-sector pay rises in the previous two years. This was abandoned, since keeping public-sector pay settlements even as low as the general rate of inflation was quite difficult enough. The proscription of RPEs was thus linked with what Sir Leo Pliatzky, a retired Treasury mandarin, called the public-sector 'crypto-incomes policy'. Although any kind of incomes policy was against the Government's principles, the use of cash limits and cost terms in public-expenditure planning resulted in an attempt to keep the going rate for public employees below that for private-sector earnings, which tended to stay 1 or 2 per cent above inflation even during the recession.

In July 1981, following Sir Geoffrey Howe's exceptionally tough Budget in March, several members of the cabinet expressed strong opposition to proposals for further spending cuts aimed at achieving the still elusive objective of reducing real public expenditure. The proposals were dropped, but a further review was carried out inside Whitehall in September 1982, suggesting radical cuts.

Mrs Thatcher circulated to her ministers a long-term study by the Central Policy Review Staff (CPRS: the 'Think Tank') showing that the share of public expenditure in the national income would continue to rise, on the assumption of slow economic growth, if drastic cuts were not made. According to Hugo Young: 'The Think Tank's proposals were hair-raisingly radical. Education cuts could be usefully achieved, it suggested, by ending state funding for all institutions of higher education ... The massive welfare budget could be slashed by stopping all benefits rising in line with inflation. On the health service, the Tank suggested its complete replacement with a system of private health insurance...'

After a rebellion by other members of the cabinet, the CPRS's ideas were put into cold storage, although in attenuated form they continued to influence policies from time to time. The Government, faced with the dilemma of either transferring public services to the private sector or substantially increasing public-sector resources, went on tinkering with each alternative, adopting neither whole-heartedly. It was after the Think Tank episode that the Government appeared to have dropped the idea of cutting real spending and settled for freezing it.

By 1983, a year in which public spending was increased because of the election, it became evident that the 4 per cent real cut in public expenditure at which the Government had aimed during its first four years had turned into a 6 per cent real increase, for reasons partly connected with the recession. During the run-up to the 1983 election Mrs Thatcher seemed to have cast constraint aside with her famous exhortation to local authorities to 'Spend, spend, spend' in order to correct previous underspending of receipts from council-house sales. The £500 million of public-expenditure cuts that the new Chancellor, Nigel Lawson, felt obliged to introduce in July 1983, just after the election, were seen as a symbolic admission that the pre-election spending spree had been somewhat overdone.

By this time the Government's more radical free-market supporters were expressing disappointment at its steady retreat from really harsh decisions about public expenditure, such as the decision to keep British Leyland going rather than shutting it down (see page 184). In a pamphlet by John Burton, *Why No Cuts?*, the Institute of Economic Affairs called for constitutional changes to force the Government to balance the Budget. It got no further than any of the many other proposals to limit the discretion of Parliament – in other words, the Thatcher Government – to change policy as it thought fit.

Some of the analysis of the CPRS document eventually emerged in a doctored form in the March 1984 Green Paper, *The Next Ten Years*, which made it clear that the Government still aimed to curb public expenditure in order to achieve its prime objective of cutting taxation, in which it had up to then scarcely been any more successful.

This Green Paper shows that without firm control over public spending there can be no prospect of bringing the burden of tax back to tolerable levels. On the illustrative framework set out in this paper the tax burden will be reduced to the levels of the early

1970s only if public expenditure is held broadly at its present level in real terms right up to 1993–94. If, on the other hand, we assume what by historical standards is a very modest rate of public expenditure growth – 1 per cent a year in real terms after 1988–89, compared with the average 3 per cent growth of the last twenty years – the tax burden would be only just below its 1978–79 level even after ten years of growth in the economy at about 2 per cent a year...

The Green Paper did hold out a ray of hope:

It would of course always be open to the Government to decide, once the virtuous circle of lower taxes and higher growth had been established, to devote some of these resources to improved public services rather than reduced taxation.

At about the same time Lawson said in a speech, 'even some modest growth of public spending might be possible. But expenditure must fall as a percentage of output.' It was some years before this view became reflected in official policy, which was still to freeze public expenditure in real terms. However, the Green Paper had set out detailed projections for a falling public expenditure to GDP ratio, which made it clear that if GDP were to grow faster, real public expenditure could increase, the burden of debt interest could fall and taxes could be cut as well. These were to be the salient features of Lawson's Chancellorship.

From the November 1983 Autumn Statement onwards the objective in successive years became to keep public expenditure 'broadly constant in real terms' in future years. The rule was softened by 'base drift', so that if spending overran in the current year, it had to remain constant relative to the overrun rather than being cut back to the figure originally planned. By the January 1985 PEWP the objective had been broadened to 'public spending ... being held constant in real terms, and amounting to a falling proportion of the nation's income'. Public spending was defined as 'general government expenditure' (GGE) of central and local government. It excluded public-corporation borrowing, included debt interest and subtracted the increasing proceeds of privatization, as did the planning total of departmental programmes. The vagaries of public accounting thus made it possible to use the decline in debt interest and the rise of privatization to combine a static or falling GGE with rising departmental programmes, satisfying both those who wished public expenditure to be cut and those who wished to increase it.

By the November 1986 Autumn Statement Nigel Lawson was able to interpret 'broadly constant' as being compatible with 'slightly rising' in real terms and was claiming credit for the achievement of a less ambitious objective: a 'continued deceleration of the growth of public spending'. This growth was scheduled to continue in future years at about 1 per cent a year in real terms, which was, as the January 1987 PEWP put it, 'significantly less than [the growth rate of] the nation's income'. It was from that year that the Treasury began to publish four-year rolling objectives for GGE to decline as a percentage of GDP of the kind that had been featured in the 1984 Green Paper. Given that GDP was by then growing relatively fast, the happy situation had been reached where GGE could also expand, not quite as fast, and thus fall as a proportion of GDP. It took ten years of hardening and softening for the public-expenditure objective to return to that originally set out in *The Right Approach to the Economy*.

By the November 1988 Autumn Statement the Government seemed to be congratulating itself on the amazing feat of both cutting public expenditure (as a proportion of GDP) and increasing it – even faster than GDP. The Statement began: 'Government spending as a proportion of national income is expected to be below 40 per cent for the first time in over twenty years. The proportion will have fallen by some 7 per cent since 1982–83.' Yet two paragraphs later: 'In real terms, the plans for the next three years allow growth in spending on programmes averaging $3\frac{3}{4}$ per cent a year. This can be afforded because of the fall in the burden of debt interest. As a result overall public spending, excluding privatization proceeds, will rise by only $1\frac{1}{4}$ per cent a year, well within the growth of the economy.' There was to be an extra £2¾ billion in capital spending that would recognize some of the suppressed claims of such disfavoured sectors as hospitals, roads, housing, prisons, London Regional Transport and the nationalized industries.

John Major, then Chief Secretary to the Treasury, warned the Treasury Select Committee that things might not always look so rosy: 'If growth in the economy turns out to be less than the growth we have planned in public expenditure, the ratio would turn upwards. It is perfectly possible in a single year, if the economy slowed down, that that could be the case.' As the following year's Autumn Statement revealed, it was in fact the case in 1989–90; the GGE/GDP ratio turned up, but partly because it had been lower than planned in the previous year. As the economy continues to slow down by more than public expenditure in 1990–91, and possibly the following year, the falling GGE/GDP ratio target may have to be put into suspense. Public expenditure may again be admitted to be what it always has been – a compromise between the Treasury and the competing claims of departmental ministers, each with his or her retinue of clients.

There was an important change in the definition of the planning total in the November 1989 Autumn Statement that had been announced in a White Paper the previous July. Instead of including all local authority expenditure, it included only that part financed by central government and excluded local authority self-financed expenditure. This was done on the grounds that the Treasury could plan only what it could control. However, it still wished to regulate GGE in relation to GDP, and this included local authority self-financed expenditure.

The Government wished to control local authority self-financed expenditure as part of its responsibility for expenditure and taxation in the economy as a whole. It was originally thought that the new community charge would be a deterrent to high local authority spending because it would need to rise steeply if additional expenditure were incurred. This proved not to be the case because local authorities were able

Figure 4. Planning totals, cash and real, 1974–88

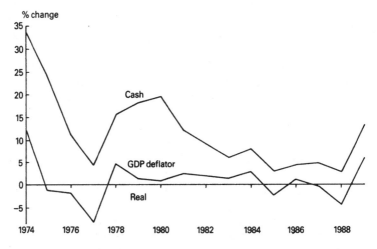

Source: Public-expenditure White Papers.

to shift the blame for the community charge to central government, whose idea it was. The Government therefore resorted to charge-capping, thus reasserting direct control over some local authorities.

The result of the change has been to reduce the information given to the public about those parts of departmental plans that are self-financed by local authorities, such as local authority education. The Treasury argued that such information, when given, was unreliable but was at least its best forecast of how much was likely to be spent by local authorities and central government combined. It remains to be seen whether the removal of self-financed local authority items from the planning total will make that easier to achieve.

Real terms and what was really spent

The public-expenditure planning totals achieved averaged an increase of 8 per cent in cash in the 1980s, less than half the 18 per cent of 1974–9 (see table 16 and figure 4). Most of the difference was explained by the fact that inflation in the earlier period, at 17 per cent, was over twice as high as the 7 per cent in the later period. The 'real' increase changed little, from 1.1 to 0.8 per cent. Just as unexpected falls in inflation caused cash plans to be higher than expected in real terms, so unexpected rises brought about real-terms cuts, even where cash plans were allowed to be exceeded. The 1970s were marked by highly erratic patterns. The planning total rose by 34 per cent in cash in 1974–5, which was still 12 per cent after adjusting for 19 per cent inflation. It was then cut by 8 per cent in real terms in 1977 as part of the IMF measures, a cut far sharper than anything seen after the change of Government in 1979. The Labour cuts left the Conservatives with less scope for further cuts without incurring even more serious damage to public services.

In the first half of the 1980s cash-planning totals were adjusted so as to give a fairly constant 'real-terms' annual growth averaging 1.8 per cent. In the second half of the decade real-terms planning totals became erratic, falling more often than rising and swinging from a fall of 4.4 per cent in 1988–9 to a rise of 5.2 per cent in 1989–90. Cash plans both tended to assume falling inflation and tried to contribute to it by reining back expenditure. The annual increases rose and fell with the current inflation rate. While the cash increase for each year's planning total generally rose during the three-year planning period as the year came closer, the cash increases set out in each year's PEWP for the next three years' planning totals tended to fall in line with hopes of falling inflation (see table 17). The outcomes were quite close to the planned figures, save in 1984–5, 1988–9 and 1989–90. The eight-year overshoot in cash plans was only 3 per cent.

While plans are made in cash, they must also be judged by their intentions and outcomes in real terms (see table 18). The Government moved away from planned real cuts after its failure to achieve them in the early 1980s, then

Figure 5. General government expenditure and GDP, 1970–88

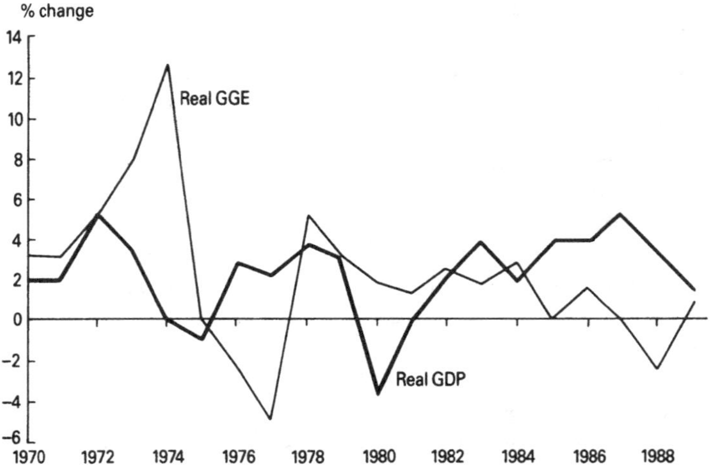

Source: The Government's Expenditure Plans 1990–91 to 1992–93, Cm 1021.

returned to them in 1985–6 and 1986–7, when excessive optimism in inflation projections caused cash-plan increases to be below the actual inflation rate. Since 1989–90 both actual and projected real-terms plans have been much higher than in previous years. There was a real-terms overshoot of 1.5 per cent in 1989–90 compared with a massive undershoot of 6.2 per cent in 1988–9. The difference between outcome and plan varied quite widely but amounted cumulatively to only just over 1 per cent in the eight years to 1989–90.

The GGE/GDP ratio fluctuated more than GGE or the planning totals themselves because its changes are the product of two variables, both of which change unpredictably (see table 16 and figure 5). It rose rapidly from 40½ to 48¼ per cent between 1970–71 and 1975–6, then fell very sharply to 42½ per cent by 1977–8. It then went up again to 46¾ per cent in 1982–3 and stayed close to that figure until 1984–5. It then fell seven percentage points to 38¾ per cent by 1989–90 – as the November 1988 Autumn Statement boasted – but is now rising again.

During the five years 1985–6 to 1989–90, while real GDP rose by an average 3½ per cent a year, real GGE was 'broadly constant in real terms', to quote the objective from the earlier period that the Government thought it had discarded in November 1986. Real GGE was held back partly because the Treasury gradually became more effective in restraining expenditure and partly because cash plans were eroded in real terms by inflation. At a time of rapid economic growth public dissatisfaction with the standard of public services increased.

The Government's 'falling ratio' objective would have been compatible with GGE growth, averaging, say, 2½ per cent a year in real terms. This would have made 1989–90 public expenditure £20 billion, or 12½ per cent higher. The difference between the ratio projected and the ratio achieved was a shortfall of over seven percentage points during the boom period of 1986–7 to 1988–9 (see table 19). The Government was so carried away by the euphoria of private-sector growth that it forgot its earlier promise to use the fruits of that growth to reverse the earlier cuts in public services. By the time it began to plan for major real increases in public expenditure from 1989–90 onwards it was too late. The boom was coming to an end, and inflation was reducing the real growth allowed for by cash plans.

There were much bigger changes within each category of GGE than in the total (see table 20). The size of the changes was persistently misrepresented in PEWPs because of the use of the GDP deflator to measure real-terms changes, ignoring the RPEs specific to each category. Fortunately, some of the RPEs and specific deflators can be derived from the national accounts Blue Book.

The most significant change was that in benefit for the unemployed, which was the main reason why public expenditure overshot in the first half of the 1980s, then undershot in the second half, as unemployment rose to a peak in 1986, then fell sharply. Because of this, social security rose from 26 to 30 per cent of expenditure by departments between 1979–80 and 1984–5 but remained at the same proportion in

1989–90. Nearly all of the real increase of 32 per cent occurred in the earlier period. The true increase was about 3 per cent higher because the negative RPE for personal transfers averaged 0.3 per cent a year in the 1980s. This is measured by the difference between the GDP deflator and the more slowly rising consumer-price deflator.

The elderly accounted for over half of total social-security expenditure, and their numbers were increasing by about 1 per cent a year (see table 21). The real increase in their benefits of 24 per cent over the last decade was about half that for the sick and disabled, for families and for the unemployed. Pensions were indexed to prices, not to earnings, as in the 1970s, which would have cost an extra £25 billion at 1990 prices (Hansard, 26 July 1990, col. 488); however, the elderly received other benefits, including housing and invalidity benefits and pensions from the State Earnings Related Pension Scheme, as well as earnings from work and occupational pensions. The average total net income of pensioners from all these sources increased by over 31 per cent in real terms between 1979 and 1987, slightly more than average labour earnings, compared with 3 per cent between 1974 and 1979 (Hansard, 25 July 1990, col. 304). Benefits for the unemployed rose £5.5 billion at 1989–90 prices over the eight years to 1986–7, then fell £4 billion in the following three years, at 1989–90 prices.

Defence spending first rose 21 per cent in the five years to 1984–5, then fell 10 per cent on the Treasury's 'real-terms' measure. Because of a relative price effect averaging 0.4 per cent a year, this is shown in the Blue Book as a volume increase of 16 per cent, followed by a fall of 7 per cent, in the corresponding calendar years (see tables 20 and 22). RPEs distorted the record of performance even more seriously in health and education. The Government claimed to have spent 14 per cent more on education and 32 per cent more on health in real terms during the 1980s, but this was a new kind of 'funny money'. The increases in input volumes were zero and 12 per cent.

The Treasury figures show a real-terms rise in education

spending of 14 per cent in the decade to 1988-9, mostly in the second half. Given a RPE of 1.1 per cent a year (7 per cent of it due to the big rise in teachers' salaries in 1986), the Blue Book figures for local authority education expenditure – nearly four-fifths of the total – show no increase at all in volume terms over the ten years to 1989. This casts doubts on such claims as that in the education chapter of the January 1990 PEWP: 'Between 1979-80 and 1988-89 pupil numbers fell by 17 per cent and expenditure per pupil rose in real terms by 42 per cent.' In volume terms, deflated by the 1.1 per cent RPE, the extra expenditure per pupil comes to 27 per cent, an increase of 2½ per cent a year. If the Blue Book figures are correct, the extra expenditure is 20 per cent.

Health expenditure is shown by the Treasury to have risen by 32 per cent in real terms during the 1980s, increasing its share of the total from 12 to 14 per cent. The Blue Book volume figure for the National Health Service (NHS) is only 12 per cent. The difference between the two estimates of about a 3 per cent versus a 1 per cent annual increase is accounted for by the NHS RPE of 2 per cent a year, due not only to pay but also to medical technology. Much of the remaining 1 per cent annual increase can be explained by the demographic rise in the number of elderly people. Hospital activity statistics suggest that the volume of expenditure per patient fell by about 1 per cent a year. It is possible that this represents in part an improvement in efficiency.

The biggest expenditure increase was in law and order, notably the police. Spending rose by 53 per cent in real terms but probably by about 40 per cent in volume terms because of the local authority current RPE of 1 per cent a year.

Employment and training programmes rose by 50 per cent during the first half of the 1980s as anti-unemployment measures such as the community programme were introduced, but they fell 11 per cent in the second half for the questionable reason given in the November 1988 Autumn Statement that 'the fall in unemployment makes savings possible on the social-security and employment and training programmes'. The cuts were based on the fallacy that training programmes are mainly for the unemployed rather than to improve the skills of those in employment (see page 222).

Transport spending appears to have been cut by 6 per cent in real terms, but here the Treasury may have failed to take credit for the negative RPE of 2.1 per cent on capital expenditure, as productivity lowered contract prices; the volume change in transport spending on roads and railways could be a rise of 16 per cent. The transport chapters of PEWPs are among the few to show RPEs because in this case they are negative and mean that unusually good value for money is being obtained – except in 1989.

The housing programme was the most heavily cut, with a 67 per cent real-terms fall, as local authorities were discouraged from building new houses. Allowing again for the negative RPE on capital expenditure, the fall in volume terms was probably nearer 60 per cent. Although the trade-and-industry programme was high on the list for cuts, it rose by 16 per cent in the first half of the 1980s because of the effect of the recession on the finances of public corporations such as British Leyland and British Steel, which could not be allowed to go under for political reasons (see page 184). In the second half of the decade real-terms spending in this area was cut by nearly 50 per cent, as the demands of the public corporations were reduced by recovery and privatization, and fewer subsidies were required by the flourishing private sector.

There was also a big swing in debt interest, which rose 11 per cent as public borrowing rose more than interest rates fell, then fell 16 per cent as borrowing turned round into debt repayment and interest rates dipped. Since the growth of programmes fell to only 1½ per cent in the second half of the 1980s while debt interest fell, GGE – which includes both – was static. The Treasury claimed that falling debt interest would allow an expansion in programmes, but the savings on public debt went into tax cuts more than expenditure increases. The big real increases in programmes pro-

Figure 6. General government expenditure: transfers, and goods and services, 1970–88

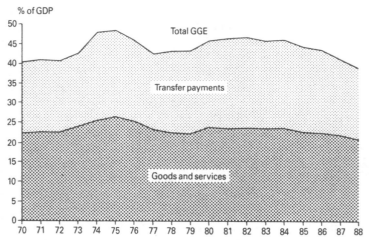

Source: *The Government's Expenditure Plans 1990–91 to 1992–93*, Cm 1021.

jected by the Treasury for 1989–90 onwards were reduced by unexpectedly high inflation.

The volume of government expenditure on goods and services – excluding social services and other transfer payments – rose by 0.9 per cent a year in the 1980s (see table 22 and figure 6), far less than the 2.2 per cent annual increase in GDP. The RPE for government expenditure on goods and services has averaged about 0.8 per cent, so this means a 'real-terms' increase of 1.7 per cent on the Treasury definition. The increase has been 1 per cent on government consumption (current expenditure: −2.1 per cent on the Treasury definition) and 0.6 per cent on capital expenditure (−1.6 per cent on the Treasury definition). Central-government expenditure has been rising 1.4 per cent a year in volume (2.4 per cent on the Treasury definition) and local government spending at 0.2 per cent (0.7 per cent on the Treasury definition).

The Government was successful in one limited aim – that of cutting Civil Service numbers by 20 per cent (see table 23). However, it was not generally understood that the 'Civil Service' consisted of a core of central-government employees, less than a tenth of all public manpower. It was, indeed, cut from 738,000 in 1979 to 585,000 in 1989. Only two-thirds of the reduction was real saving, the rest being hived off to other units outside the Civil Service, according to John MacGregor, then Chief Secretary of the Treasury, giving evidence to the Treasury Committee on the January 1987 PEWP. Civil Service cuts were nothing compared with the 60 per cent fall in public-corporation employees brought about by privatization. As a result, public-sector employment was cut by 1.4 million over the decade, falling from 29 to 23 per cent of the workforce in employment.

The cuts in general government employment were only 2.7 per cent. NHS employees rose by 6 per cent, but the whole rise took place in 1980–83. After that NHS numbers stood still, while hospital activity rose by about 2 per cent a year. Education service employees fell by 6 per cent, but the whole fall took place in 1980–83. After that numbers changed little while school rolls fell. There was a decrease in efficiency because, as the Audit Commission has argued, many small schools were kept open, and teacher–pupil ratios rose. Teachers were kept busy coping with reforms, but it is too early to say whether quality has improved. These examples illustrate the difficulties of measuring public-sector output and productivity.

How expenditure was controlled

Treasury accounting is at its most arcane when it comes to capital expenditure (see table 24). There is no doubt that public capital expenditure fell as a proportion of total public expenditure and as a percentage of GDP. This has led to serious doubts about the state of the public sector's balance sheet, notably on the part of John Hills, and about the Government's failure to manage its stock of assets responsibly. The official figures have tended to make public capital expenditure look even smaller than it really is – for example, by deducting asset sales. On the widest definition, including public corporations, it was 14 per cent of GGE in 1989–90 and on the narrowest – the planning total excluding public corporations, local authorities and defence – 4 per cent. From the point of view of the public sector's balance sheet, we can deduct £9 billion of privatizations and other asset sales from asset creation of £27 billion to get a figure of £18 billion. This is 9 per cent of GGE, and 3½ per cent of GDP, or about one-fifth of private-sector capital expenditure.

Cuts in public capital expenditure took place in fourteen out of the last twenty years. Most of the increases have been in single pre-election years by Conservative Governments, giving large but short-lived boosts against a declining trend. For example, there was a 12 per cent volume increase in 1973, a 37 per cent increase in 1983, a 7 per cent increase in 1986 and, somewhat prematurely, a 24 per cent increase in 1989. The Labour Government cut public capital spending by 40 per cent in volume in 1974–9, and the incoming Conservative Government took only three years to cut it by another 40 per cent in 1980–83. These figures do not include public corporations, whose figures have been considerably distorted by privatization.

Referring to capital expenditure, the Treasury Committee commented in its report on the 1981 PEWP:

> One cause of the past decline has been the relative ease with which, when spending cuts are required, capital spending can be reduced. Irrespective of what political view is taken about overall public spending as a proportion of GDP, the Committee believe that the decline in capital spending relative to current expenditure should be halted and reversed. Provided that the programmes are properly appraised and efficiently implemented, public-sector investment can be as desirable as private-sector investment. Major improvements of the infrastructure are necessary for the maximum effectiveness of the economy.

A Treasury official, Michael Bridgeman, attempted to justify the decline in public capital expenditure in evidence to the Committee in March 1981: 'The motorway programme is largely complete. The chronic shortage of houses of the 1950s is now a thing of the past. We are facing a fall in the school population and not a rise in the school population.' While this assessment might have appeared plausible at a time of economic stagnation, it was cast aside by the Treasury as soon as the resumption of economic growth led to demands for improvements in an overloaded infrastructure.

A Keynesian critique of the fluctuations of public capital expenditure was put to the Committee by the author, as its specialist adviser, in March 1984:

It can be argued that a more stable pattern of public capital spending would have been helpful to the construction industry and to others involved in the planning of public-sector outlays. A counter-argument can be put for varying public capital spending as a function of the business cycle. But the fluctuations in the UK in recent years are, if anything, pro-cyclical rather than counter-cyclical. The big cuts in public capital spending were in the years of maximum recession, and the big increases were in the years of recovery. Public capital spending thus contributed – in a minor way in view of its much diminished size – to the fluctuations in the economy rather than offsetting them.

Judged in terms of its own objectives, rather than those of its critics, who might have been glad to increase public expenditure, the Government was believed to have failed after its first term in office. The Treasury Committee said in its report on the PEWP in March 1984: 'Despite a succession of plans for either reduced or constant real expenditure levels, the actual out-turn has invariably exceeded the planning targets by significant amounts measured in billions of pounds.' In the following year the Committee estimated the overshoot at £11 billion, or £17 billion if various adjustments were made. It added to the criticism in its report on the 1985 PEWP: 'The historical experience is thus one of consistent failure to meet cost-terms expenditure targets, despite a succession of upward revisions to the plans.'

In its 1984 PEWP report, and on many subsequent occasions, the Committee cast doubt on the Treasury's assertion 'Finance must determine expenditure, not expenditure determine finance.' Since public expenditure was settled each year in the November Autumn Statement, it did not appear to depend on the revenue raised in the Budget the previous March or to be raised in the following year's Budget. As the Government had no up-to-date estimate of tax revenues in November, expenditure was being determined by bargaining between the Treasury and other departments to achieve the lowest figure that was politically possible. In any case the 1984 Green Paper, *The Next Ten Years*, made it clear that lower taxes were to be achieved by holding down expenditure, so this seemed to be a case of expenditure determining finance. It was a case of less expenditure requiring less finance, rather than less finance determining less expenditure.

The Committee has consistently criticized the Treasury for not supplementing its cash plans with sufficient real-terms indicators. Future plans for individual departments are given only in cash, not in real terms, so that no indication is given of the future level of service, and ministers are free to boast of cash increases that may conceal real-terms cuts. Although totals for each department are given in real terms, these are arrived at by using the GDP deflator as a general measure of inflation. Few relative price effects are given so that volumes spent or planned can be judged. Mr John MacGregor, then Chief Secretary to the Treasury, went so far as to tell the Committee in January 1987: 'I am anxious at all costs to avoid having a discussion in the survey of relative price effects.' The Committee continued to argue, as it did in February 1988, that there were advantages in using RPEs from the point of view of Treasury management, consumers and the public because they gave a better picture of the allocation of real resources.

The distortion caused by the failure to use RPEs, particularly over a long period, has been demonstrated. The suppression of RPE estimates for future years was not always effective in limiting public-sector pay rises. The result was to hold back public-sector pay in some years, which led to industrial action, followed by large catch-up increases. Including the huge 23 per cent increase in 1980 because of the Clegg awards, public-sector pay was 1½ per cent a year ahead of inflation during the 1980s – compared with 2½ per cent for earnings in the economy as a whole – but the annual pattern of increases was more variable.

The choice of priorities and objectives

Priorities in public spending were generally set by political criteria, notably the popular demand for health, education, law and order and other services. Little attempt was made to assess the relative benefits to economic welfare of different programmes, although cost–benefit analysis techniques are available. Departmental ministers are judged by their ability to obtain scarce allocations of extra finance in competition with colleagues rather than by their efficiency in achieving given objectives with fewer resources of money and manpower. Most demands are settled by 'bilaterals' between each minister and the Chief Secretary to the Treasury. The so-called 'Star Chamber', a committee of the cabinet to adjudicate between conflicting claims, does not even meet every year, and public expenditure is not normally debated in the cabinet itself.

The Treasury Committee commented in its report on the 1984 Autumn Statement: 'Against this background we recommend a reappraisal of the machinery for determining public-sector priorities, with particular reference to the need to improve the allocation across departments.' A common practice is for priority increases in expenditure by a department to be financed by cuts elsewhere in the same department, without a survey to see whether a lower-priority item in some other department might be cut.

A related criticism is that departments fail to assess whether their programmes are the most cost-effective means of meeting their often vaguely formulated policy objectives.

As the author commented in his evidence to the Treasury Committee on the January 1986 PEWP: 'Many departments' expenditure allocations are insufficient for the policy aims laid down. Either these aims will not be adequately achieved or expenditure will overrun the limits set.'

For example, is the building of new prisons the best way to deal with rising crime? Or would it be better to review sentencing policy so as to keep non-violent offenders out of prison and to give them cheaper treatment in the community, as the 1990 Criminal Justice Act attempted to do? Is lung cancer more effectively tackled by increasing hospital provision or by anti-smoking education and higher tobacco taxation? Can homelessness be reduced by building more municipal housing as an alternative to providing sub-standard boarding houses at state expense? Such questions are almost impossible to discuss within the present machinery for deciding public expenditure because they involve cutting the expenditure of one department and increasing that of another. Even if a net saving could be made, this is not how departments behave.

In its November 1986 report on the Autumn Statement the Treasury Committee commented on the Treasury's numerous changes of objective. The objectives had changed from reducing public expenditure in real terms as part of the 1980 MTFS to holding it constant in 1982, then holding it 'broadly constant' (allowing small rises) and, finally, in that year to laying down only that it should fall as a percentage of GDP. The Committee was sceptical of Nigel Lawson's claim that the policy had not changed, on the grounds that if public expenditure were cut or frozen, *a fortiori* in real terms it would fall as a percentage of GDP. The weak version of the original objective was consistent with quite rapidly rising public expenditure if GDP were rising even faster and did not appear to determine any precise target.

The objective was strongly criticized before it was even adopted by Sir Alan Walters, Mrs Thatcher's former economic adviser, in November 1985. He wrote: 'The fraction is much affected by the cyclical oscillation in income and employment. The recession increases the total value of the numerator [GGE] because of the increase in benefits paid to the unemployed, whereas the denominator, real GDP, declines as output falls.' Walters argued that both the numerator and the denominator of the ratio should be adjusted for the rise in unemployment. According to the official figures as then published, the ratio had risen from 40.5 per cent in 1979–80 to 43.5 per cent in 1982–3, but he worked out an unemployment-adjusted figure of 38 per cent.

Part of the rise in the GGE/GDP ratio in the first half of the 1980s was indeed due to the rise in unemployment and some of its fall to the subsequent fall in unemployment. The unadjusted ratio is too difficult to lower during a recession and too easy during a recovery. If it does indeed fluctuate, but around a falling trend, how far should it fall in the long run? If the reduction of public expenditure as a share of the national income is no more than a correction of its excessive rise in earlier years, should it not fluctuate around a stable rather than a rising trend, such as the 39 per cent of GDP that has now been reached? In the long run, it can be argued, the provision of current public services, such as health and education, public investment in infrastructure and public social security, should rise roughly in line with GDP, both for reasons of consumer demand and to improve the supply side of the economy.

It is inevitable that the cash plans laid down by the Treasury generally override the GGE/GDP ratio, which offers little exact guidance but rather a range of limits within which to place the total. If GDP tends to grow at $2\frac{1}{2}$ per cent, the difference between a static GGE total and one growing at the same rate as GDP is about £5 billion, which is also $2\frac{1}{2}$ per cent of public expenditure, or 1 per cent of GDP.

To measure GGE against GDP is not to compare like with like, as David Heald has argued in his survey of the wide range of possible definitions of the public expenditure/GDP ratio. Nearly half of GGE is transfer payments, notably social security and debt interest. Transfer payments are not part of GDP and have accounted for most of the fluctuations in the GGE/GDP ratio in the last ten years (see the last column of table 16). General government purchases of goods and services – final consumption plus capital expenditure – are running at only 21 per cent of GDP compared with 18 per cent for transfer payments. General government goods and services as a proportion of GDP should be given greater prominence than general government expenditure as a whole.

The verdict must be that the Treasury was better able to control public expenditure but still lacked a clear political objective for it. The Government began the decade by trying to cut it in real terms, for reasons of both political ideology and economic management, but gradually returned to the weaker objective of reducing it as a proportion of GDP. Once the weaker objective had been adopted, the Treasury inadvertently achieved the stronger aim of holding it constant in real terms and set out to increase it too late, when inflation was already taking its toll of cash plans. The result was to starve public services and infrastructure of resources at a time when they might have been expected to share in, and contribute to, the expansion of the private sector. The curbs on public expenditure made the UK a country of private affluence and public squalor. In effect the slower increase in public expenditure reduced demand on resources in the economy and allowed private consumption and investment to expand at a rapid pace, which proved to be unsustainable.

The Treasury's way of accounting for public expenditure may have made it easier to control but was thoroughly misleading about the rate at which it changed, particularly over the medium term. It seriously overestimated the volume growth of important programmes such as health and education because of its refusal to discuss relative price effects. Capital expenditure on infrastructure was in recent years maintained or increased but from a low level, to which it had been cut by two-thirds in under a decade because it was the line of least resistance. In spite of attempts to improve the efficiency of performance, there was insufficient discussion of priorities between programmes or between different types of programme, to achieve given policy objectives.

The Government hesitated to privatize essential public services, apart from a substantial part of the council housing estate. Unfortunately it did not believe in them enough to ensure that they had the resources to achieve their policy goals. It brought about some savings by persuading local authorities to contract out certain services to the private sector and hoped to do the same by hiving off some parts of the Civil Service as 'next steps' agencies. It tried experiments in crypto-privatization, such as its encouragement to schools and hospitals to opt out and its attempt to create an internal market in health and education by giving doctors and parents a wider choice of hospital or school. Such reforms were likely to fail, as they were not accompanied by sufficient increases in resources to improve quality throughout the system rather than in small, pace-setting sections of it.

At the beginning of the 1990s public expenditure was again rising faster than GDP, as it was in the early 1980s when the Government came to office. Attempts to reduce it sharply as the economy slows down are unlikely, if only because of the political unpopularity they would incur. To meet the demands of public expenditure the Government will inevitably return to net borrowing after some years of public-sector debt repayment. It is even possible that taxation will be increased if this turns out to be more acceptable to voters than cuts in public services. The reversal of all the trends of the second half of the 1980s will then be complete. The cycle may return to where it was when Mrs Thatcher came in – public expenditure rising faster than taxation and an increase in public borrowing. It would not be the end of the world, only the end of an era.

4 Taxation: piecemeal reform of the system

> 'Exorbitant taxes, like extreme necessity, destroy industry by producing despair.'
> David Hume, quoted by Colin Clark, quoted by Nigel Lawson at an Institute of Economic Affairs conference, 'The State of Taxation', 1977

A tax-cutting manifesto

Most people think that they pay too much tax and would jump at the opportunity to pay less if they could. Politicians are sure of a hearing if they offer to cut taxes and certain of defeat if they undertake to increase them. In advance of elections Government and Opposition compete for support with promises to cut taxes, only to find that the winner has to raise them once in office.

The political mythology of taxation often differs from the reality. The UK tax burden is close to the EC average, though well above that of the USA and Japan, where the scope of public expenditure is more limited (see table 25). Until the 1980s the UK tax burden was more volatile, however, as Governments of alternate parties indulged in fiscal activism to regulate demand in the economy in line with the electoral cycle.

The 1964–70 Wilson Government had raised the tax burden by 1970 to the then relatively high figure of 37 per cent, which was, in fact, the average for the 1980s. The

Budget was briefly in surplus under Roy Jenkins's prudent Chancellorship, but Labour lost the election. Under the Heath Government Anthony Barber as Chancellor cut the tax burden from 37 to 31 per cent in only three years because of tax cuts combined with, and causing, unsustainably rapid economic growth. Barber also announced the most ambitious tax reform of the post-war period, the tax-credit scheme, combining the income-tax and social-security systems. Heath was unlucky, after this, to lose the 1974 election by a narrow margin because of the energy crisis and its diverse consequences.

Denis Healey, as Wilson's Chancellor, raised the tax burden from 31 to 35 per cent in one year in 1974 because of the fall in GDP and increases in taxation. By 1978, however, he had cut the figure to 33 per cent. This was low compared with the rest of Europe, and the Conservative Opposition had to switch its attack away from the moderate-looking total tax burden to its structure, in particular the higher rates of income tax.

The Right Approach to the Economy announced four main elements in the tax strategy in 1977:

1 Lower personal taxation to restore work incentives.
2 An enterprise package of measures to stimulate business growth.
3 Stronger encouragement to personal savings and capital building on the widest possible scale.
4 Simplification of the system.

RAE pointed out that the starting rate of income tax, 34 per cent, was the highest in the world. However, by the 1979 election Labour had cut it to 33 per cent, with a promise of a further cut to 30 per cent, and a new lower rate of 25 per cent had been introduced. The document emphasized the higher rates.

The top rates, at 83 per cent on earned income and 98 per cent on investment income, stand out as a beacon of fiscal absurdity ... These tax rates ... have a catastrophic effect. They enforce the payment to senior executives of gross salaries which look enormous on paper, provoking much unjustified resentment and political propaganda – yet the net returns after tax are very low by the standards of other countries. They encourage the growth of incentives based on status, leisure and perquisites ... Meanwhile tax avoidance, moonlighting and second jobs distract effort from the basic regular work that needs doing in a healthy economy.

The Conservatives' 1979 manifesto contained a detailed set of undertakings on cutting income tax.

We shall cut income tax at all levels ...; tackle the poverty trap; encourage saving and the wider ownership of property; simplify taxes – like VAT; and reduce tax bureaucracy. It is especially important to cut the absurdly high marginal rates of tax both at the bottom and top of the income scale. It must pay a man or woman significantly more to be in, rather than out of, work. Raising tax thresholds will let the low-paid out of the tax net altogether, and unemployment and short-term sickness benefit must be brought into the computation of annual income. The top rate of income tax should be cut to the European average and the higher tax bands widened. To encourage saving we will reduce the burden of the investment income surcharge.

Undertakings were given about other taxes.

We must be prepared to switch to some extent from taxes on earnings to taxes on spending. VAT does not apply, and will not be extended, to necessities like food, fuel, housing and transport ... Cutting income tax must take priority for the time being over abolition of the domestic rating system ... We reject Labour's plan for a Wealth Tax. We shall deal with the most damaging features of the capital transfer and capital gains taxes ... We will expand and build on existing schemes for encouraging employee share-ownership and our tax policies generally will provide incentives to save and build up capital. Lower taxes on earnings and savings will encourage economic growth.

The programme had a strong element of redistributive justice in it. It set out to reverse what it saw as politically motivated injustice for those on higher incomes. More generally, it aimed to use the tax system to improve supply-side incentives to growth; incentives to work, and to invest. The two concepts were linked by the famous 'Laffer Curve', which purported to show that above a certain point increases in the tax rate yielded less, not more, revenue because of their disincentive effects. While this was clearly the case for taxpayers on marginal rates approaching 100 per cent, it never seemed plausible when applied to an economy with an average tax rate – and an average marginal tax rate – in the region of 33–50 per cent, according to sector.

However, a weaker version of the Laffer theory held that higher taxes led to lower revenue, not in an absolute sense but compared with what might otherwise have happened, because of the lower rates of growth of taxable incomes. Conversely, tax cuts might lead to higher tax revenue because of the stimulus they gave to taxable incomes.

The 1983 manifesto had little to add on taxation, but the 1987 manifesto was more ambitious. The Government still had something to prove, since the tax burden had risen from 33 per cent before it took office to 38 per cent in 1981–6. 'We aim to reduce the burden of taxation. In particular, we will cut income tax still further and reduce the basic rate to 25p in the £ as soon as we prudently can. We will continue the process of tax reform.'

Income tax comes down

In 1978 the UK was unusual among major European countries in raising as much as one-third of total tax revenue from personal income tax. Sir Geoffrey Howe, the new Chancellor of the Exchequer, moved faster than anyone had expected to rectify the position in his first Budget in June 1979, only a month after taking office (see figures 7 and 8). He cut the top rate of income tax from 83 to 60 per cent and the basic rate from 33 to 30 per cent. He increased income-tax allowances by 8 per cent more than the RPI. He introduced a new lower rate of 10 per cent alongside the 15 per

Figure 7. Taxation changes, 1979–90 (from base of indexed income-tax allowances and revalorized excise duties)

Budget year	Personal income tax: Earned	Personal income tax: Investment	Company tax	Oil tax	Indirect tax
1979	Income tax 83–33 > 60–30% Allowances RPI + 9%	Investment income surcharge 10–15 > 0–15%	Development-land tax 80–67 > 60%	Petroleum (PRT) revenue tax (PRT) 45 > 60%	VAT 8–12.5 > 15%
1980	Income tax 25 > 30% NI 6.5 > 6.75%		Enterprise zones	PRT 60 > 70% Advance PRT 15%	
1981	Allowances RPI − 13% NI 6.75 > 7.75%		Special bank c/a deposits tax 2.5%	Supplementary petroleum duty 20%	Excise RPI +
1982	Allowances RPI + 2% NI 7.75 > 8.75%	CGT indexed	NI surcharge 3.5 > 2.5% 2.5 > 1.5%	PRT 70 > 75% SPD ends	
1983	Allowances RPI + 8% NI 8.75 > 9%	Business exp. scheme	NIS 1.5 > 1%	APRT to end by 1/1/87	
1984	Allowances RPI + 7% Life-ass. premium relief ends	Inv. income surcharge ends Stamp duty 2 > 1%	CT 52 > 35% by 1986–87 Allowances reduced NIS ends		VAT take-away, alterations
1985	Allowances RPI + 5% NI 9 > 5/7/9%	Composite-rate tax on bank interest	DLT ends Employer NI UEL ends NI 10.45 > 5/7/9/10.45%		VAT press ads Excise RPI +
1986	Income tax 30 > 29%	Personal equity plans Gifts tax ends	Stamp duty on shares 1 > ½%		
1987	Income tax 29 > 27%	Profit-related pay ½ exempt Inheritance tax 60–30 > 40%			
1988	Income tax 60–27 > 40–25% Allowances RPI + 4%	Mortgage × 2 relief ends CGT indexed from 1982	1% capital duty ends		
1989	NI 5/7/9 > 2/9%				Excise 0 VAT water, fuel, construction
1990	Independent taxation Community charge	CRT ends 1991	National non-business rate		Excise RPI + Rates end

Source: Financial Statement and Budget Report, various years.

Figure 8. Main tax rates, 1978–90

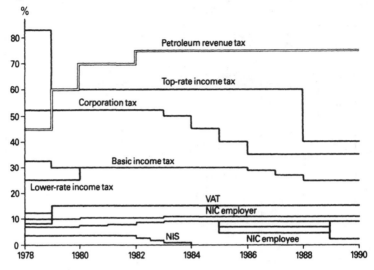

Source: *Financial Statement and Budget Report*, various years.

cent investment-income surcharge and abolished dividend controls. In order to meet most of the cost of the income-tax cuts, he raised the rate of VAT from 8 per cent (12½ per cent on some luxury goods) to 15 per cent.

Howe said in his Budget speech: 'We have over the years spent far too much time and effort trying to "level down",' and announced as his aim a basic rate of 25p in the pound. He claimed that the VAT increase would be less punitive for those on lower incomes, because a zero rate would be levied on food, fuel, public transport and housing. It would make exports relatively more attractive, since they were also zero-rated. Prices would go up by 3½ per cent on average, but people would have more money in their pockets. 'This is the only way we can restore incentives and make it worth while to work.'

The income–expenditure tax switch went part of the way

towards the reform recommended by the Institute for Fiscal Studies committee chaired by James Meade, which reported in 1978. Taking up an idea first launched by Nicholas Kaldor in 1955, the Meade Committee advocated a move from an income tax to an expenditure tax with a progressive rate structure. This would encourage saving and investment by taxing only current spending, while still redistributing income by taxing higher expenditure at higher rates. The Meade Report issued a warning that serves as a prescient comment on the 1979 Budget.

One could not expect nominal money wage rates to be reduced *pari passu* with the replacement of the tax on income by the tax on value added. This implies that there would be a corresponding rise in money costs and prices. The wage and salary earners would take home larger money pay packets as the rate of income tax was reduced, but the money price of products would have to be raised to cover the extra cost of the tax on value added. Clearly the process would have implications for incomes policies and for the control of runaway inflation.

Howe did not heed the warning that was given by critics of his Budget, and prices and wages rose by 4 per cent, contributing to a peak inflation rate of 21.9 per cent by May 1980. It was argued in *Fiscal Studies* by John Kay, then Director of the Institute for Fiscal Studies and a member of the Meade Committee, that the lowering of marginal rates of income tax had been offset exactly by the raising of marginal rates of VAT on the expenditure of post-tax income, so that 'the net effect was extremely small'. The incentive effects on higher-rate taxpayers were possibly greater, but the cut in higher rates, which swept away an anomaly, could have been carried out independently of the massive income tax–VAT switch that affected all taxpayers.

In the 1980 Budget Howe abolished the lower income-tax rate of 25 per cent, so that the starting rate was raised to 30 per cent. Lawson marked his first Budget in 1984 by abolishing the 10–15 per cent investment-income surcharge; since investment income was not made subject to employee

National Insurance Contributions (NICs), the result was that it was treated more favourably over a wide range of income than was earned income from work. There were no further changes in the basic rate until 1986, when Lawson cut it to 29 per cent, and 1987, when he rewarded the voters in the run-up to the election by cutting it again to 27 per cent. The major reform came in 1988, when Lawson finally fulfilled Howe's promise of a 25p basic rate. More surprisingly, he abolished all the higher rates save the lowest 40 per cent one, which became the top rate. The UK moved from being in line with the European average of top rates to well below it, but Lawson was spurred on by the rate competition with the USA, which had in the 1986 tax reform cut its top rate to 28 per cent (but with a 34 per cent band at lower levels).

When Conservative Chancellors did not cut tax rates they raised tax allowances above the statutory RPI indexation. This occurred in every Budget between 1979 and 1985, with the outstanding exception of the harsh 1981 Budget, when allowances were not changed even in nominal terms and were thus cut by 13 per cent in real terms. Allowances were again over-indexed in 1988 but in no other year after 1985. The result was that between 1978 and 1980 they rose by 24 per cent in real terms, while average earnings rose by $33\frac{1}{2}$ per cent.

Keeping up with the NICs

A main target of UK tax reformers has been the anomalous coexistence of separate income-tax and social-security systems. The income-tax system has numerous allowances and reliefs that are similar in effect to social-security benefits, while the social-security system has NICs that are similar in effect to income and payroll taxes, according to whether they are levied on employees or employers. The main anomalies occur with regard to marginal rates of tax/contribution and eligibility for allowances/benefits.

Barber proposed to tackle the matter by his tax-credit

scheme, published in 1972. This would not have integrated the tax and social-security systems – an administrative nightmare – but it would have aimed at the substitution of tax credits for both tax allowances and social-security benefits, with everyone becoming either a net taxpayer or a net tax-credit recipient but not both at once. Mrs Thatcher said in Liverpool in December 1976: 'We still see tax credits as the most hopeful way ahead.'

The 1979 manifesto welcomed child benefit, which Labour had just substituted for child tax allowances, as 'the first stage of our tax-credit scheme'. But, it warned, 'Further progress will be very difficult in the next few years, both for reasons of cost and because of technical problems involved in the switch to computers. We shall wish to move towards the fulfilment of our original tax-credit objectives as and when resources become available.'

The ideas behind the tax-credit scheme had bipartisan support. Although Howe made little progress with it during his Chancellorship, a sub-committee of the Treasury Select Committee, chaired by the Labour backbencher Michael Meacher, took much evidence and drafted an important report, *The Structure of Personal Income Taxation and Income Support*. Some of the details were controversial, and the Treasury Committee was unable to agree on it in time for the dissolution of Parliament in May 1983. It was published as a draft.

The Meacher Report claimed that 9 million adults were at risk from the poverty and unemployment traps in 1979. These occur when the marginal rates of tax implied by income tax and the withdrawal of benefits approach or exceed 100 per cent. In Kay's words: 'The poverty trap refers to the way in which people on low incomes see most or even all of any increase in their incomes absorbed by tax and lost benefits. The unemployment trap is the result of benefits providing incomes for those out of work which approach, or exceed, the net earnings after tax from a job.' To avoid the traps, the report recommended a fuller integration of the tax and social-security systems. It also said:

'Employees' national insurance contributions ... should be replaced by a social-security tax with a similar structure to income tax.'

To begin with, the Conservatives gradually increased the rate of employee NICs from 6.5 per cent in 1979 to 9 per cent in 1983. This raised the combined marginal rate of tax by 2.5 per cent for all those below the NIC upper-earnings limit, almost fully offsetting the 3 per cent cut in the basic rate of tax in 1979. The combined marginal rate of basic tax had changed by 1983 only from 39.5 to 39 per cent. Since NICs were less visible than income tax and were held, without much justification, to be related to benefits, the political impact was less than that of maintaining the basic rate.

It was only in 1985 that the Government made its first move to reform NICs. Unusually, it took up an idea put forward by Professor Richard Layard of the London School of Economics, who had in that year founded the Employment Institute to examine alternatives to Mrs Thatcher's policies (see page 240). Lower rates of 5 and 7 per cent were introduced for part-time and other lower-paid workers. The same structural changes were made for employers' NICs: new rates of 5, 7 and 9 per cent were brought in underneath the existing 10.45 per cent rate. The upper-earnings limit for NICs remained in place for employees but was removed for employers, who now had to pay the top rate of 10.45 per cent right up the income scale.

Unemployment was still rising, and the Government was keen to adopt any measure that might contribute to lowering it. These reforms, said Lawson in his 1985 Budget speech, 'will significantly improve the flexibility of the labour market and the prospects for jobs ... The radical restructuring I have announced will encourage employers to take on the young and unskilled, and give them, in turn, an incentive to seek work at wages that employers can afford.'

The effect of the measures was hard to predict. Although they lowered the costs to employers of some forms of labour, notably part-time women workers and juveniles, they raised the cost of managers and highly paid skilled workers. The supply response by lower-paid workers to the lowest contribution rates was likely to be less than the demand response by employers, although it might be more in areas of high unemployment. This meant that, although hirings might increase, the average wage in this part of the labour market might rise.

One unfortunate side-effect was the creation of new 'traps'. There had always been a trap at the NIC lower-earnings limit because any employee whose pay moved from just below to just above the limit suddenly had to pay 9 per cent on all earnings, not just on those above the limit. There was thus a marginal tax rate of infinity at the lower-earnings limit. The reforms created new traps of this kind on the frontiers between the 5 and 7 per cent and the 7 and 9 per cent bands. Similar traps existed for the employers. An important rigidity therefore remained.

The lower NIC employee rates made a minuscule contribution to the alleviation of the poverty trap by lowering some marginal tax rates by 2 or 4 per cent. The main measure to combat the poverty and unemployment traps was contained in the extensive but unambitious social-security review announced in 1986 by Norman Fowler, then Secretary of State for Health and Social Security, and implemented in 1988. By basing means testing for benefits on income net of tax rather than gross income, it lowered the effective marginal rate, so that it could not exceed 100 per cent. At the same time it spread high marginal rates of more than 80 per cent over a wider range of lower incomes. The poverty trap became wider and shallower but easier to climb out of.

The unemployment trap was alleviated by a number of different measures. By 1982 earnings-related supplement was phased out, and benefits were subjected to tax. Benefits rose more or less in line with prices, while earnings rose by $2\frac{1}{2}$ per cent a year more on average. Tax thresholds, while rising more slowly than earnings, rose faster than prices. Benefits were awarded more selectively, thus not only reducing the number officially counted as unemployed but also increasing those who were still *de facto* unemployed but not tempted to remain so by the loss of benefits that they were no longer getting. The incentive to work, or at least to seek work, was increased, even if jobs remained difficult to find until the great post-1986 expansion.

Lawson had a second bite at the cherry of NIC reform in his last Budget in 1989, which went some way towards the Meacher proposals of 1982 for an NIC allowance similar to an income-tax allowance. A new 2 per cent rate was introduced for all income up to the lower limit for employee NICs, and the 5 and 7 per cent rates were swept away, to be replaced by a single 9 per cent rate, which applied only to income between the lower and upper limits, not to that below the lower limit. It was an expensive reform, costing £2.8 billion in a full year at a bad moment in the inflation cycle, but not as expensive as a completely tax-free allowance on the pattern of income tax:

The second Lawson reform got rid of the NI traps for employees but, illogically, maintained the old structure of multiple rates and traps for employers' NICs, mainly because of the additional cost of abolishing them. The reform also failed to tackle the long-standing problem of the dip in combined income tax/NI marginal rate – from 34 to 25 per cent – for the range of incomes between the upper NI earnings limit and the threshold of the higher 40 per cent rate of income tax.

Tax allowances – his and hers

Family taxation took longer to implement than any other tax reform under the Thatcher Government. It was ten years from the issue of the Green Paper *The Taxation of Husband and Wife* in 1980 to the implementation of so-called 'independent taxation' of husband and wife from 1990 onwards. The Green Paper set out the reasons for making a change:

1. Social change meant that half of all married women were 'economically active' (the official euphemism meaning either working or unemployed), making up a quarter of the total workforce.
2. Wives were still subordinate to their husbands in tax matters and had no privacy in their own financial affairs.
3. There was discrimination against wives because they did not get as much in earned-income allowances as their husbands and no separate allowance at all for investment income.
4. There was discrimination against one-earner couples in favour of two-earner couples because the wife's (earned-income) allowance was available to the latter but not the former (unless the earner was the wife, who got her wife's allowance and the married man's allowance – the strange anomaly of the 'breadwinner wives').

The Green Paper suggested a system of either partially or fully transferable allowances as between husband and wife (see table 26). It was assumed that the married man's allowance would be abolished and that each partner would have a single allowance. If the allowances were the same as the existing single allowance, the husband would lose out if his wife were working because she would use up her own allowance and he would not have the higher married man's allowance. If she were not working, a partially transferable allowance would mean that she could give him, say, half her allowance, restoring his single allowance to the level of the married man's allowance. A fully transferable allowance would make the husband of a non-earning wife even better off than under the existing system, with double the single allowance.

The Green Paper proposals thus appeared to discriminate against two-earner couples compared with the existing system and to encourage wives to work in the home rather than in paid employment, particularly with a fully transferable allowance. They seemed calculated to alleviate unemployment at the cost of setting back the emancipation of women. No action was taken for some years. Then the House of Lords Select Committee on the European Communities reactivated the subject in response to a European Community recommendation, issuing in November 1985 a report on *Income Taxation and the Equal Treatment of Men and Women* (significantly not *Husband and Wife*).

The House of Lords said that 'a system with transferable allowances would be difficult to understand and expensive to administer, and would create a substantial disincentive to wives in seeking paid employment. Independent taxation with fully transferable allowances would be identical to joint taxation in most important respects.'

The House of Lords had understood that full independence could not be achieved if husband and wife had to compare their earnings in order to decide how much, if any, of the wife's allowance to transfer to the husband. It was also clear that if transferability depended on the marriage relationship, the system would discriminate in favour of married as against unmarried households. This was not a point to worry the Thatcher Government, though the Dutch had shown that it was possible to have transferable allowances within unmarried households.

The next Green Paper, in 1986, attempted to overcome the difficulties of the previous one by proposing to raise the single allowance to make it equal to $1\frac{1}{4}$ of the existing ones. A two-earner couple would then get $2\frac{1}{2}$ allowances, as now, though equally split between husband and wife. It would make no difference whether the couple was married or not if both were working. There would still be a discrimination in favour of marriage for one-earner couples: wives could fully transfer all allowances to husbands and would not have to go out to work to get them.

The Green Paper scheme was about 25 per cent more expensive than the existing system (see table 26) because it meant raising all single allowances by a quarter in order partly to remove the discrimination in favour of marriage and creating new allowances for non-working wives. The cost of up to £5.5 billion was to be met partly by letting inflation erode the real value of allowances and partly by phasing in the changes. Faced with the choice, the Government preferred to spend a similar sum cutting the basic rate of tax from 30p to 25p between 1986 and 1988.

The promise of independent taxation, once mooted, could not be dropped, however. In the 1988 Budget Lawson promised that it would be introduced in 1990. His stated objectives were: 'First, to give married women the same privacy and independence in their tax affairs as everyone else. And, second, to bring to an end the ways in which the tax system can penalize marriage.' The scheme that was announced in 1989 was far less ambitious and expensive than any of the Green Paper plans. Its main feature was the separation of part of the married man's allowance into a married couple's allowance, which the husband could transfer to his wife to set against her income if he did not have sufficient income to absorb it. The new system thus broadly replicated the existing one but with important differences affecting mainly high-earning couples.

Higher-rate couples were helped in two ways by not having to aggregate their income for tax purposes. With both spouses paying higher rates, the husband was able to keep the married couple's allowance instead of, as before, having to give it up if the couple opted for separate taxation. Even if only the husband were paying higher-rate tax, his wife's earnings no longer incurred tax at his marginal rate but only at her marginal rate – in most cases the basic rate. Couples were also allowed to be separately taxed on their investment income. This gave non-earning wives a use for their new tax allowances and offered an incentive for spouses to distribute income-bearing assets more equally. In general, it gave women a new sense of dignity, although it retained discrimination in favour not only of marriage but also of the husband within it. It also created the need for an extra 4.7 million women to fill in tax returns, thus raising compliance costs for both taxpayer and tax collector.

Three main defects remain. First, taxation of couples is not totally independent, since a couple must collude to maximize the advantage of the married couple's allowance. Second, there is discrimination in favour of married couples as against others, although this may be a desired policy goal. Third, there is discrimination in favour of one-earner married couples without young children as against those with them. The married couple's allowance given to such couples is not required for any purpose save to keep a wife who could earn an income outside the home if she chose to. The Government has been deaf to appeals to increase substantially child benefit for couples with young children as a substitute for the married couple's allowance. Discrimination between children of married and non-married households would automatically disappear. Instead the Government has cut the real value of child benefit by either freezing it in nominal terms or raising it by less than inflation in most recent years. (It was raised only from £4 in 1979 to £7.25 in 1990, a real cut of 21 per cent.) The House of Lords rightly pointed out that the tax and social-security systems must be considered in conjunction with each other in assessing their impact on the family.

Tinkering with tax on savings

The Government carried out many detailed measures to encourage saving and capital accumulation. The abolition of the investment-income surcharge in 1984 has been mentioned. The most important were reforms of capital gains tax (CGT). In 1982 CGT was indexed, so that an indexation allowance for RPI inflation from that date could be subtracted from the taxable gain. There was no indexation of pre-1982 gains, in which there was often a large element of inflation, so a new anomaly was created. In 1988 this was dealt with by ignoring gains made before 1982, and taxable gains were aggregated with other income, although still with a separate CGT allowance. Higher-rate taxpayers were put out to find that their gains were to be taxed at 40 per cent rather than the formerly uniform 30 per cent rate. In 1987 the tax on lifetime gifts was abolished, and in 1988 the multiple tax rates of 30–60 per cent on transfers at death were replaced by a new inheritance tax rate of 40 per cent.

Bill Robinson, Director of the IFS, pointed out that these could be seen as steps towards a comprehensive income-tax system, such as reformers had been advocating for many years. CGT, he pointed out, still had many loopholes. It was payable in arrears, enjoyed a big exemption allowance, gave rollover relief on retirement, could be deferred on gifts and was extinguished on death. There is much still to be done to integrate CGT and inheritance tax, which needs to be based on the amount received by the donee rather than on the amount given by the donor, so as to encourage the wider dispersal of wealth. 'Nothing can be said to be certain, except death and taxes,' as Benjamin Franklin wrote, but nothing is more uncertain than the relationship between them.

The Business Expansion Scheme, an improvement on the 1981 Business Start-up Scheme, was introduced in 1983; private investors escaped tax – notably at the higher rates – on investments in approved schemes. Stamp duty was halved to 1 per cent on all transactions in 1984 and halved again to ½ per cent on share transactions in 1986. Personal Equity Plans (PEPs) were introduced in 1986, allowing equity investors to receive both dividends and capital gains tax-free on investments held for at least five years by plan managers – mainly the clearing banks, as it turned out. In 1987 Profit Related Pay (PRP) was introduced to allow up to half of pay, up to a limit, to be tax-exempt in defined profit centres. Composite-rate tax on building society deposits, which was extended to bank deposits in 1985, was abolished by the 1990 Budget, to take effect in 1991, so that non-taxpayer savers would not have irrecoverable tax deducted from their interest. From January 1991 a boost was given to bank savings deposits by the introduction of Tax-Exempt Special Savings Accounts (TESSAs), with interest free of tax if the deposit were held for up to five years. For the impact of these and other measures on personal share ownership, see page 168.

The problem with such selective measures to encourage savings, as John Hills pointed out in 1984, was that they widened the scatter of different degrees of 'fiscal privilege' on different assets. Fiscal privilege is defined as the taxpayer's marginal rate of tax minus the tax rate on the real return on an asset. At a time of high inflation assets whose value rises out of proportion to the tax on them enjoy high fiscal privilege, and those whose real return is eroded by more than the tax charge have negative fiscal privilege. For example, houses and pension schemes have high fiscal privilege, bank and building society accounts and gilts low fiscal privilege. The creation of special saving schemes with high fiscal privilege may only divert savings from vehicles with low fiscal privilege rather than increasing the total amount of savings. Any reform of tax on savings should seek to create an equal degree of fiscal privilege for a wide range of savings media, if not for all equally.

The Government shrank from abolishing areas of high fiscal privilege. Lawson was prevented by Mrs Thatcher from ending mortgage interest relief on housing or at least limiting it to the basic rate of tax (see page 149). Nor did it improve areas of low fiscal privilege – for example, by taxing only the real, rather than the nominal, return on deposits. Lawson dropped the idea of removing tax exemption from pension contributions in his 1985 Budget but imposed a ceiling of £60,000 pensionable salary for tax-free contributions on new entrants in 1989.

The introduction of personal pension plans in 1988, after a successful campaign led by Philip Chappell, a former merchant banker, looked like an attractive move towards the Thatcherite entrepreneurial society. It would encourage economic independence by making it easier for people to change jobs or set up on their own, and it would encourage individual savings and thus reverse the trend towards giant collective funds.

By April 1990 over 4 million people had been persuaded to leave the State Earnings Related Pension Scheme (SERPS), eight times the number assumed by the Department of Social Security. Unfortunately, the cost to the Treasury of the National Insurance Contribution rebates, and the additional 2 per cent incentive, was also far higher than anticipated. The National Audit Office reported in November 1990 that the gross cost to the National Insurance Fund up to April 1993 would be £9.3 billion, offset by savings of SERPS pensions in respect of the same period of £3.4 billion, giving a net cost of £5.9 billion. The cost in 1991–2 alone was estimated at £2.5 billion (Hansard, 19 December 1990 col. 236). Even worse, it turned out that members of personal pension schemes had the option of contracting into SERPS again as and when it suited them, notably if the rebates and incentives were to be reduced.

In a leading article entitled 'The pensions débâcle', the *Financial Times* (4 January 1991) concluded: 'The real failure here was to allow the pensions agenda to be hijacked by the personal pensions lobby when a more fundamental rethink of the role of state pensions was called for.' More generally, this was an example of the unwisdom of providing savings incentives in isolation without working out any general relationship between taxation and savings of all kinds.

The Meade Report, advocating an expenditure basis for taxation (see page 113), showed a way of giving tax incentives to savings that was far more radical than anything ever contemplated by the Thatcher Government. Tax measures to encourage savings amounted to sporadic tinkering rather than fundamental reform. The Government also failed to provide proper savings incentives for those receiving welfare benefits. For example, benefits are withdrawn at a high rate from pensioners and other recipients with savings of over about £8,000. This is an incentive to live on capital, not to accumulate it and pass it on.

Incentives a shaky foundation for tax cuts

Assessments of changes in income tax and in NICs and social-security benefits are best considered jointly. Tax changes can be distinguished as changes in the marginal rates of tax, applied to gross income, and changes in the tax allowances whose value to the taxpayer is their amount times the marginal rate of tax, so that it goes down if tax rates are cut. For the average male earner real income rose by 33½ per cent between 1978 and 1979, while his basic rate of tax fell by 22 per cent, from 32p (a weighted average of the 25p and 33p rates) to 25p in the pound. There was therefore a 4 per cent real rise in this component of income tax because (133.5 × 0.25) is 4 per cent more than (100 × 0.32). The tax allowances went up by 24 per cent in real terms, but the cut in the tax rate caused their value to the taxpayer to fall by 3 per cent in real terms, leading to a further rise in tax. Tax paid rose by 9 per cent in real terms, while falling by four percentage points as a proportion of gross income.

The average rate of tax fell by 18 per cent, less than the basic marginal rate, from 21.3 to 17.5 per cent of male earnings. However, employee NICs fell less than income tax because of the rise in rates in the early 1980s. The combined marginal rate fell from 39.5 per cent to 34 per cent, a drop of 14 per cent; the combined average rate fell only from 27.8 to 25.5 per cent, a drop of 8 per cent (see table 27). There was no allowance for NICs, so the tax allowances for the two systems combined were less than for income tax alone.

The incentive effects of tax changes are ambiguous because they depend on two separate effects, the substitution effect and the income effect, corresponding to the two parts into which we have divided tax changes. The substitution effect works through a lowering of the marginal tax rate and leads the taxpayer to substitute work for leisure at the margin, as the price for each extra hour of work rises in terms of after-tax income. The income effect works through the value of tax allowances, which give the taxpayer a lump-sum gain like a tax-credit and lead him to work less in order to achieve a given income target.

The incentive effects of tax cuts thus depend on how they

are split up between rate reductions and allowance increases. From the point of view of stimulating effort, the preference for allowance increases over rate cuts from 1980 to 1986 was misconceived; in view of the high unemployment, this may have been a blessing in disguise, even if it was not what the Government intended. A tax system designed to maximize incentives abolishes all allowances and has a proportional tax, with one basic rate on all income that is both the average and the marginal rate. This would at present be about 25 per cent, including NICs.

The degree of incentive from the taxpayer's point of view is the inverse of the income elasticity of the tax system from the tax gatherer's side. The income elasticity is the percentage by which tax paid increases for each extra 1 per cent on gross income; the lower the elasticity, the higher the incentive. It can be calculated by dividing the marginal tax rate by the average tax rate. The minimum possible figure is 1 – good for incentives, bad for revenue collecting. The net result of the changes in the 1980s was that this ratio for income tax/NICs for the average married male earner fell from 1.42 to 1.33 and by more for higher-income earners. In theory there was a slight improvement in incentives.

The evidence on incentives is somewhat mixed. The Treasury commissioned a major study from Professor Chuck Brown of Stirling University and a team of experts but was not pleased with the results. Instead of publishing them, it placed them in the House of Commons Library and left publication to Stirling University. Brown looked at the supply of labour by households, basing his findings on data collected in 1980; allowance must be made for the fact that it was a recession year. He found that, with no constraint on the demand for labour, a tax cut from 29 to 25 per cent had no effect on hours worked, while a 25 per cent increase in tax allowances would cause a drop of twenty-five minutes in weekly work. A revenue-neutral tax-rate cut, financed by a cut in allowances, would cause an increase of twenty minutes in time worked. He concluded: 'The changes in predicted hours are very largely the effect of the change in the level of demand constraint. Little of the change in predicted hours is the result of the changes in taxation.'

Similar conclusions were reached in an IFS study by Richard Blundell and Ian Walker, which concluded that women, with more of a choice about whether to work, were more responsive to tax changes than men and that they were more likely to be affected by the move to independent taxation and by benefit changes than by the basic rate cuts. 'The labour-supply response of secondary workers in general and married women in particular is much greater. This is where we need to worry about the efficiency costs of high tax rates incident, under a system of joint taxation, on the wives of high-earning men. Separate taxation of husbands and wives may be a simple reform, but it is an important one.'

Blundell and Walker were sceptical about the incentive effects of even the large cuts in the higher rates in 1979 and 1988, yet Lawson saw these as almost the crowning glory of his Chancellorship: 'The reason for the world-wide trend towards lower rates of tax is clear. Excessive rates of income tax destroy enterprise, encourage avoidance and drive talent to more hospitable shores overseas. As a result, far from raising additional revenue, over time they actually raise less. By contrast, a reduction in the top rates of income tax can, over time, result in a higher, not a lower, yield to the Exchequer.' Lawson said: 'The top 5 per cent of taxpayers today contribute a third as much again in real tax as they did in 1978–9 . . . while the remaining 95 per cent of taxpayers pay about the same as they did in 1978–9.'

Professor Patrick Minford presented econometric evidence in favour of the higher-rate cuts. In a typical case of a high earner a cut from 60 to 40 per cent in his marginal rate would increase his marginal earnings by 50 per cent, and he might then increase his hours worked by 25 per cent. His total income might rise by 20 per cent, and he might as a result reduce his hours worked by 10 per cent. These substitution and income effects working in opposite directions would cause a 15 per cent increase in hours worked.

However, it was unlikely that the tax paid on even such a large increase in hours worked could compensate the Inland Revenue for the tax lost on the income from hours already being worked.

Others were more doubtful. Blundell and Walker wrote: 'Higher rates of income tax are paid by high-earning men whose labour supply is fairly unresponsive to changes in after-tax wage rates. Different people may adopt different value judgements about the equity arguments for high tax rates on big earners, but the efficiency or deadweight burden argument for cutting these rates is weak.'

It was pointed out that there were not enough hours in the week for high earners to respond in such a way as to increase total tax revenue. More important, the increase in tax paid by high earners appeared to be caused by large real salary increases due to performance-related pay structures, including some connected with privatization (see page 165). The cuts in tax rates in 1979 may have caused some companies to switch from other forms of remuneration to taxable earnings for their top executives, so the salary increases were neither independent of the tax cuts nor very closely linked with actual – as opposed to expected – improvements in performance.

Whether top-rate cuts have increased tax revenue or not, they have certainly increased the after-tax income of recipients. As table 27 shows, the proportionate gain from tax/NIC changes since 1978–9 has risen with income, from 0.7 per cent of pre-tax earnings for those on two-thirds of average earnings to 28.7 per cent for those on ten times average earnings, or from £1.42 to £872 a week. For the average earner the gain has been 2.3 per cent, or £7 a week. The same estimate is made by Paul Johnson and Graham Stark, but they also take benefit changes into account. They point out that the average household lost out as a result of combined tax and social security changes from 1980 to 1982 and that only by 1987 was it showing any gain on 1978. The main gain came in 1988 and reached an average £7 per household in 1989. However, the average was pulled up by a £19-a-week average gain for the richest one-tenth, and the poorest 50 per cent had small losses of a pound or two a week. Single parents and the unemployed lost out most, while one-earner couples with no children made the biggest gains.

The income-tax cuts between 1978–9 and 1990–91 were worth £27 billion (this figure was slightly surpassed by 1988–9 – see table 27). Of this £5 billion was due to cuts in allowances, which were worth an average of £190 to each of 25.7 million tax units, and £22 billion to cuts in tax rates, of which half went to the 1.4 million earning over £30,000 a year and the other half to the 24.3 million earning under that sum.

Top executives and members of the professions are motivated as much by interest in their work, pride in achievement, a sense of duty and public recognition as by salary. Their choice between different posts in the UK is also likely to depend on such factors. However, if rewards become so high in top companies, particularly in the City, that they are difficult to refuse, scarce talent may be drained away from the production industries, the universities, the Civil Service and politics to the detriment of the country's performance as a whole. Similar considerations may apply to smaller numbers of posts in other countries, but free trade in executives may be seen as a valuable adjunct to free trade in goods and services.

Marginal tax rates may have some influence on decisions about whether to work longer or shorter hours in the same job or whether to take on additional part-time work. In so far as financial considerations determine the choice of one post rather than another, as opposed to hours worked in the same post, the average rather than the marginal rate of tax is important. Cuts in marginal rates entail reductions in average rates, but ones that are not so sharp. In the last resort there is rough justice in the thought that a person should be allowed to keep at least half of every extra pound he or she earns. With marginal tax rates limited to 50 per cent average tax rates will at most be a good deal less than that. On grounds of equity, if not efficiency, a cut in the top income-tax rate to 50 per cent might have been sufficient.

The corporation tax that wished inflation away

When the Conservatives took office in 1979 the UK system of company taxation was 'in a state of complete chaos', according to an Institute for Fiscal Studies lecture in late 1978 by Lord Cockfield, who became a Minister of State at the Treasury. During their first few years their main action in this area was to dismantle the National Insurance Surcharge on companies by salami tactics, in slices of 1 or ½ per cent, from 3½ per cent in 1981 to zero in 1984. As a payroll tax it had become counter-productive at a time of sharply rising unemployment.

The next step was to publish in 1982 a Green Paper on corporation tax that listed the defects of the existing system. It made a modest contribution to revenue, although this was also due to the low rate of profit; it was not adjusted for inflation; it contained big unused tax losses due to 'tax exhaustion' from allowances exceeding profits; and it discriminated in favour of some kinds of investment, notably plant and machinery, and against others, particularly commercial buildings.

By 1984–5 twice as much tax was being raised from the North Sea in oil and gas taxes of all kinds as was coming in corporation tax from the rest of the corporate sector put together. The Government ruthlessly raised existing tax rates, and piled on new taxes as the oil price went up, to extract its maximum share from the oil rents determined by OPEC: Petroleum Revenue Tax (PRT) was raised in three stages from 45 per cent in 1978 to 75 per cent in 1982. A new Advance PRT was introduced in 1980 and a new Supplementary Petroleum Duty in 1981. The new taxes were phased out as the oil price fell again.

Similarly, the Government imposed a one-time windfall tax on the clearing banks in 1981, raising £355 million by means of a 2½ per cent levy on their non-interest-bearing deposits, since they were thought to be making economic rents out of the high interest rates required by official monetary policy and were known to be, quite legitimately, deferring mainstream corporation tax by using their capital allowances to lease assets to their customers.

The Green Paper was greener than most, since it did not put forward any proposals. Lawson achieved a surprise effect with his 'radical tax-reforming Budget' in 1984. His aim, he said, was 'to encourage the search for investment projects with a genuinely worthwhile return, and to discourage uneconomic investment'. He started from the premise that the 100 per cent allowances on plant and machinery encouraged wasteful use of capital, on which the post-tax return might actually be higher than the pre-tax. He therefore reduced them in three annual stages to 25 per cent while over the same period reducing the rate of corporation tax from 52 to 35 per cent. By changing the allowances and at the same time cutting the marginal tax rate, he was apparently improving incentives and bringing the marginal and average tax rates closer together, as he was later to aim to do in personal taxation.

Simultaneously Lawson ended stock relief, which had been introduced by Healey to protect company finances from inflation. He called it 'a form of emergency help to business facing the ravages of higher inflation. Those days are past; and the relief is no longer necessary.' He spoke with the boundless confidence of a member of a Government that had reduced inflation from nearly 22 per cent to under 4 per cent in three years and could not imagine it rising again.

The reforms were logical, but they were subjected to damaging criticism from the IFS and company representatives. The previous structure had tended to favour capital-intensive industries, notably manufacturing. Critics argued that this feature should have been preserved because the high exchange rate and trade-union practices had created a bias against manufacturing. The effect of the reforms was to give equal advantages to less capital-intensive service industries, notably finance and property, in which the UK already played a leading international role, although the transition period accelerated some manufacturing investment to take advantage of the higher allowances while they lasted (see page 189). This was hardly an argument in favour of the reform in the long run.

The reforms brought in more tax revenue and resulted in more companies paying mainstream corporation tax, as opposed to the Advance Corporation Tax they could not avoid paying on dividends. The CBI argued that the reform was not revenue-neutral and called for a rate cut to 30 per cent to prevent their tax burden from rising. Corporation tax revenues did, in fact, rise strongly in the late 1980s, making it easier to cut personal taxes, but this was a consequence as much of the rise in the rate of return as of the increase in the average tax rate.

The main complaint against the reform was that it dismissed inflation in a cavalier manner. The IFS showed that at any rate of inflation over 7 per cent companies would be worse off as a result of the reform. The 100 per cent allowances had been a rough-and-ready form of compensation for the rise in the replacement cost of capital assets, but no form of inflation-accounting for corporate profits had been put in its place. The accounting profession did not help matters with its prolonged and Byzantine disputes about the merits of rival forms of inflation-accounting. The Government itself, instead of taking the initiative, lost interest in inflation-accounting in the mistaken view that inflation would no longer be a problem.

The reform was supposed to make equity finance less unattractive in relation to debt by lowering the tax rate on it, but any increase in inflation had the opposite effect. As three IFS authors concluded: 'The amount of tax that UK firms must pay in relation to their real profits increases with the rate of inflation. Inflation non-neutralities in the corporation tax discourage firms from engaging in worthwhile investment activity, especially where that investment involves higher holdings of inventories or is financed from equity sources.' Inflation also made debt finance less attractive, however. Any rise in the inflation rate also raised the cost of debt capital by raising the nominal interest rate, since a higher proportion of the principal was, in effect, being repaid early in the life of the loan (see page 32).

A further business tax reform was the new national non-domestic rating system introduced in 1988 as the counterpart of the replacement of domestic rates by the community charge. The object was to prevent local authorities from imposing penal rate poundages on captive businesses by introducing a uniform national poundage and assigning the proceeds to local authorities. The accompanying revaluation caused some dramatic rate increases in the South-East, driving many small businesses out of existence, and some windfall gains in other regions. The Confederation of British Industry (CBI) complained that the starting point had been set too high and that the tax had been too rigidly indexed to inflation as measured inappropriately by the RPI rather than by the lower producer price index. Business interests were also deprived of any influence that their position as ratepayers might have given them over local authority policy.

Poll tax – the peasants' revolt

'Community charge' is the euphemism invented for the particular version of poll tax carried out by the Thatcher Government. The Government used to call it 'poll tax' in official papers, and in her last appearance at the Dispatch Box as Prime Minister Mrs Thatcher referred to it as 'the poll – er, the community charge'. A poll is a head. A poll tax is a per head tax on people. It is about as closely related to a fair personal charge for local authority services as National Insurance Contributions are to benefits received. So poll tax let it be.

The poll tax involved Mrs Thatcher, in a personal way, in a long-drawn-out Greek tragedy culminating in her political downfall. It was she who, as Shadow Environment Secretary, got the commitment to abolish domestic rates into the Conservatives' 1974 election manifesto. It was still there, but pushed down the list of priorities, in the 1979 manifesto (see page 109). The next step was the Green Paper *Alternatives to Domestic Rates*, published by Michael Heseltine as Environment Secretary in December 1981.

The objections to domestic rates were numerous. They were unfair because they were related neither to the number of people living in a property nor to their ability to pay. They were inflationary because local authorities, faced with cuts in central-government finance, maintained their spending by raising the rates by more than the RPI. They were based on out-of-date valuations, but revaluations were sure to cause a political storm, especially in the South-East, where house prices had risen rapidly.

The main alternatives surveyed by the Green Paper were a local sales tax, a local income tax, a poll tax, revenues assigned by central to local government, and a reform of the rating system. In 1976 the Layfield Report had proposed a local income tax either instead of, or in addition to, domestic rates, and many regarded it as the fairest solution. The Thatcher Government, dedicated to cutting national income tax, was not going to undo the good work by introducing a local income tax, particularly if local authorities were free to set the tax rates.

The background to the debate was the running battle over expenditure between the Treasury and the mostly Labour urban local authorities, with the Department of the Environment (DoE) caught in the cross-fire. By the 1983 election there was no agreement on any alternative to domestic rates, and the DoE was given the unenviable job of trying to control them. The 1983 manifesto took the battle on to new ground by undertaking to abolish the Greater London Council and the other metropolitan councils altogether.

On rates the manifesto said: 'There are ... a number of grossly extravagant Labour authorities whose exorbitant rates demands have caused great distress both to businesses and domestic ratepayers. We shall legislate to curb excessive and irresponsible rate increases by high-spending councils, and to provide a general scheme for limitation of rate increases by all local authorities to be used if necessary.' After the election the new Environment Secretary, Patrick Jenkin, had the thankless task of carrying out these commitments under the eagle eye of Mrs Thatcher. In August 1983 he issued a White Paper, called simply *Rates*, that set out the rate-capping proposals and concluded: 'No consensus can be found for an alternative local tax to replace domestic rates.' The long-delayed revaluation was to proceed. The White Paper waxed eloquent about its rediscovery of the merits of rates.

The Government recognize that rates are far from being an ideal or popular tax. But they do have advantages. They are highly perceptible to ratepayers and they promote accountability. They are well understood, cheap to collect and very difficult to evade. They act as an incentive to the most efficient use of property. No property tax can be directly related to ability to pay; but rate rebates, now incorporated in housing benefit, together with supplementary benefit, have been designed to reduce hardship. The Government have concluded . . . that rates should remain for the foreseeable future the main source of revenue for local government.

The *status quo* did not last because the rating revaluation, applied first to Scotland, caused a storm of political protest there that seemed to bode ill for a similar revaluation south of the border. Mrs Thatcher's advisers were taken with a pamphlet by Douglas Mason, *Revising the Rating System*, published in 1985 by the Adam Smith Institute. It made two main points:

Domestic rates should be replaced with a simple per capita tax on all adults over the age of 18. Such a uniform charge reflects the fact that individuals' consumption of local services is roughly equal.

The cost of financing police and education services, already subject to considerable central direction, is almost exactly balanced by the rate support grant, and the finance of these services should be transferred to the centre, with the rate support system being ended.

In September 1985 Jenkin was dismissed and replaced by Kenneth Baker, who, as Jenkin's Minister of State for Local Government since 1984, had been working on ideas for replacing the rates. It was Baker's first cabinet job, and he was determined to make his mark as a policy activist. In January 1986 he brought out another Green Paper, *Paying for Local Government*, coming down strongly in favour of the poll tax, now dressed up as the community charge.

Mrs Thatcher pushed the proposal through a cabinet committee in the teeth of opposition from the Treasury. In a May 1985 paper Lawson fired a broadside that should normally have been enough to sink it without trace, as he revealed in his Stamp Memorial Lecture in November 1990:

I pointed out, with examples, that a flat-rate poll tax (for that, incidentally, was what it was officially called at that time) would be politically unsustainable; and that we would be forced to give so many exemptions and concessions that we would be in danger of ending up with a surrogate income tax. I pointed out, too, that local authorities would seize the opportunity of the transition from rates to poll tax to bump up their spending and revenue and blame it all on the imposition by the Government of an alien system of taxation. I concluded (lest there should be any doubt about where I stood) that the proposal for a poll tax would be 'completely unworkable and politically catastrophic'. Unfortunately, I received no support from any of my colleagues on the committee.

Instead Lawson put forward a radical reform of the rating system. There would be a gradual transition from rental to capital valuations, to come into force only when a property changed hands, with a system of banding, and a fixed discount for pensioners. Central government would take over 'complete responsibility for the financing and key aspects of the management of education'.

The proposal went forward none the less. The community charge, like domestic rates, would cover about a quarter of local authority spending. This meant that every 1 per cent increase in a local authority's spending above the level agreed with the DoE would have to be paid for by a 4 per cent increase in the charge. At one bound Baker appeared to have escaped from the twin horrors of property revaluation and rate-capping. The community charge would apply to all adults, not just to heads of households, and, so the theory ran, this would make local authorities more accountable for spending increases, which would at the same time become more visible. The business, or non-domestic, rate would be set by the DoE, on the basis of a revaluation, and assigned to local authorities on the basis of agreed expenditure rather than rate yields. (This part of the plan was carried out, with big relative changes in business rates in favour of the north and against the south.)

The proposal was, however, to be implemented with caution. 'Domestic rates should be phased out over a period of up to ten years and replaced by a flat community charge.' One worrying feature was that the rates were the only tax on domestic property. Even if they accounted by then for a much higher proportion of total tax revenue than similar taxes in other countries, there could be an undesirable boost to the already worrying rise in house prices if the only tax on housing were suddenly swept away. In concentrating its attention on local government finance the Government was in danger of losing sight of the other problem of how to tax housing, which fell between the local remit of the DoE and the national remit of the Treasury.

After eight months in charge of one of the most complex portfolios in Whitehall Baker moved on to deploy his activism in Education in May 1986, handing the DoE over to Nicholas Ridley, who was close to Mrs Thatcher in his political sympathies.

The 1987 manifesto was clear and confident.

We will now tackle the roots of the problem. We will reform local government finance to strengthen local democracy and accountability. Local electors must be able to decide the level of service they want, and how much they are prepared to pay for it. We will legislate in the first session of the new parliament to abolish the unfair domestic rating system and replace rates with a fairer community charge.

The Conservative Party suffered a rush of blood to the head at the victorious October 1987 post-election party conference, as a result of a speech by Gerry Malone, a defeated ex-MP from Scotland, where the rating revaluation was causing great unpopularity. He called for the community charge to be introduced in one move rather than phased in. In November Mrs Thatcher and Ridley persuaded a cabinet committee, against the better judgement of Lawson and others, to respond to the party conference by adopting the 'big bang', with only transitional reliefs for hard cases, rather than 'dual running' of the community charge and the rates for some years.

A typical critique of the poll tax was that by Stephen Smith of the IFS, who listed its defects in February 1988. It was more expensive to collect than rates because there were more people than properties, and they could and did move frequently. It would raise house prices. It was regressive. The higher incidence on lower incomes could be offset at a cost by rebates, but the lower incidence on higher incomes was a windfall gain that would be allowed to stand – with huge income-tax cuts to be added later. The poll tax was capricious in its incidence, though in a different way from rates.

The poll tax was implemented first in Scotland in 1989–90 and then in England and Wales in 1990–91. It quickly became clear in early 1990 that Lawson's warnings were sound. Local authorities, far from limiting their expenditure, were increasing it – partly because of unexpected pay inflation – and blaming the Government. Their grant was raised so that the poll tax would not need to raise more than the rates had, but the result was an increase of 27 per cent – still

17 per cent net of rebates, which had been raised by 81 per cent to soften the impact. Instead of a flat rate of £278 in England, based on the difference between the DoE standard spending assessments and central government grant, the average came out at £363, with huge variations, from less than half that figure in Tory Wandsworth to 50 per cent more in Labour Haringey.

The fairness of a flat rate across the country, which was part of Mason's original proposal, was lacking from the start. Nor was there the degree of accountability to allow local electors to force local authorities to reduce the tax; indeed, many of them stood to suffer if local spending were cut. By now Chris Patten, who had inherited the DoE from Ridley in July 1989, had to sort out the mess. As the poll tax was manifestly failing to control local government expenditure, he reverted to the bad old ways of capping – the poll tax, not the rates now – thus short-circuiting the supposedly democratic mechanism that had been one of the main arguments in favour of the tax.

In November 1990 the Government's Autumn Statement showed that Patten had extracted an extra £4 billion from the Treasury for local authority grant so as to reduce the need to raise poll tax again. For 1991–2 the average for England was supposed to rise from £357 to £380, only 6½ per cent. The poll tax, according the the 1981 Green Paper, had the advantage that it would reduce the inflation rate. While rates were an expenditure tax, which was therefore included in the RPI, the poll tax was a charge on income and would therefore be omitted from the RPI. When it came to the point in 1989 the Treasury scored an 'own goal' by accepting the advice of its Retail Prices Advisory Committee that the poll tax should be included in the RPI because it was replacing the rates. The 27 per cent increase in poll tax over rates then added a full 1 per cent to the RPI increase in 1990–91, pushing it over 10 per cent in summer 1990. Only if the increase could be held to 6½ per cent in 1991–2 would the RPI increase fall again by 1 per cent.

When Michael Heseltine challenged Mrs Thatcher for

the leadership of the Conservative Party in November 1990 he was able to point to his opposition to the poll tax when he was Environment Secretary in 1979–83. His promise to abolish the tax contributed to his high standing in the public opinion polls and thus to his achievement of 152 votes of MPs against Mrs Thatcher's 204. This result led to her downfall. It was poetic justice that Heseltine then found himself back at the Department of the Environment, with the responsibility, agreed with the new Prime Minister John Major, of carrying out a fundamental review of the poll tax. As in 1381, the peasants had revolted and won their point. Those who do not learn from history are condemned to repeat it.

The changing structure of taxes

The UK's average tax burden rose from 34.3 per cent in the 1970s to 37.4 per cent in the 1980s (see table 25). However, the average EC tax burden rose from 33.1 per cent in the 1970s to 39.0 per cent in the 1980s. The UK has done better than other countries in maintaining a relatively stable, rather than a rising, tax burden in the 1980s partly because of public-expenditure restraint. The UK's total tax burden rose sharply in the early 1980s; although it then fell, it was higher at the end of the decade than when Mrs Thatcher took office.

The tax burden for households was similar to that for the economy as a whole in 1987 (see table 28). Income taxes were progressive, rising with income as a proportion of income, though certainly less so since the 1988 tax cuts. Indirect taxes were regressive, falling with income as a proportion of income. The two together gave no clear reading, with those on average incomes paying more tax as a percentage of income than those on lower incomes but also more than those on top incomes.

The changes have been in the structure rather than in the size of the tax burden (see table 29). Personal income taxes fell from 33.0 per cent of total taxation in 1978 to 26.5 per cent in 1989, the same as in Italy, lower than in the USA (35 per cent, but lower since the reform there) and West Germany (29 per cent) but higher than in France (12 per cent) and Japan (23 per cent). Employee NICs rose from 7.7 per cent in 1978 to 9.0 per cent in 1988 but were cut back to the earlier level by the 1989 reform. Employer NICs fluctuated at just over 9 per cent, and the two together were well below the 1988 average of 29 per cent for the EC, Japan and the USA.

Corporate income taxes rose from 7.5 per cent of total taxation in 1978 to 12.3 per cent in 1989, well above the EC average of 7.5 per cent and below only Japan (24 per cent) among major countries. The 1984 reform thus overdid the quest for a better revenue-raising system. UK taxes on property (all but 2 per cent in rates) averaged 12.5 per cent in the 1980s, equally divided between domestic and non-domestic sectors; this was well above the EC average of $4\frac{1}{2}$ per cent and comparable only with the USA (10 per cent) and Japan (11 per cent).

There was a big rise in VAT, from 9.1 to 16.9 per cent of total taxation, between 1978 and 1989 because of the 1979 Budget switch and the rising weight of VAT goods in consumer spending. The UK thus moved up to the EC average, which is an ironic comment on the Treasury's refusal, on grounds of principle, to harmonize VAT with Britain's EC partners. Excise and other indirect taxes fell from 17.5 to 14.2 per cent because of the less buoyant spending patterns on goods such as tobacco. The UK's total indirect taxation of 31 per cent was again almost the EC average, though much higher than that of the USA and Japan.

Between 1978 and 1989 personal taxes of all kinds were cut from 46.6 per cent to 40.8 per of total taxation. Total corporate taxes fluctuated around an average of 27.6 per cent with no clear trend. Indirect taxes rose 4.5 points from 26.6 per cent to 31.1 per cent. The trend was reversed in 1990 by the poll tax, which switched about 2 per cent of GDP from indirect taxes to personal income taxes. The record on taxation can be judged against the four objectives set out on page 108.

1 The cuts in personal taxes went mainly to middle- and, even more, to high-income groups, and it is doubtful how much effect they had on work incentives.
2 The economy was stimulated more by the demand than by the supply effects of changes in the tax structure. The rise in VAT, the boost to demand and the switch from rates to poll tax made the control of inflation more difficult. In spite of business expansion schemes, enterprise zones, freeports and so on, business growth suffered in the end from the failure to inflation-proof corporation tax and from the burden of the national non-domestic rate.
3 In spite of the proliferation of special savings schemes, the personal-saving ratio sank to its lowest level for many years in 1989 because the tax incentives to borrow were even greater. The growth of personal wealth (see table 35) was due more to the rise in the price of houses and shares than to any new tax incentives to savings.
4 Far from being simplified, the tax system became more complex than ever. Lawson sought to justify this when he wrote: 'I had no intention of reforming *all* the distortions in the tax system . . . While the general presumption should be invariably in favour of fiscal neutrality, in practice there will always be a case for some carefully considered tax incentives.' As a result there are still too many tax privileges for special-interest groups distorting the free market. Tax reform has been piecemeal and incoherent rather than being based on a long-term blueprint.

5 Privatization: progress on some fronts

> 'The government of business is not the business of government.'
> Nigel Lawson, Cambridge Energy conference speech,
> 1982

Origins of a novel policy

It was a master-stroke of public relations on the part of the Thatcher Government to coin and put into world-wide circulation the concept of 'privatization'. It had a positive ring, as opposed to the much more negative-sounding 'denationalization', which conjured up the dreary image of adversary politics, with the two main parties shifting the frontiers of state control back and forth across vital sectors such as steel, which became more and more reminiscent of pointless exchanges of shell-holed territory in the trench warfare of the First World War.

Privatization was not part of the Thatcherite vocabulary during the years of Conservative Opposition. It subsequently came to cover a wide range of policies affecting different parts of the economy. First there was the right of sitting tenants to buy their homes from councils. Then there was the contracting out of central and local government services to private sub-contractors. Most central, but slowest to emerge, was the sale to the private sector of state shareholdings, nationalized industries and other public corporations. Finally, and most hesitantly, there were attempts to boost the small private component in largely public services such as education, health and social services.

Even in its most radical flights of fancy, the Thatcher Government never considered privatizing the NHS or the education service, but piecemeal measures to extend private medicine and education tended to undermine assurances that the much larger public services were high on the list of priorities. It was only late in the 1980s that serious attempts were made to introduce some of the disciplines of the market system into health and education but in the face of suspicion that the aim was to reduce costs rather than to improve the quality of service.

There were many different motives for privatization, some more political than economic and some more important than others at different times or in different sectors. They were:

- to reduce the role of the state in the economy and restore powers of decision to the individual;
- to implement the ideal of the property-owning democracy, partly as a way of increasing political support for the Conservative Party as the champion of private ownership;
- to improve productive efficiency by promoting better management of public assets, whether in industry or in housing;
- to introduce allocative efficiency by substituting competitive free-market pricing for administered prices and controlled rents;
- to finance the PSBR and at the same time remove claims on it arising from public-corporation deficits or investment programmes;
- to promote wider share ownership so as to spread wealth and subject company management to more democratic control;
- to encourage employee share ownership so as to bring about better industrial relations.

Own sweet home

Conservative housing policy was set out fully in *The Right Approach* in October 1976.

> There are three main reasons why we should do more to encourage home ownership. First, it gives people independence; the ownership of their home buttresses a family's freedom. Second, largely for this reason, most people want to become home-owners, and are happier as home-owners than as tenants. Third, helping people to become home-owners represents an excellent bargain for the taxpayer; the average subsidies on a newly built council house add up to about £1300 in the first year, while tax relief on an average new mortgage is around £300.

The document endorsed assisted-deposit and shared-purchase schemes for first-time buyers. It assumed, rather than stated, the continuation of mortgage-interest relief and advocated 'a maximum mortgage rate, which the Government ensures by adjusting as necessary the composite rate of tax paid by the building societies' – an odd notion for a party seeking to restore market freedom.

The novel feature was the expansion of the sale of council houses, which was happening only on a small scale where councils wanted it and were not prevented by the minister.

> We wish, once and for all, to get rid of the unfair restrictions on the sale of their homes to council tenants and new town tenants. We believe they should have the statutory right to buy their homes ... Local authorities are expensive and not always efficient providers of homes ... Much local authority new building is essentially an expensive process of bull-dozing neighbourhoods into piles of rubble, with a switch within the rented sector from private into public.

Help for public housing was to be concentrated on 'areas of serious housing stress', and there was to be a tenants' charter setting out the responsibilities of local authorities and the rights of their tenants. The decline of the private rented sector was to be halted, but this depended on 'the creation of a climate in which private renting is once more seen as sensible and acceptable'.

The proposals were spelled out in detail in the 1979 election manifesto. Even more important than the right to buy was an affordable mortgage rate. 'The prospect of very high mortgage-interest rates deters some people from buying their homes and the reality can cause acute difficulties to those who have done so. Mortgage rates have risen steeply because of the Government's financial mismanagement. Our plans for cutting government spending and borrowing will lower them.'

Then came the right to buy. 'We shall give council house and new town tenants the legal right to buy their homes . . . The terms we propose would allow a discount on market values reflecting the fact that council tenants effectively have security of tenure. We shall also ensure that 100 per cent mortgages are available.' The private rented sector was to be revived. 'There are now hundreds of thousands of empty properties in Britain which are not let because the owners are deterred by legislation. We intend to introduce a new system of shorthold tenure.'

The 1983 manifesto reaffirmed the right-to-buy policy already being implemented, extending it to leaseholds, improving on the discounts and widening the tenants' charter. The 1987 manifesto had to confess failure in reversing the decline of the private rented sector and introduced the 'right to rent'. New private investment was to be attracted into rented housing by extending the systems of assured and shorthold tenancies, with further liberalization of rent control. (Sir Geoffrey Howe, when Deputy Prime Minister from 1989 until his resignation in 1990, liked to recall that he and Colin Jones had proposed the relaxation of rent control in a seminal Bow Group pamphlet, *Houses to Let*, published in 1956.)

Local authorities were to be shifted out of rented housing by giving tenants the right to form co-operatives able to nominate housing associations or private-sector bodies to take over as landlords, and Housing Action Trusts were to be given powers to the same end. Instead of the landlord choosing tenants, tenants were to choose their landlord.

Mortgaging the future

The mortgage rate was crucial to the Thatcher Government's policies and fortunes. The monetarist approach to macro-economic policy made it impossible to keep the promise of lower mortgage rates. Thanks to the separation of the mortgage market and the money market, the building societies were able to hold the mortgage rate down to 15 per cent all through 1980, while bank base rates were raised to 17 per cent, then 16 per cent (see figure 2). After that, deregulation in financial services made the building societies compete more directly with the banks for both deposits and mortgages. The mortgage rate was on average 0.9 per cent higher than bank base rates during the 1980s as a whole (see table 13), far lower than other personal-loan rates.

The belated reduction in public borrowing did not reduce interest rates as much as had been hoped. Mortgage rates fell into single figures only once during the 1980s, for a few months in summer 1988. They were reduced to around 10 per cent for six months before the 1983 election and to just over 11 per cent for a few months before the 1987 election. This played a part in the restoration of the Conservatives' popularity.

If the Government could not keep interest rates down, it could and did act to maintain a ready supply of mortgages. In 1982 the banks were given the green light to enter the mortgage market, and the monetary targets were raised to allow them to do so (see page 46). The banks and other non-building society lenders more than doubled their share of the market in mortgages outstanding, from 18 per cent at the end of 1979 to 40 per cent at the end of 1989. The building societies were stimulated to do better by the competition. Mortgage rationing became a thing of the past, and purchasers were able to borrow up to 95 or even 100 per cent of the valuation of their property, amounting to two and a half or even three times their annual incomes. Mortgage debt rose by 11 per cent a year in real terms in 1980–89.

Mortgage-interest relief (MIR) became the sacred cow of Mrs Thatcher's housing policy. It effectively reduced the average mortgage rate in the 1980s from 12.7 to about 9.5 per cent, or 2.5 per cent after inflation, thus softening the sharp edge of monetary policy. She refused all entreaties from the Treasury to abolish it or at least limit it to the basic rate of tax. Its effect was mitigated by the £30,000 ceiling (raised from £25,000 in 1983), by the abolition in 1988 of double relief for non-married members of the same household, and of relief for home improvements, and by the reduction of tax rates.

The Duke of Edinburgh's inquiry into British housing recommended in 1985 that MIR should be phased out and the money used on a needs-related rent allowance to encourage the revival of the rented sector. The author, in evidence to the inquiry, pointed out that it would be unfair to give tax relief on industrial but not on mortgage borrowing and recommended the abolition of only higher-rate mortgage relief. The cost of MIR more than doubled in real terms during the 1980s, reaching nearly £7 billion in 1989–90, the equivalent of 4p in the pound income tax (see table 30).

Although local authorities had to be lenders of last resort for the right-to-buy scheme, the private sector quickly took over and increased its share of this market from 43 per cent in 1981–2 to 95 per cent in 1988–9. The right to buy was implemented by Michael Heseltine, Mrs Thatcher's first (as he was Mr Major's first) Secretary of State for the Environment. He described it in his book *Where There's a Will* as 'an irreversible shift of wealth in favour of working people and away from the state'. Reluctant Labour urban authorities adopted delaying tactics at first, but Heseltine won a test case against Norwich. He felt that the success of the policy was assured when the Labour Party later dropped its threat to repeal the Act in view of its obvious electoral popularity.

The right to buy was given to public-sector tenants of three years' standing. The discount started at 33 per cent, rising to 50 per cent after twenty years' tenancy. In the event of a resale within five years, the discount had to be partly repaid. The 1984 Housing and Building Control Act extended the right to buy to leasehold property and increased the discount to 60 per cent after thirty years. The 1986 Housing and Planning Act increased the discount to 43–70 per cent for flats, according to length of tenure.

The original target of 1 million homes was reached in September 1986. The great majority were sold to sitting tenants under the right to buy. The peak year was 1982, when 240,000 public-sector homes were sold (see table 30). By 1989 the cumulative total reached 1.5 million, with new towns and housing associations contributing about one-tenth, local authorities the other nine-tenths. As a result of the 1986 Act, sales of flats rose from 6 per cent to 18 per cent of all right-to-buy sales.

The 1988 Housing Act belatedly attempted to do for the private rented sector what earlier legislation had done for the owner-occupied sector. Rent control was abolished for new lettings under assured or shorthold tenancies, including those by housing associations. Local authority and existing private rents, while still controlled, were in many cases allowed to be increased by more than inflation. Housing-benefit expenditure had to be increased, against the opposition of the Treasury, to allow lower-income families to meet higher rentals. Business Expansion Schemes, giving tax relief on personal investments, were extended in 1988 to cover rented housing.

Shrinkage of the rented sector

The result of these policies was a rise of 3.8 million in the number of owner-occupied homes, from 55 per cent of the total in 1979 to 67 per cent in 1989 (see table 31). Of the extra homes, 1.5 million came, mostly under the right to buy, from the public rented sector, 0.7 million from the private rented sector and 1.6 million from new construction. The right to buy thus accounted for two-fifths of the increase in owner-occupation. New construction for the private sector came to slightly more and moved up from 57 per cent of all new construction in 1979 to 87 per cent in 1989. There was a corresponding drop of 1 million in public rented homes, from one-third to one-quarter of all tenures. New construction in the public sector, which fell from 80,000 in 1979 to just over 20,000 in 1989, made up for only about one-third of the 1.5 million homes transferred to owner-occupiers. The biggest setback to policy was that the decline of the private rented sector, far from being reversed, continued – from 12 per cent of tenures in 1979 to 7 per cent in 1989. This meant a loss of 800,000 homes, mostly conversions into owner-occupation, because selling was so much more profitable than letting, and about 90,000 slum-clearance demolitions.

The desirability of owner-occupation, like motherhood, is often taken for granted, yet there is no correlation across economies between the general standard of living and the owner-occupation ratio. The UK's two-thirds is paralleled by that of the USA. On the European continent the relationship is almost inverse. It is 77 per cent in Spain, 59 per cent in Italy, 51 per cent in France and 40 per cent in former West Germany. The UK is also unusual in that 30 per cent of under-25 households are owner-occupiers. In other countries the rented sector, public or private, is relatively more attractive, either because of the better condition of the housing or because of the structure of subsidies.

Owner-occupation is a second-best for some households, which cannot obtain affordable rented accommodation. Yet a recent survey found that there were still 10 per cent of households in rented accommodation who would prefer owner-occupation. Owner-occupation in the UK has become increasingly attractive as an investment as well as a type of tenure. It also tends to improve the housing stock, as owners spend more than tenants on home improvement. Its disadvantages are that it reduces labour mobility, to the detriment of the labour market and thus the control of inflation, and it subjects recent purchasers to disproportionate hardships when interest rates are increased because of monetary policy.

Owner-occupation is impossible for some: the homeless, the elderly, single parents, the unemployed and those on low or irregular earnings. It is undesirable for others: students, young mobile workers and the disabled. Rented, often subsidized, accommodation is needed for such households. The right to buy has debased the average quality of the remaining public rented housing stock. As Christian Wolmar wrote in *Search* in November 1990: 'The best of the council stock has been sold, leaving behind a high proportion of flats and defective homes. There is simply no resale market for such homes, and therefore no incentive to buy them, whatever the discount.' He pointed out that the reduction of the council stock had reduced the chances for those on waiting lists. 'Waiting to fill dead men's shoes may not be very salubrious, but it's an awful lot better than waiting for Godot.'

The rise in homelessness is the product of many factors, which cannot all be attributed to government policy. Household formation, some of it latent, is increasing faster than the housing stock, which rose by 2 million, or 0.9 per cent a year, in the 1980s. More young people leave home; more families break up; more people fail to qualify for social-security benefits; and some fail to take them up. Housing policy cannot, of itself, correct these trends. Homeless households rose from 16 per cent (42,000) of new local authority tenants in 1981–2 to 31 per cent (73,000) in 1988–9. Because not all the homeless are recognized as voluntarily so by local authorities, some are without such accommodation. The total number of homeless households is estimated by John Greve and Elizabeth Currie at 140,000 a year (400,000 people, of whom half are children); this is the number recognized by local authorities, and many have to be accommodated in private bed-and-breakfast accommodation at considerable expense. About 1 million households were homeless for some period during the 1980s.

The characteristics of the homeless are such that they are unlikely to be able to afford private accommodation in either the owner-occupied or the rented sector. The rundown in the rate of public housing construction made it more difficult for local authorities or other public landlords both to accommodate all the homeless decently and to find space for other deserving tenants, who were increasingly crowded out by the homeless because of their statutory priority. Local authorities particularly resented the successive forms of Treasury control over their right-to-buy receipts, which they were prevented from fully reinvesting in new housing so as to maintain their stock. In 1990 local authorities could spend only 25 per cent of housing sales receipts and had to spend the other 75 per cent on debt redemption.

The private rented sector could, if its decline had been reversed, at least have accommodated some of the higher-income groups from the public rented sector. Unfortunately, the 1988 Act did not make the return on private rented investment attractive enough to compare with the return on either owner-occupation or financial investment. The average house price nearly trebled in the 1980s, from £21,000 to £62,000, while the general price level only doubled. Housing thus increased in value by 50 per cent in real terms, or 4 per cent a year, a return bettered only by equities, certainly not by private rental. The opportunity cost of building for rent rose correspondingly, so that the yield required on the price of housing, without being outrageous in percentage terms, put free-market rents out of reach of all but those on relatively high incomes.

The sales of homes by the public sector in England brought in £17.5 billion in the 1980s. Together with similar sales in Scotland and Wales and other sales of government land and buildings, asset sales were £30.6 billion (see table 30). Another £3 billion or so was realized by new-town and housing association sales. The whole of this sum was less than the cost of mortgage-interest relief, which came to £39 billion. It could be argued that the average discount on housing sales of 40 per cent, rising by the end of the 1980s to 50 per cent, meant that public assets had been sold too cheaply; but the fact that most of them were sold to sitting tenants would have reduced the market value, so the discount must be accepted as a recognition of reality.

Moving on from the nationalized-industry battleground

The Conservative approach was originally to discipline the nationalized industries rather than to privatize them. The intellectual case against the nationalized industries was set out in an article in the *Lloyds Bank Review* in April 1976 by John Redwood, then a Fellow of All Souls, later to become head of Mrs Thatcher's policy unit, then an MP and Minister of State for Corporate Affairs. They misallocated capital, distorted demand by under- or over-pricing, added to the money supply because of their borrowing, got their funds at below market rates and suffered from poor industrial relations.

A controversial report of a policy group written by the Thatcherite MP Nicholas Ridley was leaked to the *Economist* of 27 May 1978. Its essence was to set the nationalized industries strict rate-of-return targets, freeing them from government interference in prices and pay but imposing penalties on management if the targets were not met. The main legislative proposal was to end statutory monopolies and introduce competition by allowing new entrants into coal, steel, electricity, posts and telecommunications. The group was particularly concerned with the strike threat in the public sector and was pessimistic about the prospects of resisting it in such vulnerable areas as water, gas, electricity and the NHS. 'The eventual battleground should be on ground chosen by the Tories, in a field they think should be won.' There followed a prophetic passage mapping out a plan for the most crucial episode of the whole Thatcher Government, the 1984 coal strike:

The group believes that the most likely battleground will be the coal industry. They would like a Thatcher Government to: (a) build up maximum coal stocks, particularly at the power stations; (b) make contingency plans for the import of coal; (c) encourage the recruitment of non-union lorry drivers by haulage companies to help move coal where necessary; (d) introduce dual coal/oil firing in all power stations as quickly as possible. The group believes that the greatest deterrent to any strike would be 'to cut off the money supply to the strikers, and make the union finance them'. . . There should be a large, mobile squad of police equipped and prepared to uphold the law against violent picketing.

There was no more than a hint of privatization in *The Right Approach to the Economy*. 'The long-term aim must be to reduce the preponderance of state ownership and to widen the base of ownership in our community. Ownership by the state is not the same as ownership by the people.' The 1979 manifesto was concerned mainly to avoid further nationalization and to make the existing nationalized industries more effective, but it did make some specific commitments, mainly to reverse the most recent Labour measures: 'We will offer to sell back to private ownership the recently nationalized aerospace and shipbuilding concerns ... We aim to sell shares in the National Freight Corporation to the general public.'

Howe gave a clearer pointer to the future in a little noticed passage of his 1979 Budget speech:

Sales of state-owned assets to the private sector . . . are not justified simply by the help they give to the short-term reduction of the PSBR. They are an essential part of the long-term programme for promoting the widest possible participation by the people in the ownership of British industry. This objective – wider public ownership in the true meaning of the term – has implications not merely for the scale of our programme but also for the methods of the sales we shall adopt.

By the 1983 manifesto the Government was able to point to the transfer to private ownership, in whole or in part, of Cable and Wireless, Associated British Ports, British Aerospace, Britoil, British Rail Hotels, Amersham International and the National Freight Corporation (see table 33). The next batch was to be British Telecom (51 per cent), Rolls-Royce, British Airways, British Steel, British Shipbuilders, British Leyland, as many airports as possible, the National Bus Company and British Gas's oil interests (later named Enterprise Oil).

Competition of a kind had already been provided for Telecom by means of Mercury (a partly, and later wholly, owned subsidiary of another privatized company, Cable and Wireless) and the end of British Gas's monopsony power to be the sole seller of gas to industry. The biggest privatization, that of the gas industry itself, followed these others in 1986. Only British Shipbuilders proved to be impossible to sell or even to give away.

By the 1987 manifesto the Government was looking for fresh fields to conquer and added water and electricity to its auction catalogue. Privatization was now presented as 'popular capitalism' under the heading 'a capital-owning democracy'. 'We will continue to extend share-ownership as we have done with home-ownership ... We will privatize more state industries in ways that increase share-ownership, both for the employees and for the public at large.'

How the monopolies were taken private

During the early years of the Thatcher Government the political debate was still much more about the nationalized industries than about privatization. In the recession the nationalized-industry deficits contributed to the over-run of the PSBR, and their performance became more abysmal than ever. The Treasury Select Committee conducted a major inquiry entitled *Financing of the Nationalized Industries*, to which the author was a specialist adviser. The inquiry started with high hopes that a way could be found of financing some nationalized-industry borrowing for worthwhile investment projects, by means of private capital, in such a way as to exclude it from the definition of the

PSBR. The idea was to privatize the financing rather than the ownership, the debt rather than the equity, of the nationalized industries.

The Committee's report, published in July 1981, found that the real return on capital of the industries (without subsidies) had fallen from zero in 1970 to −2 per cent in 1979, although there was a wide scatter of performance. It found that there was no physical crowding out because of nationalized-industry investment (hardly surprising in a recession) and that financial crowding out was much less than 100 per cent. In other words, the demands of the industries for both physical and financial capital could be met without undue strain on the economy. The Committee suggested (3.16): 'If the Government is satisfied that proposals for investment from the nationalized industries satisfy the investment criteria in terms of expected rate of return then they should usually be allowed to go ahead.' Unfortunately, the nationalized-industry chairmen giving evidence could not point to more than a few hundreds of millions pounds' worth of 'frustrated investment'.

The findings on financing were a non-event, since the Committee was persuaded by the impeccable logic of the 'Ryrie rules' put forward in evidence by Mr (now Sir) William Ryrie, then second permanent secretary at the Treasury. The essence of the rules was the following.

(a) Only worthwhile investment projects by nationalized industries would receive government approval.
(b) Guaranteed government loans were the cheapest form of finance, so the net return on such projects would be higher if they were used.
(c) Since the government had to limit its borrowing, it could not automatically approve all nationalized-industry loans just because the projects passed the rate-of-return test.
(d) Even if a way could be found of excluding from the PSBR private-sector loans to nationalized industries, they were still effectively guaranteed by the government, so there was no point in paying higher private-sector rates.

These 'rules' emerged in the course of tortuous verbal fencing between the Treasury and the Committee. The report concluded (6.9): 'The arguments put to us for greater freedom for nationalized industries to borrow more on the private market do not seem to us to be convincing.' However, it then went on: 'Not one of [the industries] appears to regard the system under which they are controlled as ideal, nor has it seemed to us designed to give the maximum incentive to their efficiency or effectiveness. The respective merits of public and private ownership, and shifts in the existing balance between them, are contentious issues . . .' In other words, the Committee could not tackle the much wider question of transfer to private ownership without departing from the consensus it normally sought and dividing on party lines. The impasse that it reached was a clear signal to many in Whitehall and Westminster that it was time to break the mould of the nationalized industries.

About half the total £29 billion proceeds of privatization came from the energy sector, and the additional £11 billion expected from the electricity industry raised the proportion still higher. About £6 billion was raised by selling shares in BP, a publicly quoted company in which private-sector investors already held 49 per cent of the shares. Since BP was already efficiently managed, like any other private-sector oil company, the main point of selling the government's 51 per cent holding was to raise finance for the PSBR. The coincidence of one of the BP offers with the stock-market crash of October 1987 led to the insertion of a floor price by the Bank of England. The Bank had to buy in only 2 per cent of the shares sold because of the purchase of 21 per cent of BP by the Kuwait Investment Office, which was later forced to divest itself of all but 10 per cent. The Government received an unpleasant reminder that one reason for nationalizing a company such as BP in the first place had been to prevent it from falling into foreign hands.

Nigel Lawson, then Secretary of State for Energy and an enthusiast for privatization on ideological grounds, pioneered the sale of Britoil (formerly the British National Oil

Corporation), the 100 per cent government-controlled North Sea oil company, in 1982, raising over £1 billion. In 1989 the Government felt obliged to authorize the takeover of Britoil by BP. This was one of many examples of privatization that was not accompanied by any increase in competition. Another was the takeover by British Airways, shortly after privatization in 1987, of British Caledonian, which had a few years earlier been given some of BA's routes to create more competition.

Economists had debated for years which public corporations were 'natural' monopolies, able to achieve higher efficiency as single units, and which were only *de facto* monopolies, likely to become more efficient by being broken up and having to compete. As Michael Beesley and Stephen Littlechild pointed out in a 1983 article in the *Lloyds Bank Review*, most of the public utilities, notably electricity, gas, and telecommunications, were 'natural' monopolies on the distribution side but not on the production side. There was therefore a case for first ending the vertical integration of production and distribution, then privatizing the distribution side as a monopoly subject to regulation and the production side after breaking it up into several competing units so as to make regulation unnecessary. The Government's eagerness for substantial asset sales within a short time closed its ears to this argument in the cases of British Telecom and British Gas, whose managements argued that profits, and thus the share price, would be higher if their vertically integrated monopoly structure were retained. The argument was later accepted in the cases of electricity, which had a less well integrated structure before privatization, but only in attenuated form.

British Telecom was 51 per cent privatized in 1983, raising £4.7 billion. This was the first such sale of a major public utility with a monopolistic position by share offer. Efficiency was to be enhanced, and monopoly curbed, by a regulator, Oftel, and by a licensed competitor, Mercury. The idea of selling off local area networks separately, or allowing competition against them, as had happened in the USA, was not seriously considered. Pricing was based on the $RPI - x$ formula, with x set at 3 per cent (increased to $4\frac{1}{2}$ per cent in 1989). This meant that prices could rise by the RPI, less 3 per cent for the estimated annual gain in productivity; $RPI - x$ was a weighted average of different tariffs, allowing scope for lower or higher increases in different markets. The degree to which British Telecom's profits were based on restrictive pricing agreements became known only in 1990, when the *Financial Times* revealed the workings of the cartel of national telephone companies in the international calls market (see page 192).

The next such sale of a monopoly was that of British Gas in 1986. There were several possible combinations of horizontal and/or vertical disintegration. British Gas's North Sea gas production could have been sold off in one or several companies, as its North Sea oilfields were under the name Enterprise Oil. The gas-pipeline grid could have been hived off as a common carrier network and sold as a unit to the private sector but with utility regulation. The local distribution of gas could have been separated from production and the main grid and broken up into regional companies, as it was when first in public ownership and still was in name.

Sir Denis Rooke, the powerful chairman, traded his support for privatization for the retention of the existing integrated structure. Ineffective provisions were made for outside suppliers to have access to British Gas's pipelines on terms that were guaranteed to be unacceptable to them. A regulator, Ofgas, was set up with powers that turned out to be more effective in practice than they had looked on paper. The principle of $RPI - x$ was applied, with x set at 2 per cent. British Gas could also add a y factor for cost changes and with little obligation to buy in the cheapest market.

The water boards, privatized in 1989, were kept as separate regional companies, but sold simultaneously on a variety of yields reflecting divergent profit prospects. They were subjected to two regulators: one, on river maintenance, was hived off from them to become the National Rivers Authority, and the other, Ofwat, was set up to regulate their prices. Here the new formula $RPI + k$ was introduced to allow for the fact that there was not much scope for productivity increases but a need to finance long overdue and expensive capital works, as far as possible from internal sources.

The Government decided to try to avoid the same monopoly structure for electricity that it had set up for gas. Generation, the national grid and distribution were separated from other other. There was a good case for setting up about half a dozen generating companies in competition with each other. In the end only two were set up, because one, National Power, had to be large enough to absorb the risks of the nuclear industry, which did not at first deter the Government from privatizing it. The other, PowerGen, was to be given only about one-quarter of the market. In 1989 the Government pulled out the nuclear industry because it was advised that National Power would be unsaleable if it were included, and put it into a separate state corporation. The Government refused, however, to reconsider the structure of the industry on the grounds that it was too late to do so, although the withdrawal of the nuclear stations removed the main obstacle to the creation of several generating companies. In summer 1990 the prospects for PowerGen looked so poor that the Government toyed, amid embarrassing publicity, with the idea of selling it privately to Lord Hanson. Some months later the chairman, Robert Malpas, resigned.

The prospects for the twelve regional electricity companies ('recs') and the integrated Scottish companies, Scottish Power and Scottish Hydro-Electric, looked rather better, with a regulator, Offer, due to apply a $RPI - x + y$ formula similar to that for gas. The creation of a market structure linking the generating companies, the recs and the grid jointly owned by them proved highly complex, and at least one false start was made. The preservation of a merit order, giving preference to power stations in ascending order of marginal cost, was difficult to reconcile with free competition – allowing stations to price below cost if they wished –

and the obligation to maintain supplies to customers at all times. It was also hard to determine to what extent generators should be allowed to sell direct to customers, short-circuiting recs, and to what extent recs or outsiders should be licensed to compete with the main generating companies in the generation of electricity. The sale of the recs in December 1990 realized £5.2 billion, and another £2.8 billion came from debt sales. The sale of 60 per cent of the generating companies in February 1991 was expected to bring in another £2 billion or so.

Apart from the monopoly utilities, the privatization of a wide range of industrial enterprises was relatively simple and uncontroversial. After British Aerospace and Cable and Wireless, the main ones were British Airways, Rolls-Royce and British Steel (see table 33). British Airports Authority was privatized as a unit, although there was a case for privatizing each airport separately and allowing them to compete; the basis of competition, however, would have been landing rights, which were, and still are, set by government on a non-market basis. The privatization of the motor industry was also controversial. Jaguar, hived off from British Leyland and privatized in 1984, made a good start but fell on hard times and was taken over by Ford in 1989 after a Monopolies Commission inquiry. The rest of BL, by then called Rover, was sold to British Aerospace in 1987, but with a host of opaque inducements offered by Lord Young, the Trade and Industry Secretary, that aroused the wrath of the EC Commission, and with property assets that turned out to be worth more possibly than the car-manufacturing operation.

The £29 billion raised by privatization up to 1989–90 incurred a number of substantial costs. These were less for sales by private treaty than for share offers, except that it was hard to be sure that more would not have been realized by a public offer. (The Government was heavily criticized by the Public Accounts Committee for undervaluing property assets in private treaty sales.) The costs of underwriting, marketing, money transmission and advice came to anything betwen 3 and 7 per cent of the proceeds and amounted to about £1 billion. The average discount at which shares were sold was 14 per cent, which amounts to a cost of about £3 billion compared with selling them at the immediate post-flotation price. The Government could have established a fair market price for the shares by selling a few at the outset and then selling other shares at the market price, as they were able to do in the case of the already quoted BP shares.

The Government has also incurred a cost by writing off £15 billion of public-corporation debt to facilitate privatization. This can be too easily dismissed as an accounting transaction within the public sector. However, if the privatized corporations had kept their debt, they would be paying interest to the taxpayer unless the debt had been sold to the public; either way the new shareholders would have been worse off, and the Government would have received less on privatization for the equity, although it could have recouped by privatizing the debt, as it did in part in the cases of Telecom, British Gas and the recs.

Privatization reduced the size of the public-corporation sector by about half in a decade. This was a remarkable achievement, yet some of the most difficult and loss-making public corporations remained to be tackled. While it was easier to sell the more profitable corporations first, those that were most difficult to sell on financial grounds would have benefited more from private-sector disciplines. Since the Government had prepared the ground for a major confrontation with the National Union of Mineworkers, it seems a pity in retrospect that the £3 billion cost of the coal strike to the economy was incurred only to accelerate pit closures and raise productivity rather than returning the whole industry to private ownership. Coal is not a natural monopoly. Competing mining companies could have been set up and the price of coal reduced to world levels, thus laying a far better basis for the privatized electricity industry, which inherited long-term contracts to buy British coal at above world prices.

British Rail and London Regional Transport were also

made to improve productivity, but the standard of service to the public was so poor as to justify privatization, and possibly some degree of disintegration, following one of the several different patterns that have been endlessly discussed but never decided. The Post Office could and should have been privatized years ago, along with Telecom, but for reservations on the part of the royal family about the so-called 'Royal Mail' which the Government should have been able to assuage.

Private does not make perfect

The most important aim of privatization was to improve the performance of the public corporations. The removal of the 'queries and quibbles of a stage army of second-guessers in Whitehall' was argued to be beneficial by John Moore, formerly a stockbrocker in the United States, who was responsible as Financial Secretary to the Treasury for launching the privatization programme in 1983–6. Yet for the key industries there are still large numbers of civil servants who follow their performance at arm's length because of their importance to the economy. The new breed of regulators for the monopolies represent a different form of state control, which may actually be more irksome to management, although the hope is that it will be more beneficial to the consumer. As the OECD commented in its 1988/89 *Economic Survey* on the UK: 'The monitoring of the privatized enterprises by a regulator is subject to all the difficulties involved in monitoring a public enterprise by the Government.' The Government's reply was given by Nicholas Ridley, then Secretary of State for Trade and Industry, when he told the *Financial Times* on 6 November 1989: 'We can achieve better regulation when the utility is at arm's length.' The jury will be out for some time on this.

Since UK private-sector industry's performance had fallen well below international standards, it might be asked what was to be gained by transferring the public corporations to it. As Cento Veljanovski put it in *Selling the State*:

'The nationalized industries and the private corporation share many common characteristics and face similar problems.' The divorce between shareholder ownership and management control common to both public- and private-sector corporations is particularly marked in the UK and in the USA and is not healed by changing the identity of the shareholder – in either direction – as between the state and private investors.

The difference is held to lie in the twin fears of bankruptcy and takeover that operate in the private but not in the public sector. However, it is inconceivable that a public utility transferred to the private sector would be allowed to go bankrupt (although one coal mine or power station might well do so). The threat of takeover has been removed in some cases of privatization by the 'golden share' in the hands of the Government, allowing a veto, yet the reality is there, since golden shares have been waived in cases such as Britoil and Jaguar. The Government has thus had the worst of both worlds: no takeover threat to improve performance, yet no real barrier to the removal of competition and national control by takeover either.

Both managers and employees have received better pay incentives to perform after privatization. From Matthew Bishop and John Kay's figures, top-executive salaries in privatized companies rose three and a half times between 1979 and 1988, while those in the private sector rose by 85 per cent, both in real terms. This raised privatized salaries from 40 to 75 per cent of those in the private sector. The pay of privatized employees rose by 67 per cent in real terms, compared with 25 per cent in the private sector, and thus moved from 90 to 120 per cent of private-sector pay.

According to a study by United Research, 'employees in many instances outperformed all previous expectation.' The privatized-industry executives contributing believed that the essential benefit of privatization was the change from the non-commercial, trade-union, Civil Service culture of public corporations, which had to be turned round from facing towards government and away from the customer. They also found it easier to discuss and satisfy their financial requirements with banks in the City than with bureaucrats in Whitehall. Some of these comments apply equally to private industry as it emerged from the 1970s, and many of the improvements in manning and productivity claimed for privatization took place in public corporations before privatization and in those not privatized.

The most spectacular improvements happened before privatization in British Steel under the chairmanship of Ian MacGregor, in British Airways under that of John King and, without privatization even being on the agenda, in British Coal, again with Ian MacGregor as chairman. The managements' victories in the steel strike in 1982, and in the coal strike in 1984, might not even have been achieved had these two industries then been in the private sector because they were due to the Government's willingness to fund the short-term losses in the long-term national interest. If private-sector companies can go bankrupt, this may improve their performance, but it also makes them more vulnerable to strikes. Private-sector companies have been notably weaker in resisting pay demands during the 1980s than has the public sector, for this reason.

Some of the increase in productive efficiency is common to all British industries irrespective of ownership. Allocative efficiency, which depends on competitive pricing, is a separate question, particularly for the privatized monopolies. Moore said in 1983: 'The primary objective of the Government's privatization programme is to reduce the power of the monopolist and to encourage competition.' In the cases of Telecom and British Gas, however, there has not yet been enough competition to create a rational pricing structure, although the regulators have made more headway than might have been expected. However, if more competition had been introduced, neither privatization nor the regulation that accompanied it would have been necessary. In the absence of sufficient competition, privatization does not change matters fundamentally; regulation is needed, but it could be applied as well to public as to privatized corporations.

Some of the standard measures of performance are inconclusive (see table 34). Allocative efficiency can be measured partly by the return on capital employed (ROCE), productive efficiency by total factor productivity (TFP). British Gas's ROCE fell, but this may reflect lower energy prices; its TFP rose, probably because of demanning. British Steel's ROCE has risen sharply, partly because of better market conditions, but its TFP was rising sharply under improved management before privatization and continued to do so afterwards. Telecom's ROCE increased strongly to a far higher level than that of manufacturing industry, a sign that its monopoly power was still excessive, but its TFP did no better than that of manufacturing industry, with only a slight improvement.

In the public sector performance was equally diverse and not that different from that of the privatized sector. British Coal (thanks partly to the captive electricity market) has always had an ROCE similar to that of the private sector but a radically improved TFP since the strike. British Rail had a dramatic rise in ROCE because it was encouraged to raise fares and an equally good increase in TFP. The Post Office's ROCE fell because of price restraint, and there was little change in a reasonably good TFP increase. The same point was made by the Hundred Group of accountants, which is afraid that the important remaining public corporations may get Cinderella treatment. They revived the old call for them to be allowed to borrow from the private sector without guarantee.

The performance of the privatized sector improved, but so did that of the private sector and the remaining public-corporation sector. This was due partly to supply-side improvements in management ability and industrial relations throughout the economy, partly to the recovery in demand after 1982, which again affected all British industry favourably but was followed by recession in 1990. There are no controlled experiments in economics. Much of the improvement due to privatization might have been secured in its absence, and there could have been an even greater improvement in all types of companies' performance had competition policy had more of a cutting edge (see page 194). Given the beliefs of the Thatcher Government, it was more likely that it would achieve results in the public-corporation sector by means of privatization than by freeing the nationalized industries from official interference and installing a structure of regulation, given that it believed neither that they could perform efficiently nor that they could be trusted not to require constant ministerial interference.

Popular, but was it capitalism?

Wider share ownership, like home ownership, is an important aim of Conservative policy. It is supposed to give citizens an extra source of income for use in unemployment or retirement and to encourage them to take a intelligent interest in the health of the corporate sector on which the economy and their livelihood depend. It is also believed to make company managements more responsive to popular opinion, as represented by a wider universe of small shareholders.

The percentage of shares held by the personal sector fell steadily after the Second World War, from 54 per cent in 1963 to 28 per cent in 1981 and 20 per cent in 1988, with the life-assurance and pension funds (LAPFs) acquiring shares from personal investors (mostly on death) and holding them on behalf of the persons who contribute to their funds. The tax incentives have continued to favour investment through pension funds. The Government's two main attempts to redress the balance were Personal Equity Plans (PEPs) (1986), offering tax freedom for investment income, of which there were 850,000 by 1990, and Tax-Exempt Special Savings Accounts (TESSAs) (1990), which offer tax relief for bank deposits but not equities. The French Loi Monory, giving exemption from tax on the principal invested, found no favour in the UK, except in the case of the Business Expansion Schemes, although it would make personal investment as attractive as pension funds. Personal pension plans have increased to over 4 million (see page 124), but they are managed investments, which do not allow individuals to act as shareholders.

It was only at the end of the 1980s that the Government belatedly responded to pleas to give further tax concessions for employers' contributions to Employee Share Ownership Plans (ESOPs). There are about 1.5 million employee shareholders under various profit-sharing and share-option schemes, which offer considerable advantages in terms of improved industrial relations compared with wider share ownership of a more general kind. The successful privatization of National Freight Corporation by means of an employee buy-out in 1982 was not destined to be repeated because of the difficulties of financing such an operation on the much larger scale required for most other privatized companies. There was also a number of management buy-outs of private-sector companies, with similar advantages but also with high risks where the gearing of debt to equity has been excessive.

Privatization widened the number of individual shareholders but did not deepen their proportion of total holdings, which continued to fall in the 1980s (see above) as large inherited personal shareholdings were sold to the institutions, which held 65 per cent of all shares in 1988. Because the average privatization shareholding is so small, the value of total personal holdings can continue to fall even while the number of shareholders increases. There were over 9 million shareholders in 1988 compared with 3 million in 1979, and they were 21 per cent rather than only 7 per cent of the population, according to the General Household Survey for 1988.

The extra 6 million shareholders were mostly owners of privatization shares or shares in Abbey National and Trustee Savings Bank, which had between them as many shareholders as all the privatized companies put together. Abbey National had 4 millon shareholders, British Gas 2.5 million, TSB 1.8 million, Telecom 1.2 million. There were 5.7 million owners of privatization shares, and 5.5 million

Figure 9. Share ownership, 1988

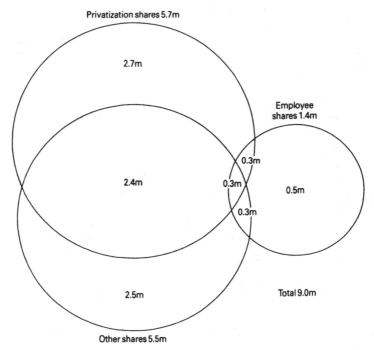

Source: General Household Survey, 1990.

owners of other shares, with an overlap of just under 50 per cent (see figure 9), and another 3 million unit trust holders. 'Manual' socio-economic groups, which were 53 per cent of the population, formed only 28 per cent of the owners of non-privatized shares but 39 per cent of those who owned privatized shares only. Share ownership became more 'democratic' – more like the football pools and less like the bridge table.

Shareholders were attracted by the post-issue premiums on privatization shares, which averaged 33 per cent. Even after the costs of financing applications and dealing, which were high on a unit basis for small parcels of shares, millions of people made a quick profit on flotations, but many were disappointed because the discounts caused nearly every issue to be vastly over-subscribed. There was a rapid fall-away of shareholders, usually between one-third and two-thirds of the original number, as stags sold out, but others stayed in, if only because of the fringe benefits gained by holding. There was some justification for staying in, since privatization shares outperformed the equity market on average by 29 per cent, partly because they were so cheaply sold. There was widespread criticism of the discounts offered, which encouraged stags rather than long-term shareholders, and of the fragmentation of shares into millions of small holdings, which raised companies' register costs and discouraged serious higher-income investors from building up significant holdings. It was popular, but was it capitalism?

Of the new shareholders, 60 per cent owned only one share, 22 per cent only two shares. Such holdings were likely to be small save in the case of employee shares, of which much larger holdings were made available on attractive terms. Risks cannot be adequately spread in a portfolio of one or two shares, and unit trusts and LAPFs are more suitable for such investors. Had the Government had the sole aim of spreading share ownership, it could have given shares away, as John Redwood, now Minister for Corporate Affairs, suggested in a radical pamphlet, *Equity for Everyman*. Holders could then have been given a diversified portfolio of public-corporation stocks.

Lawson also tried at one stage to encourage major private-sector companies to make special issues of new shares to individual investors, thus extending the concept of shareholder democracy exercised by millions of small holders, in parallel with the Government's other aim of making trade unions more democratic. The companies themselves were lukewarm, and the idea was stymied by the unwillingness of the main institutional shareholders to give up their pre-emption rights, which they could use to prevent companies from increasing their share capital by more than 5 per cent without getting their prior approval.

Personal wealth rose during the 1980s, but this was due only to a very small extent to privatization of homes and shares (see table 35). Total personal wealth rose by 80 per cent in real terms, while real earnings went up by 25 per cent. The real value of housing rose by 90 per cent, while that of shares rose by 160 per cent in real terms. The proportion of housing increased slightly from 40 to 42 per cent of personal wealth. That of shares also went up, but only from 5½ to 7½ per cent, as the rise in capital values and in privatization holdings was offset by the net annual sale of shares held by the personal sector. The part of personal wealth held in LAPFs rose from 12 to 21 per cent, while that of farmland and other non-financial assets halved to 12 per cent. The policy of wider share ownership had less effect on the structure of personal wealth than the tax privileges maintained for housing and for pension funds. The reform of the Stock Exchange at Big Bang in October 1986 did little to facilitate private-client business. Many brokers gave it up as uneconomic, but the banks took it up, offering discount broking services and PEPs through their branch networks.

Selling the family silver

In the *Alice Through the Looking-glass* world of Treasury accounting sales of public assets are neither revenue nor a method of financing but negative expenditure. Thus sales of council houses and other government land and buildings are deducted from capital expenditure and purchases of assets to give a net capital expenditure figure (see table 24). Since government capital expenditure was in any case cut, the figure net of asset sales makes it look even smaller than it really is. Other privatization proceeds are similarly treated as a deduction from the planning total or general government expenditure.

Asset sales raised a total of £60 billion in the 1980s, about half land and buildings and the other half privatization proceeds (see table 32). If other privatization proceeds are added back to the PSBR as though they were a means of finance, then the PSBR is brought closer to the true financial deficit of the public sector. If sales of land and buildings are also added back, then the true deficit is two and a half times the PSBR, and the public sector was in small surplus for only one year, 1988–9.

Asset sales were able to finance a rising addition to government expenditure, peaking at 7 per cent more than the recorded total, or £13 billion, in 1988–9. Treasury arithmetic resulted in a large understatement of both government expenditure and public borrowing. It was possible to allow public expenditure to rise by more than the announced figure and to claim credit for a sharper reduction in net borrowing than actually took place. This was done by a reduction in assets, which avoided the need for an increase in liabilities.

The use of asset sales to finance current expenditure was regarded critically by many, including Lord Stockton (formerly Harold Macmillan), as 'selling the family silver'. Mrs Thatcher retorted that she was 'selling it back to the family' – although, if it was theirs, it was not clear why they had to pay for it. In a February 1984 *Fiscal Studies* symposium David Heald referred to 'the always dubious practice of selling capital assets to meet a revenue problem, best described as following the pawnshop principle'. However, raising money was only one of several motives for privatization. It is the arcane method of accounting rather than the process of privatization itself that should be criticized on financial grounds, as the Treasury Select Committee argued throughout the 1980s.

Treasury accounting is misleading in another way, in that it is based on cash flows rather than on net present values. If the price at which public assets is sold equals their net present value to the Treasury, then there is no loss or gain to the public finances because the cash flow from the sales is offset by the net present value of the discounted future income stream from the asset, in terms of interest or trading surplus. The same argument applies to the Treasury's avoidance of cash outlays on public-corporation investment because the future returns on the investment are also removed from the account. In the extreme case, almost that of Rover cars, the Treasury has to pay someone take the 'asset' away and disposes of the net present value of a discounted future stream of losses.

This basic position needs to be modified in two ways. First, the Treasury has sold the assets at a discount to the assumed net present value, so there is a loss. This does not apply to council houses because the market itself would impose a discount for a sitting tenant. It does apply to the discounts on share sales, amounting to about £3 billion, and to other privatization costs of about £1 billion. On the other hand, if the net present value of the shares is based on the income stream under private ownership, this is sometimes assumed to be higher than under public ownership, so the act of privatization may increase the market value of public assets. Our analysis of performance suggests that there is little evidence to support this view. The Government could, and in some cases did, increase the net present value of its assets by installing better management and regulation in the public-corporation sector.

It could also be considered that wider share ownership offered society gains justifying the share discounts. Certainly there are gains to individual shareholders and to City institutions. The losses on privatization can thus be seen as a form of subsidy to share ownership, just as mortgage-interest relief is a subsidy to home ownership.

There is no doubt that privatization reduced the share of the public sector in the economy (see table 36). The public sector's share in the net national capital stock fell from 44 per cent in 1979 to 31 per cent in 1989. Its share in annual gross domestic fixed-capital formation fell from 29 per cent to 14 per cent, that of the local authorities fell from 10 to 4 per cent and that of the public corporations from 15 to 5 per cent. The public sector's share of GDP fell rather less because employment incomes were better maintained in local government than was capital spending. It fell from 27 to 20 per cent, with the public corporations' income share in GDP dropping from 10½ to 4½ per cent. The public sector's share of employment fell from 29 to 23 per cent, mainly because that of the public corporations fell from 8 to 3 per cent (see table 23).

For those who take the view 'private good, public bad', privatization was a success. It must be seen in the context of the reduction of the state's share in the economy in general (see chapter 3). If, as suggested there, the Thatcher Government saw the public sector as an enemy country, then the nationalized industries were its commanding heights, some of which were conquered by privatization. Privatization can be judged both by how efficiently it was carried out and by how effective it was in achieving certain economic objectives. The implementation was mixed; it improved with experience but is yet to be tested on British Coal and British Rail. It is too early to judge the full economic effects, which will depend on the trade-off between competition and regulation applied by future Governments. With monopolistic utilities, under public or private ownership, the government of business is still the business of government.

In the last resort the justification for privatization is a matter of political economy rather than pure economics. It was well put by Cento Veljanovski of the Institute of Economic Affairs in *Selling the State* (p. 206):

This justification of privatization does not derive from its economic attractiveness. It simply interprets the policy as a radical change in the institutional structure which shifts the locus of decision-making to individuals and private organizations because that provides a more democratic basis for society and is necessary for a society based on individual autonomy. Private property permits individuals to exercise their freedom and enables their preferences to determine where resources are allocated and what is produced. The link between private property, markets and liberty is a strong one and is the primary defence of privatization.

The question of how best to limit the monopolistic abuse of

power remains without a final answer. The Thatcher Government's attempts to answer it were no more impressive in the public sector than in the private sector (see chapter 6).

6 Industrial performance: miracle or mirage?

> 'There are three statements that you should never believe. First, "I shall respect you even more in the morning, darling." Second, "The cheque is in the post." Third, "I'm from the Government, and I'm here to help you." '
>
> Denis Healey (author's notes)

'General post' at the DTI

There have always been two conflicting views about government policy towards industry in the UK in all the political parties and in business itself. The first is that the Government can make a positive contribution to industrial success through a whole range of policies in such fields as infrastructure, the regions, taxation, credit, trade-union reform, exchange rates, trade and training and, more directly, through industrial policy itself, subsidizing research and development (R&D), backing long-term winners in the new-technology stakes and giving support in export markets. The second is that official subsidies distort the market and that the Government can make only a negative contribution by sweeping away obstacles to industrial expansion, such as pay, dividend, price and foreign exchange controls, planning and use regulations, restrictions on working hours and conditions, and the whole accumulated panoply of bureaucratic red tape and form-filling that imposes such high compliance costs. In the words of the 1988 Blue Paper on Mergers Policy, the Government is 'more likely than private sector decision-makers to make mistaken commercial judgements'. It depends whether one thinks that British industry is itself subject to the inertia of tradition and requires external stimulation to galvanize it into effective action or that it is a Gulliver roped to the ground by armies of Whitehall pygmies, asking only for a chance to get up and flex its muscles.

Mrs Thatcher and her various ministers, like most of their predecessors, have displayed a mixture of the two attitudes, and it is easy to point to examples of each of the two types of business culture in the UK. The dilemma occurs in an acute form in relation to the issues of nationalization versus privatization (see chapter 5) and labour relations (see chapter 7). In the departments of Trade and Industry matters were not helped by the presence of twelve different cabinet ministers during a decade – not to mention the hosts of junior ministers who came and went – in an area that more than most might have been thought to require some long-term continuity of purpose (see figure 10). Sir Keith Joseph was the shadow industry secretary in Opposition, and it was a measure of Mrs Thatcher's originally negative attitude to the matter that she made him her first Industry Secretary.

In *The Right Approach to the Economy* in 1977 Joseph and his colleagues stressed the need for higher profitability by means of deregulation and, if possible, without subsidy. 'Industry is about competition – and risks . . . Risks will not be taken unless in the long run there is on balance a fair chance that a profit can be made . . . Profitability is now so low as seriously to restrict investment . . . We aim to reduce the volume of new legislation as well as to remove current restrictions.' They opposed the use of industrial development certificates and other planning machinery to force industry to locate in the regions. 'Attempts to steer firms to particular places may actually have reduced the net development of industry in the country taken as a whole.' They had a bias towards small firms and against large companies,

Figure 10. Ministerial changes at economic departments, 1979–90

	1979	1980	1981	1982	1983	1984	1985	1986	1987	1988	1989	1990
TREASURY	HOWE				LAWSON							MAJOR
ENVIRONMENT	HESELTINE				KING	JENKIN	BAKER	RIDLEY				PATTEN
TRADE	NOTT	BIFFEN	COCKFIELD	PARKINSON	TEBBIT	BRITTAN	CHANNON	YOUNG		RIDLEY	LILLEY	
INDUSTRY	JOSEPH		JENKIN									
EMPLOYMENT	PRIOR		TEBBIT		KING		YOUNG		FOWLER			HOWARD

particularly those in the public sector, requiring subsidies. 'Ill-considered rescue schemes take money from the more efficient to give it to the less efficient.'

The 1979 manifesto had little to say about industry.

Government strategies and plans cannot produce revival, nor can subsidies. Where it is in the national interest to help a firm in difficulties, such help must be temporary and tapered. We all hope that those firms which are at present being helped by the taxpayer will soon be able to succeed by themselves; but success or failure lies in their own hands. Of course, government can help to ease industrial change in those regions dependent on older, declining industries ... there is a strong case for relating government assistance to projects more closely to the number of jobs they create.

By the 1983 manifesto there was a complete change of tack, with Kenneth Baker, the Minister for Information Technology at the Department of Industry from 1981 to 1984, boasting about how much the Government was spending on backing new technology. Promises for the future covered the Alvey programme for research into advanced information technology, university-based science parks to bring research to the market, new product-launch aid through public purchasing, micro-computers in schools and IT centres for the unemployed, and cable networks 'for the whole new world of tele-shopping and tele-banking'. Regional policy was to be promoted by duty-free 'freeports', following the creation of twenty-four 'enterprise zones' free from local authority rates and from a certain number of regulatory constraints. By 1987 these echoes of Harold Wilson's 'white-hot technological revolution' of twenty years before had faded, as some of the 'winners' turned out to be 'losers' (cable networks and home banking, for example). Any resemblance between Kenneth Baker and Tony Benn, who had once run the Department of Industry under the label 'Department of Technology', was purely coincidental. The 1987 manifesto was long on self-congratulation on industrial performance but short on new policies, which were perhaps not thought to be required. There was a detailed blueprint for the reform of education, the department to which Baker had by then moved, and rather less on training.

Four Department of Trade and Industry policy areas can each be considered separately over the Thatcher decade. They are subsidies, mergers and takeovers, competition and deregulation. The performance of British business in the light of these policies can then be assessed. The understanding of these policies depends on the changing characters of the various ministers at the helm. Joseph, in his heart of hearts, believed that his real aim was to do himself out of the job of Industry Secretary by getting the Government out of the business of industrial support. It was his personal tragedy that he took over during the severest recession since the war; his principles were put to the test and failed it. His successor, Patrick Jenkin, took a much more positive attitude. In 1983 he put out a document on *Strategic Aims* that began: 'British industry is moving in new directions at a time when many of its critics are preoccupied with the problems of the past. It was to establish the place of the Department of Industry in this new industrial framework that Industry Secretary Patrick Jenkin called for a thorough self-analysis by the department of its aims and objectives . . .'

The central aim was a 'profitable, competitive and adaptive productive sector in the UK'. There were three subsidiary aims:

1. CLIMATE. A climate for UK industry as conducive to enterprise as anywhere in the OECD.
2. EFFICIENCY. Using the power of Government selectively to help raise industrial efficiency to internationally competitive levels.
3. INNOVATION. Technology available and applied on the scale necessary to ensure UK competitiveness.

After the 1983 election, the strategic aims were somewhat blurred by the re-merger of the two departments into the Department of Trade and Industry (DTI). The merger affected only the very top level, with a single secretary of state and his ministers responsible for supervising eight mini-empires, each headed by a Civil Service deputy secretary who had responsibilities as wide as those of a permanent secretary in many other departments. The interests of industry – government support – often conflicted with those of trade: free competition internally and externally.

There were no fewer than four Trade and Industry secretaries in 1983–7. Cecil Parkinson, an accountant by training, looked well suited to the job and took the important decision to exempt the Stock Exchange from the Restrictive Practices Court after a 'plea bargain' by which it would reform itself within a new framework set by the Government. A rising star, as it seemed, he found his career interrupted after only four months at the DTI by Miss Sara Keays. Norman Tebbit then spent two years in the job. A safe pair of hands, he seemed glad to move closer to the centre of power when Mrs Thatcher appointed him Party Chairman in September 1985. Leon Brittan, with a more intellectual, lawyer's approach, lasted only eight months until he was sacrificed – perhaps to avoid the greater sacrifice of the Prime Minister herself – over the Westland affair in May 1986. The Government had a difficult decision over Westland, in which it was involved both as a shareholder and as a customer for military helicopters. Mrs Thatcher and Brittan decided in favour of a takeover by the US Sikorsky company, but their refusal to back a proposal for a co-operative European solution brought about the resignation of its main supporter, Michael Heseltine, the Defence Secretary. Paul Channon served out the year or so to the 1987 election with some competence but did not have time to leave a distinctive mark.

When Lord Young took over in June 1987, he brought with him responsibility for the inner cities, which had until then been exercised by the Department of the Environment. The DTI had become, as he saw it, 'a Department of Disasters ... a Department that had lost its way'. He put a new stamp on it by issuing a White Paper in January 1988 entitled *DTI – the Department for Enterprise*. Young, a successful former property developer, saw the spread of information as the key to the creation of wealth. He broadened the range of advisory services to business and was criticized for the amount of government money he spent on advertising them. He tried to restructure the DTI along functional rather than industrial lines, giving pride of place to the marketing function and downgrading the idea of divisions sponsoring particular branches of industry. His position in the House of Lords, and his lack of political experience, weakened his impact, and he had to share the job with Kenneth Clarke, representing the DTI in the House of Commons. Young was philosophically committed to deregulation and competition and was also close to Mrs Thatcher as an adviser.

After two years Young gave up when he fell foul of the brewers, who successfully went over his head to soften the Monopolies Commission recommendations against too much vertical integration with the 'tied houses' in their industry. Ridley, a throwback to the Joseph tradition of wishing his departmental responsibilities out of existence, lasted only a year before he was forced to resign, to the Prime Minister's evident reluctance, because of a *Spectator* interview in which he abused the Germans. At the time of Mrs Thatcher's resignation Peter Lilley had held the job for four months and had already shown signs of a more adventurous approach to market freedom than had some of his predecessors.

One of the few Tory ministers not to have served a spell at the DTI was Heseltine. Since Mrs Thatcher regarded his activist views about the need for an industrial strategy as akin to socialism, she took good care to keep him away from the one department where he might have had a chance to try them out. The fact that there has been continuity of policy in a number of important areas shows that civil servants play a vital role, particularly when ministers change so frequently that few of them have time to learn the job.

Subsidies – the sun also rises

The British tradition has been to subsidize either sunset industries, mostly in the public sector, such as steel, coal, railways and shipbuilding, or sunrise industries, involving new technology, such as space, jet aircraft and computers. Relatively little support has been given to run-of-the-mill manufacturing industries. There has also been for many years some kind of regional policy aimed at offsetting the competitive disadvantages of the north and the 'territories' – Scotland, Wales and Northern Ireland. Mrs Thatcher's new broom, wielded at first by Joseph, made remarkably little difference to the broad lines of policy. It simply meant less money and the demoralization of civil servants who were made to feel that they were acting against her true beliefs.

Government expenditure on trade, industry and energy (mainly coal) doubled in real terms (at 1989–90 prices), from £5.5 billion in 1978–9 to £11 billion in 1982–3, before falling again by 40 per cent to £6.6 billion in 1989–90, one-fifth higher than at the outset. Joseph found that he could not prevent nationalized-industry deficits from rising during the 1980–81 recession, even though the resulting increase in the PSBR made it impossible for the Government to achieve its monetary targets (see page 44). In 1980 his department sent him into cabinet committee with a rescue plan for British Leyland, the nationalized motor manufacturer. He spoke against his own department's plan but was overruled by Mrs Thatcher on pragmatic grounds, although she made it clear that she supported him in principle.

The public-corporation deficits were reduced by a combination of economic recovery, better management and privatization (see chapter 5). Yet those with the largest deficits were the most difficult to privatize, and the public sector was still left with British Coal, British Rail and British Shipbuilders. Privatization in itself does not absolve the Government from granting subsidies – for example, launch aid for new models by British Aerospace. During the 1990–91 recession public-sector financial deficits were again increasing, as they did ten years before.

Government support continued to be given for innovation, although that for micro-electronics, software and fibre-optics was withdrawn in 1987. Nearly half of all official R & D money was spent on defence, and the R & D spending by industry did not rise in line with profits. In 1988 the R & D programme was switched away from near-market, single-firm programmes to collaborative research for groups of firms. Total R & D was then £10.3 billion or $2\frac{1}{4}$ per cent of GDP, low by international standards, of which the Government funded 37 per cent, the private sector 54 per cent and overseas sources the rest.

Regional support was reduced, and its basis changed. In November 1984 the old scheme of Regional Development Grants (RDGs) ceased to give automatic assistance to industrial projects in certain areas. It was extended to cover service industries, and projects became subject to DTI approval. No RDGs were awarded after March 1988, and their place was taken by regional selective assistance (RSA), on a similar basis, with the emphasis on job creation. In

April 1988 a new scheme of regional enterprise grants (REGs) was introduced, with emphasis on technological innovation. The reduction of regional support was slowed down by vigorous lobbying by the CBI and by the availability of EC regional aid, which helped to reduce the UK's net contribution to the EC budget.

Regional policy can be judged by its success in attracting new investment that might not otherwise have been made. By this criterion the old RDGs contained an element of deadweight loss, since they offered windfall gains – for example, to North Sea oil companies investing in onshore facilities in Scotland. They did, however, help to attract to the UK foreign investments that might have gone to competitor countries offering similar subsidies. Although subsidies to assisted areas are subject to EC-imposed limits, the UK has the additional attraction of relatively cheap labour. Tebbit regarded it as a success when in February 1984 he signed up the Japanese car firm Nissan for a major investment at Washington, in the North-East. Five years later its rival, Toyota, agreed to make a similar investment at Derby in the Midlands, which had locational advantages in spite of not being in an assisted area. The example of the British Steel plant set up in 1957 at Ravenscraig in Scotland, which could not be closed without a political storm in spite of privatization, shows that regional policy may have negative results if it overrides, rather than encourages, sensible decisions about location.

The Treasury made a virtue of necessity by arguing that the high cost of housing in the South-East, aggravated by high mortgage-interest rates, was in effect an unintended fillip for regional policy because it gave people an incentive to move to other parts of the country. For those who regarded their homes as an investment rather than just part of the cost of living, the argument did not hold water.

Other subsidies included the small-firm loan-guarantee scheme, set up in 1981; the enterprise zones launched in 1981; the freeports started in 1983; and the Business Expansion Schemes, also introduced in 1983. After 1987 the emphasis was on advisory schemes and on trade promotion, notably in the context of the DTI's Europe 1992 initiative. Expenditure on trade subsidies rose because of the difficulty of getting repayment of guaranteed export loans to developing countries by the Export Credit Guarantee Department. An attempt by the Treasury to query the cost-effectiveness of tied-export loans in a report by Ian Byatt, then its Deputy Chief Economic Adviser, came to nothing.

Government expenditure on trade and industry other than public corporations was cut by a quarter in real terms over the decade to £1.7 billion (see table 37). The cuts were higher on regional and industrial subsidies, and the main increases were on statutory and regulatory functions and, above all, export credit subsidies. Administration expenditure went up, as DTI officials were targeting and monitoring the use of their smaller allocations to try to make them effective. According to the OECD, UK subsidies were cut from 2.7 per cent of GDP in 1975–9 to 2.3 per cent in 1980–84 and to 1.7 per cent in 1985–8, contrary to the general trend; subsidies in OECD Europe rose from 2.5 per cent of GDP in the first period to 2.7 per cent throughout the 1980s. UK subsidies remained proportionately higher than those in the USA and Japan. The question remained whether the UK needed not just to get better value for money but to spend more to catch up with more advanced industrial rivals.

Takeovers – dangers of the middle way

Takeovers and mergers are a difficult area for advocates of the free market. At one extreme, advocates of competition argue that any merger above a certain size requires justification of positive benefits – such as economies of scale – if the reduction in competition is to be justified. At the other, advocates of freedom maintain that businesses should be free to expand by integration and that mergers should be prevented only if there is positive proof that they will reduce competition. Competition can be defined in terms not only of existing home market competition but also of the European or world market and of the ease of entry of potential competitors ('contestability') rather than the existence of actual competitors. Many other factors – to do with employment, research, regional policy, debt leverage, and foreign ownership – can be adduced for or against particular mergers on public-interest grounds.

The ground rules were set by the Competition Act 1980, which laid down that the Director-General of Fair Trading (DGFT) should decide whether a proposed merger, or any other practice, was anti-competitive and, if so, to refer it to the Monopolies and Mergers Commission (MMC). (Any MMC report, which can be guaranteed to impose several months' delay, is referred to the Secretary of State for Trade and Industry, who can accept or reject it.) The Tebbit guidelines of 1984 stressed that competition was the primary criterion for assessing a merger or takeover; others included consumer interests, new products and employment. The MMC had to be satisfied that a merger was not against the public interest rather than that it was in the public interest. From time to time the Secretary of State was accused of using his discretion in an arbitrary manner. As Mrs Thatcher said to Kenneth Harris in a different context: 'Standing in the middle of the road is very dangerous; you get knocked down by the traffic from both sides.'

Mergers can be referred if the result would be to give control of at least 25 per cent of the market – however that is defined – or would create a grouping over a certain size; this size was raised from £5 million to £15 million in 1980, then to £30 million in 1984. The result was that the Office of Fair Trading (OFT), which was obliged to assess about half of all known corporate mergers in 1979, had to assess only about a fifth of them in 1989. In the 1980s the OFT referred to the MMC only 3½ per cent of all the 2,400 mergers qualifying under these rules – a total of eighty-six, and the majority of them were cleared, some with conditions.

The Bank of England took the view that the takeover and

merger regime in the UK, in which the City takeover panel participated to protect the interests of shareholders, was 'designed neither to inhibit nor to encourage takeovers, but to encourage competition and ensure fair treatment'. Gordon Borrie, the DGFT, was suspicious of the argument, often used by industry, that international competition both requires integration of domestic companies and frees it from the taint of monopoly. 'Often there will be barriers to trade ... It is not enough to claim that the UK is part of some wider international market. The facts have to be demonstrated in the particular case.' Borrie was also critical of conglomerate mergers: 'Some such mergers are motivated more by the prospect of quick returns than by a determination to build up a company's long-term health and competitiveness.'

In the 1990s the UK merger regime was changed fundamentally by a 1990 EC directive that gave the Brussels Commission power to vet all proposed mergers resulting in a combined world-wide turnover of over 5 billion ecu, with at least two of the firms having a turnover of 250 million ecu in the EC unless two-thirds of either was in one member state. Other mergers will continue to be the responsibility of the UK authorities, but it may not be possible to draw a neat dividing line between the two types of merger or to avoid 'double jeopardy', when a merger has to be vetted twice over.

The second half of the 1980s saw an unprecedented surge in UK mergers, of which only about 5 per cent were contested takeovers (see table 38). In 1989 merger expenditure on industrial and commercial companies amounted to £27 billion at current prices, about 5 per cent of the value of their equity, and the same proportion of GDP. Among companies' preferred methods of expansion, mergers rose from about a tenth of expenditure in the early 1980s to nearly a third in the late 1980s, the share of spending on new capital assets falling from three-quarters to a half. The share of overseas investment fluctuated around an average of about 15 per cent.

A surprising number of large mergers was outside the traditional industrial areas, in natural resources, food, drink and retailing (see table 39). Those involving foreign ownership were highly controversial, notably Nestlé–Rowntree and Guinness–Distillers. In 1989, a vintage bid year, some even bigger ones got away: the £7 billion bid by the Metsun consortium for GEC and the £13.4 billion bid by Hoylake for BAT would have strained the financial system to its limits. In 1988 there were also two UK takeovers of over £5 billion for US companies: the GrandMet takeover of Pillsbury and the BAT takeover of Farmers' insurance.

It was not that spending on new assets slackened, contrary to widespread complaints about the lack of investment. Fixed-capital spending rose by 40 per cent in real terms in the two years 1984 and 1985 because of the phased withdrawal of the old capital allowances and by 35 per cent in the two years 1987 and 1988 because of fears of capacity shortage to meet the boom in demand. Fixed-capital spending by industrial and commercial companies doubled in real terms between 1983 and 1988, but expenditure on mergers multiplied eightfold. Some companies may have reckoned that, with new UK capital programmes at the limit, they could achieve their ambitious expansion plans by some combination of merger and overseas investment alone.

The Government appears to have welcomed mergers and takeovers as part of the shake-up by which British industrial performance was being improved in the 1980s. The threat of takeover may have made some companies perform more efficiently – provided that their shares rose enough to make them unattractive to a bidder and that they did not actually get taken over; BTR's bid for Pilkington was a case in point. The reality of takeover was also good for victim companies' shareholders, who have had windfall gains in the value of their shares – at the cost of sacrificing any future gains from the same source. Share prices benefited from takeover speculation ranging over far more companies than were ever bid for. The equity market became a market in corporate control, not just in dividend income streams.

Agreed mergers, on this argument, are bad news for shareholders, who benefit more from a contested bid, particularly if there is more than one contestant.

The main argument against takeovers is that economies of scale or scope are seldom achieved by the successful bidder, whose shareholders are therefore unlikely to benefit. This is particularly true of the mega-mergers of the second half of the 1980s, of which each pre-merger company was already large enough to have exhausted any possible such economies (see table 39). The management time and energy spent on bids or defences might in most cases have been better spent running the company, and the large sums paid to merchant-bank advisers may do more for the profits of the financial-services industry than for those of its clients. Smaller companies are particularly vulnerable because the cost of an anti-bid defence varies little with size and may make it more advantageous to agree to a merger than to resist. The Government's complaisant attitude towards mergers was at odds with its bias in favour of small rather than large firms and its belief in self-employment and independent economic decision-making for as many people as possible.

The DTI Blue Paper on mergers policy issued by Lord Young in 1988 was on the whole in favour of 'leaving it to the market', intervening only when necessary and, in such cases, speeding up the time-consuming reference procedures, which were often enough in themselves to abort a proposed merger. Yet at some points doubts crept in: 'The commercial performance of enterprises post-merger has, more often than not, failed to live up to the claims of the acquiring firm at the time of the merger.' John Redwood, the DTI Minister for Corporate Affairs, was reported as making a similar point in the *Independent* of 8 December 1990: 'Evidence is rising that, except in the very short term, takeovers can all too often damage the wealth of shareholders of the bidding company rather than improve it.' Borrie took issue with the prevailing permissive line in the Government when he wrote in 1987:

The doubts about post-merger performance living up to expectations have been reinforced. The question therefore is whether this further evidence suggests that, irrespective of the effect of a merger on competition, those contemplating a merger should be required to demonstrate positive benefits flowing from it if the merger is to be cleared ... A change in the burden of proof would certainly blow away the froth from the 'frothy and almost hysterical' merger boom.

The 1988 Blue Paper, for all its doubts about the effectiveness of mergers, rejected the argument put forward by the chief official operating the policy: 'It would be ... inconsistent to reverse the burden of proof and to require those proposing a merger to demonstrate that their proposal would be positively in the public interest. This would make takeovers much harder to carry out and would have a damaging effect on efficiency by weakening the discipline of the market over incumbent company managements.' A strange reversal of the common-sense view had come about. Takeovers, it seemed, were bad news for the bidder but good news for the victim company.

The Blue Paper set out to show that all was well because the degree of concentration had declined between the mid-1970s and the mid-1980s. After taking account of increased market penetration by imports, the market share of the five leading firms (the 'C5 ratio') had fallen from an average of 39 per cent in 1979 to 34 per cent in 1984. It is possible, however, that the merger wave of the second half of the 1980s reversed the trend. The Blue Paper also revealed a very high C5 ratio in some industries: 98 per cent in tobacco, 84 per cent in cement and 83 per cent in margarine. The degree of concentration itself is less the problem than the possibility of market-sharing and price-fixing agreements when relatively few firms dominate the market.

Price competition – the paper tiger

If the Thatcherite belief in the free market meant anything, it meant that competition should ensure that prices were competed down, whether by internal or by external competitors. This should, indeed, be the main way in which the free market prevents inflation. Yet the priority attached to the restoration of profits appears to have weakened any resolve that ever existed to install a tougher price-competition regime. The Bank of England estimates that the increase in profit margins accounted for over one-third of the increase in manufacturing output prices between 1982 and 1988. Pre-tax margins in the non-oil economy doubled, from 4.4 per cent to 8.8 per cent, between 1982 and 1987. Business incomes also contributed proportionately more than pay to domestic inflation (see table 14). The Bank's figures show that, as in some other countries, manufacturers' output prices would have fallen (by 0.8 per cent) in 1986 with constant margins because of the sharp fall in oil prices: the rise of 4.1 per cent that occurred was more than accounted for by the 4.9 per cent increase in profit margins – the highest in any year in the 1980s. The rise in margins was also due to the effect on export profits of sterling depreciation – another mistake that the Government could have avoided.

The regime that the Government inherited was clearly inadequate to prevent restrictive trade practices designed to maintain prices among a group of producers. Restrictive agreements have to be registered with the DGFT, who is empowered to, and does, approve most of them as harmless. There is no penalty for not registering an agreement except an order to 'cease and desist', although clearly the more obnoxious ones are the least likely to be registered. Unregistered agreements have no legal validity and cannot be enforced by law – which is not to say that the participants do not have other ways of ensuring compliance. One example of such an agreement, unearthed by the *Financial Times* in 1990, was that between the telephone companies of various countries to maintain prices of international calls at a high level, thus securing monopolistic profits at a cost to their customers of £6 billion a year. The *Financial Times* revealed that British Telecom had made a profit of £445 million on international-call revenue of £770 million in 1987–8, a profit margin of 58 per cent. The Bank of England's study on profit margins showed that those in telecommunications had fallen from 31 per cent in 1982 to 20 per cent in 1984, only to rise to 23 per cent in 1987. These were much the highest margins in the UK and nearly three times the average of 8.75 per cent. With an average margin, BT would have made about £400 million less profit on international traffic.

During the review of competition policy that took place in 1987 Borrie said that the 1956 Restrictive Trade Practices Act, although it had successfully outlawed resale price maintenance, was 'not likely to be the most effective legislation possible'. He went on:

The obvious alternative approach is to prohibit agreements which restrict or prevent competition, no doubt with some provision for exemption in specified circumstances. Such an approach could bring greater clarity. It would have the additional benefit of allowing the OFT to concentrate its resources on the truly anti-competitive agreements . . . It would involve some change in my own investigatory powers and could provide greater scope for private actions.

Borrie's call for a 'radical reappraisal of the law' was followed by the publication of the Green Paper *Review of Restrictive Trade Practices Policy*, published in March 1988 as the outcome of the policy review chaired by Hans Liesner, the Chief Economic Adviser at the DTI. It pointed out that the present penalties were ineffective and started from the premise that 'the promotion of competition . . . is at the root of the Government's economic philosophy; and since it is anti-competitive agreements which have to be suppressed, the law should be targeted on these at the outset.' The Green Paper argued that the prohibition should be general rather than confined to specific types of agreement but should still specify the types of agreement prohibited: price-fixing, collusive tendering, market sharing, restrictions on information, refusal to supply or to deal with suppliers. The Green Paper would hardly have referred to such agreements had the authors not been sure that they were alive and well in Mrs Thatcher's free-market Britain.

It was another sixteen months before the Green Paper was followed in July 1989 by a White Paper along similar lines, *Opening Markets: New Policy on Restrictive Trade Practices*. The White Paper proposed that powers to deal with obnoxious agreements should be given not to the DGFT but to a new restrictive-trade-practices tribunal formed from ten new part-time members of the MMC – something of a put-down to Borrie's crusading zeal. It laid down that there should be forcible-entry powers and fines of £250,000 or 10 per cent of turnover but with resort to the High Court for fines of over £1 million. While well-intentioned, the proposed legislation looked less than Draconian. It would bring the UK into line with Article 85 of the Rome Treaty on restrictive agreements but would fall well short of the US anti-trust regime, with prison sentences for price-fixing. It would still not match Article 86, dealing with the abuse of dominant market positions, which can also result in monopolistic pricing.

The publication of the White Paper was almost Young's last act before he resigned in July 1989 after coming off worse in his encounter with the brewers (see page 182). He announced in the preamble to it: 'The introduction of this legislation, when the parliamentary timetable permits, will advance the operation of competition in many sectors and enhance the measures already taken by the Government to improve efficiency throughout the economy.' Yet between then and Mrs Thatcher's resignation in November 1990 nothing happened, whether because of the parliamentary timetable or for other reasons about which one can only speculate.

It is amazing that it took the Thatcher Government ten years to formulate a simple piece of legislation against restrictive-pricing agreements that might have been thought central to its policy of free competitive markets and that even then it was not implemented. One can conclude only that the Conservative Party has the same kind of relationship with the companies that finance it – or sometimes fail to do so – that the Labour Party has with the trade unions that are its main source of funds. The Government carried out far-reaching reforms of restrictive practices on the trade-union side of industry (see chapter 7) but not on the employers' side. Samuel Brittan's jibe about 'monetarism without markets' seems amply justified in this case.

Deregulation – the U-turn

The attempt to abolish unnecessary legislation has a respectable pedigree on the liberal free-market wing of the Conservative Party. In 1979 Ralph Harris, the Director-General of the Institute of Economic Affairs, was made a life peer and was able to carry on to the floor of the House of Lords his campaign for the repeal of outdated laws. A good example was the 1831 Truck Act. This was intended to protect workers from being paid in kind rather than in cash but had become an obstacle to the payment of wages by cheque or by automated transfer, which the unions were able to prevent, even though there were savings available to be shared between employer and employee. It was repealed in 1984.

Yet Mrs Thatcher's Government brought in 660 Acts of Parliament to the end of 1989, compared with 360 by the Labour Government in 1974–9; her average was sixty-two a year, only a fraction less than Labour's sixty-seven a year. Trade-union reform and tax reform alone imposed big demands on parliamentary time, and the abolition of outdated legislation often needed new and more complex legislation to take its place. It was ironic that Mrs Thatcher objected to so much EC legislation from Brussels, as in many cases the object was to make it unnecessary for the UK and the eleven other member states to pass their own laws – on environmental protection, for example. Whatever her doctrinal position on government intervention, the Prime Minister's temperament led her to centralized control of many aspects of economic life.

Young became the main champion of deregulation in the

Government and was particularly anxious to reduce red tape for small firms. His first White Paper as Minister without Portfolio, *Lifting the Burden*, was presented in July 1985 mainly as a way of removing obstacles to the creation of jobs (see page 239). It presented a diverse, and sometimes trivial, list of changes either carried out or in process. It referred in particular to proposals for simplifying the system of planning regulations for new-business development and to attempts to break into anti-competitive self-regulation by the professions – for example, opticians and lawyers.

Perhaps the showpiece of deregulation was the enterprise zones created by the 1980 Budget: companies could get 100 per cent capital allowances and de-rating on industrial and commercial buildings and exemption from development land tax and many of the usual planning and other regulatory constraints. The London Docklands area was the best known of the twenty-five set up during the 1980s. It is hard to say how much investment in the zones was diverted from elsewhere and how much was additional. It is not hard to see that in many cases the location was not optimal and imposed big infrastructure costs on the public sector over and above the loss of tax revenue and control of the urban environment. The zones were a classic example of planning by omission rather than by commission.

Young's second White Paper on deregulation, *Releasing Enterprise*, appeared in November 1988. He was able to point to more substantial achievements: private housing rentals, air transport, London buses, radio frequencies and personal pension plans. The White Paper did not mention the important new regulatory structures that had been brought into being as a result of privatization and the opening up of the Stock Exchange. There was a huge increase in delegated regulation designed to discipline privatized monopolies by bodies such as Oftel, Ofgas, Ofwat and Offer.

Financial deregulation was one of the Thatcher Government's main policies. Regulation was uneasily divided up between the DTI, the Treasury, the Bank of England, the

Stock Exchange and the Building Societies Commission, which were each responsible for some aspects. Deregulation began with the abolition of exchange control by Howe, the Chancellor, in October 1979. It allowed companies and pension and insurance funds to invest abroad at will and to borrow freely in foreign currency. This led to the abolition of the banking 'corset' in July 1980 and, soon afterwards, to the easing of qualitative guidance on bank lending (see page 39).

Parkinson took the decision to reform the Stock Exchange in 1983. This required the passage of the Financial Services Act in 1986. The Act established a new regulatory body, the Securities and Investments Board, supervising a new group of self-regulatory organizations (SROs), including the Stock Exchange itself. There was also a Building Societies Act in 1986 and a new Banking Act in 1987, replacing that of 1979, which had already been shown up as inadequate by the Johnson Matthey collapse of 1984.

Deregulation brought about rapid growth of economic activity, employment and profits in the financial and business services industry (see table 4). Yet it required a complex new structure of regulation and self-regulation to supervise the vast expansion of both old and new financial products. The DTI was shown to be not up to its side of the regulatory task by episodes such as the Barlow Clowes and Levitt affairs, in which gullible investors were swindled by unscrupulous investment managers. Compliance costs for the financial institutions soared. The increased scale of activity was not sufficient to bring down prices for the individual consumer of banking or Stock Exchange services, and the main benefits went to the big insurance and pension-fund investors. In spite of the show trial of the Guinness affair, it was widely felt that the new Serious Fraud Office was up against unfavourable odds in tracking down malpractice in the newly liberated and globalized City environment. It was perhaps fortunate that the building societies were too busy 'doing what comes naturally' and pushing out mortgage money to have time to abuse their new powers as the US thrift institutions had. Deregulation nevertheless left the UK financial system exposed to a wide range of new risks arising from the huge increase in credit in boom times that borrowers were ill-equipped to service in recession.

Company statistics over-extended

The Government's aim was to stimulate companies to increase their profits. Gross trading profits and income from self-employment rose at 2.4 per cent a year in real terms during the 1980s, but if the much reduced appreciation of stocks due to inflation is deducted, the figure rises to 3.4 per cent (see table 40). If the slightly slower 2.5 per cent growth of rent is added in, total business income rose by 3.2 per cent in real terms, significantly faster than the 2.3 per cent increase in GDP as a whole.

Profit performance was highly variable between different sectors. The energy sector, including North Sea oil and gas, and coal, experienced a real 3.4 per cent a year decline in profits, most of it due to the 40 per cent drop in 1986 caused by the sharp fall in the oil price. The sector's share of total business income rose to 21 per cent in 1981–4, then fell to 8 per cent in 1989. Manufacturing was hit by a real profit fall of 38 per cent in the 1980–81 recession, which was only just offset during the subsequent recovery, with another fall beginning in 1989; there was no net increase in real profits between 1979 and 1989. The construction industry did well, increasing its real profits by nearly 60 per cent during the 1986–8 boom in housebuilding and property development and experiencing an average real increase over the decade of 7.3 per cent. The distribution sector, including retailing, did almost as badly as manufacturing in the 1980–81 recession but profited more from the consumer boom to show an average of 1.5 per cent. Transport and telecommunications did rather better, with an average 2.8 per cent rise.

Financial and business services were the outstanding performers, with a 7.4 per cent annual increase; this sector covers banks, building societies, securities firms, investment management, insurance, accountancy, law, advertising and estate agency. The share of these services in total business income rose from 15 to 24 per cent, while that of manufacturing fell from 21 to 17 per cent – a striking role reversal. Other services also did well, with a 5.5 per cent real increase.

Profit growth is related loosely to the growth of output and investment, so the changing composition of profits mirrors the shift in the structure of the economy towards finance and construction and away from energy and manufacturing. The restructuring is also reflected in the very different growth of the various types of business income (see table 41). The main feature has been the growth in self-employment income at a real rate of 5.2 per cent, from 23 to 29 per cent of total business income. The growth in self-employment has also made a major contribution to the fall in unemployment (see page 247) and goes hand-in-hand with the rise in the financial and other service industries, in which self-employment is increasingly common – and lucrative.

The growth of the financial-services sector has also caused an annual increase of nearly 7 per cent in real net bank and other interest, which is due as much to the Government's monetary policy as to the improvement in the banks' own performance. Rent, including imputed rent from owner-occupation, has risen in line with business income as a whole. Surprisingly, this means that gross trading profits hardly rose at all, strictly speaking, and their share of total business income fell from 50 to 40 per cent. Private-sector profits did slightly better with an annual real increase of 1 per cent because of the transfer of some of the most profitable public corporations by privatization, which exaggerated the drop in public-sector trading surpluses. The two sectors must be added together to give a fair picture. If falling energy profits are excluded, non-energy gross trading profits rose by about 1 per cent a year in real terms.

Profitability, as distinct from profits, is measured by the rate of return on capital (see figure 11). For UK industrial

Figure 11. Rates of return: industrial and commercial companies, 1960–89

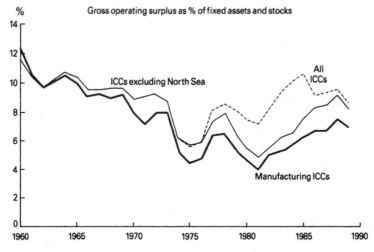

Source: CSO, *Business Bulletin*, October 1990.

and commercial companies the gross return averaged about 10 per cent in the 1960s, then fell to a low of 5.7 per cent in 1975. It recovered to 7.8 per cent in 1978, then fell to its lowest recorded level of 4.8 in 1981. It improved to a new peak of 9.1 per cent in 1988, similar to that of 1972, and then began to fall again. The figures for manufacturing, which were in line with those for other industries in the 1960s, were not as good in the 1980s.

As the Bank of England showed, the UK's rates of return in the later 1980s caught up with those in other industrial countries as a consequence of a combination of a bigger share of profits in the national income and a higher productivity of capital. The UK did better than major competitors on the first and worse on the second. The inclusion of North Sea oil and gas pushed the UK's return on capital above 10 per cent for two years in the mid-1980s, but the return on oil and gas then fell into line with that for all industrial and commercial companies.

Higher profits were seen by the Government as a necessary condition of increased industrial investment (see table 42). Gross domestic fixed-capital formation rose by 3.7 per cent a year in real terms in the 1980s, faster than the 2.3 per cent increase in output as a whole but in an erratic manner in relation to the movement of output. It fell by 14 per cent in the 1980–81 recession, then rose by 26 per cent in the 1987–8 boom. It fell again in the 1990–91 recession. The 1980–81 recession hit hard investment in agriculture, manufacturing, construction, housing, distribution and transport, while the boom had a particularly marked effect on construction, distribution, transport, telecommunications and financial services. While the recession affected production industries most, it was service industries that reacted most favourably to the boom.

Miss Rosy Scenario brings financial headaches

The short-lived investment surge of the late 1980s was achieved at the expense of a widening balance-of-payments deficit (see page 21) and a sharp deterioration in industrial and commercial company finances (see table 43). The national accounts for companies in 1989 give a more extreme picture of what had already begun in 1988. UK taxes took 18 per cent of total company income, or 22 per cent of income earned in the UK; this rose to 50 per cent after deducting interest, payments abroad, full depreciation and stock appreciation, which demonstrates the extent to which the 1984 corporation tax reform failed to allow for inflation or the replacement of capital (see page 131). After deduction of taxes and the other items listed, the remaining UK income was less than all monies paid out in dividends. The rise in dividend payments was seen by companies as necessary in order to maintain their share prices as a defence against takeovers, although in the longer run it may have made them more vulnerable. J.W. Lomax of the Bank of England, writing on dividends, found that 'in large measure, recent increases are attributed to the development of hostile mergers and acquisitions activity'.

The result was that the whole of companies' new net expenditure on capital and financial assets had to be financed externally. They spent more on overseas investment than on fixed-capital spending at home, almost as much on merging and taking over the shares of other companies (more if payment by the issue of shares is included) and over half as much building up liquid and other financial assets. So less than a third of their funding requirement was for new capital expenditure and stockbuilding, and it came to three-quarters of their total internal income. About two-fifths of their funding came from the banks and the rest from a variety of sources; much less was raised from the equity market after the 1987 crash than before it.

The so-called financial deficit (the amount by which total capital expenditure, including depreciation and stock appreciation, exceeds undistributed cash flow) rose to £25 billion following a run of surpluses from 1980 to 1986. The net borrowing requirement was over twice as high, at £52 billion because of the need to finance overseas investment and mergers and takeovers. Total funding was even higher, at £77 billion, because of the additional finance for liquid assets and a large unidentified item most likely to consist of unrecorded inwards overseas investment.

The resulting deterioration in companies' balance sheets is shown in table 44. Tangible assets, or capital stock, rose by 3.2 per cent a year in real terms, as companies invested more than what was needed to replace worn-out equipment. Overseas investment rose by nearly 10 per cent a year in real terms, thanks to the lifting of exchange controls in 1979. Financial assets rose by 6.4 per cent a year in real terms, and holdings of shares in other companies increased even faster than bank deposits. On the liabilities side bank loans outstanding rose by nearly 10 per cent a year in real terms, mainly because of a real increase of over 60 per cent in 1988 and 1989 alone. The value of equity rose by 13 per cent a year in real terms; although most of this was related to the rise in share prices rather than to the issue of new equity, it entailed dividend expectations from shareholders that companies were hard pressed to meet. Inward overseas investment rose nearly 6 per cent a year in real terms. Total real liabilities thus rose by 8.8 per cent a year compared with 4.3 per cent for assets.

There was thus a deterioration in a number of significant ratios. Bank loans were twice as high as bank deposits in 1979, improved to one and a half times in 1983–7, then went back to twice in the two years to 1989. Financial liabilities were one and two-thirds financial assets from 1979 to 1984, then rose to twice in 1987–9. Financial liabilities rose from 54 per cent to 82 per cent of total assets, leaving net wealth of only about £200 billion at the end of 1989 – the difference between assets of £1,100 billion and liabilities of £900 billion. The market valuation of equity rose from 46 per cent of net wealth in 1979 to 2.6 times net wealth at the end of 1989, or from 31 per cent to 78 per cent of tangible assets. The gearing ratio of bank loans to equity, which peaked at 45 per cent in 1981, was only 28 per cent in 1989, but all that this showed was that the market's expectations of companies' earning power had exceeded even their enormous increase in bank borrowing.

The improvement in labour productivity by manufacturing industry – rather than by companies in general – is widely regarded as the main industrial achievement of the Thatcher era (see chapter 7). Yet it generated a euphoria in financial markets that led, in the new world of deregulation, to dangerous levels of company debt and equity prices. In 1990 bankruptcies, bad debts and bank provisions were also increasing. The picture given here is that of the whole industrial and commercial-company sector; some individual companies are better, others worse, than the sector as a whole. While the management of production improved, the management of finance was in some cases overwhelmed by an *embarras de richesse* in terms of new financial products – but the riches were, in many cases, borrowed. The recession of 1980–81 was a severe test, which many companies failed. The recession of 1990–91 was an equally severe, but different, test in which excessive ambition rather than inadequate dynamism was often the fatal flaw.

Some of the responsibility for the financial over-extension of UK companies must be shared between lenders and borrowers. Never had credit been so freely available in the UK, and it was inevitable that some on both sides would abuse their new-found freedom. The British banks, which had been accused in the 1970s of lending too little to industry, were criticized in the 1980s for lending it too much. Some of the most imprudent loans, especially for property development, were made by Japanese and other foreign banks that had been attracted to the City by its position as the world's leading international financial centre. The British banks tried to escape from the burden of their enormous provisions for doubtful overseas lending by increasing the share of more profitable domestic lending in their balance sheets, only to find that this too required unforeseen bad-debt provisions. While mortgage and consumer loans to personal borrowers proved relatively sound, many companies – large, medium and small – misjudged their capacity to service loans taken on at the height of the expansion of their business. Few actually went so far as the farmer who sued his bank for lending him more than he could safely afford to borrow; the legal proceedings usually ran in the other direction.

The Government must also bear its share of the responsibility. After 1986 monetary targets were abandoned, and nothing was put in their place, so that credit ceased to be controlled effectively. The exchange rate might have provided the necessary discipline had the UK joined the ERM in 1985 (see chapter 2). High interest rates, which were supposed to choke off the demand for credit in a free market, did not do so because profits appeared to be rising fast enough to cover them, and banks were offering corporate borrowers 'caps', 'collars', 'forward-rate agreements' and other devices to shield them from the effects of higher interest rates. The Bank of England's prudential capital-ratio controls on lending sometimes had the opposite effect to that intended when banks resorted to riskier lending in an attempt to earn margins sufficient to provide the extra capital required.

The resurgence of inflation, which the Government failed to prevent, made matters worse. In a July 1990 analysis the CBI pointed out:

A rise in inflation, accompanied by an equivalent rise in interest rates, causes cash-flow problems for companies. In fact the inflation rate reduces the real value of debt and so what is happening is effectively that companies are paying back debt at a faster rate in real terms. To offset this, companies could increase their borrowings but many may be unable or unwilling to do so. Research by Sushil Wadwhani at the LSE suggests that, as a result, each one per cent on the annual inflation rate adds 5.8 per cent to the number of bankruptcies.

The same argument had been used the other way round by the Government to argue the case for lower inflation when Howe gave his 1983 Budget speech as inflation was falling to 4 per cent: 'Lower inflation encourages higher spending by companies, both in stocks and in investment. For lower inflation contributes to lower interest rates, so improving cash flow.'

The Government was guilty of inducing over-optimism about the future on the part of borrowers by making exaggerated claims about the improvement in performance by British business, which suggestible businessmen were only too prone to believe – awarding themselves unjustified increases in pay and benefits on the strength of it (see page 231). The main improvement took place in manufacturing, which in 1990–91 was no longer exposed so starkly to recession as it had been a decade earlier. This time the deficiencies in performance were more evident in some of the rapidly growing service industries, including the banks and the securities houses themselves, some of which were in a weaker financial state than were many of their own borrowers.

The Government was taken in by its own propaganda about the supply-side miracle supposedly brought about in British business by tax cuts, deregulation, trade-union reform and so on. It was misled by the length of the recovery into thinking that the UK had somehow escaped from the age-old business cycle and was entering into a new, long-term growth path at 3 or 4 per cent a year instead of the more normal 2¼ per cent that actually obtained for the 1980s as a whole. It was therefore not surprising that British businessmen, who in many cases also had a personal faith in the charismatic powers of Mrs Thatcher, should be seduced by Miss Rosy Scenario. Even the October 1987 stock-market crash did no more than dent their optimism and was later dismissed by the Government as a false signal of impending recession that had led to an unfortunate cut in interest rates, later to be reversed.

The balancing act collapses

The Government's other misjudgement, with which Lawson as Chancellor was particularly identified, was to take the view that the balance-of-payments deficit was not its responsibility because its own finances were in surplus and it was repaying debt. If the private sector ran a deficit, it could finance it by overseas borrowing just as if it were domestic borrowing. Lawson told the IMF in Berlin in September 1988: 'Private-sector behaviour is by its nature self-correcting over time . . . there is a limit to the amount of debt which the private sector will be willing – or can afford – to undertake. Once that limit has been reached, the savings ratio will rise again.' He put forward the same thesis at greater length in his July 1988 Institute of Economic Affairs (IEA) lecture, 'The State of the Market'.

While Lawson may have been technically correct, his analysis said nothing about the fall in the exchange rate, the rise in the interest rate or the number of business failures that could occur as part of the process of 'self-correction'. To adapt Healey's phrase, it was not 'sado-monetarism' but 'masocho-monetarism'. It so happened that the industrial and commercial company deficit of £25 billion in 1989 was similar in scale to the £19 billion balance-of-payments deficit on current account.

By accounting identity, the current-account deficit had to be financed by a capital-account surplus. Unfortunately, the long-term capital account was also in deficit because of the continuing high level of net direct investment by industry overseas. So the total surplus of short-term funds required from abroad was £46 billion, or about 9 per cent of GDP. Most of this came in the form of short-term sterling deposits in UK banks at high interest rates dictated by the Government's monetary policy, which the banks then competed to lend to British business and personal borrowers. The Government could not fail to become involved in the private sector's deficit, having responsibility, as it did, for interest rates, the exchange rate, the rate of inflation and the rate of economic growth.

Concern about the prospect of a balance-of-payments deficit in manufactures had been expressed in 1985 by the House of Lords Select Committee on Overseas Trade, chaired by Lord Aldington. The Committee quoted a projection published in the *Lloyds Bank Economic Bulletin* for September 1984, 'The UK's vanishing surplus', showing the current account moving from a £1 billion surplus in that year to a deficit of £13.6 billion in 1990. The main defect of this projection, only £0.2 billion out for 1990, was that it underestimated the size of the non-oil-trade deficit due to the boom in 1988 and 1989 (see table 45). Lawson gave his contemptuous reaction in his Mansion House speech in October 1985: 'The Government ... wholly rejects the mixture of special pleading dressed up as analysis and assertion masquerading as evidence which leads the Committee to its doom-laden conclusion.' Yet it turned out to be uncomfortably close to the truth. The Committee called for a wide range of policies in support of competitiveness in manufacturing industry, but these were ruled out by Lawson as protection by 'a cocoon of subsidies'.

Heseltine, publishing his memoirs from the backbenches in 1987, sided with the House of Lords against Lawson: 'A year or two ago the Chancellor of the Exchequer offered the House of Lords the Government's opinion: "It is industry's job to make itself competitive." So it is, but the implication that it is not also in part the Government's no longer carries conviction.'

Even when the Committee's forecast turned out to be correct in 1988, the Government shrugged it off as unimportant and gave priority to getting the rate of inflation down. Lawson's studied indifference to the balance of payments was not shared, however, by some of his more conventional colleagues, including his successor as Chancellor, John Major. One reason for worrying about the balance of payments is that it conveys messages about the strengths and weaknesses of the British economy. If particular sectors are not able to meet international competition in a world of increasingly open trading, they will not survive in the domestic economy either, and output and jobs will be lost. Unfortunately, there is inadequate understanding of the international performance of many sectors of the economy, partly because so many of them are lumped together under the all-embracing term 'manufactures', which accounts for over four-fifths of all British exports.

The current account was roughly in balance only twice in the period under review, in 1979 and again in 1986. There was a large swing into a surplus of £6.7 billion in 1981 (3.1 per cent of GDP), then into a deficit of £19.1 billion (4.4 per cent of GDP) in 1989 (see figure 12). The surplus was caused as much by the effect of the 1980–81 imports recession as by rising net exports of North Sea oil, which did not reach their peak of £8.1 billion until 1985. The 1989 deficit was caused by an excess of domestic demand in the UK relative to other countries as well as by the decline of the oil surplus.

In the 1980s (see table 46 and figure 13) exports of non-oil goods increased at 3.7 per cent a year in volume, not far short of the 4.1 per cent growth of world exports, but imports rose by 6.4 per cent a year, nearly three times as fast as the 2.2 per cent growth of British GDP (twice would

Industrial Performance

Figure 12. Current external balances as percentage of GDP, 1979–89

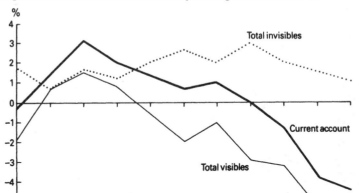

Source: Pink Book, 1990.

have been in line with the international norm). In value terms the result was improved by a rise in the UK terms of trade, with non-oil export prices rising at 5.2 per cent compared with 4.4 per cent for import prices, which reflected partly an improvement in the quality composition of exports, partly a loss of price competitiveness.

The export trend accelerated after 1981 in line with the world economic recovery and the fall in the UK exchange rate. Non-oil export-volume growth moved up from −4 per cent in 1981 to 10 per cent in 1989 and the first half of 1990. In the 1980–81 recession imports fell almost as much as exports but then moved into an accelerating trend, somewhat bumpier than that of exports. Non-oil import growth peaked at over 10 per cent in 1983 and 1984 and again at nearly 15 per cent in 1988. In 1989–90, as in 1985, imports rose less than exports.

The picture was less reassuring for services, which account for one-third as much again as goods of UK exports. The volume of services exports rose by only 1.2 per cent a

Figure 13. Non-oil trade volumes, percentage changes, 1980–89

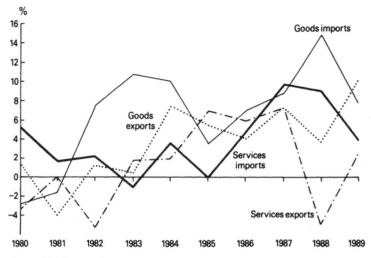

Source: Pink Book, 1990.

year in the 1980s, one-third of the figure for non-oil exports of goods. The volume of services imports rose by 3.9 per cent a year, three times as fast as services exports. Again, the terms of trade moved in the UK's favour by 1 per cent a year, but the result was disappointing in an area of traditional British strength.

Exports of services were highly erratic, with negative growth in 1980–82, good volume increases of over 6 per cent a year only in 1985–7 and a surprising fall of 4 per cent in 1988, the *annus terribilis* of Britain's external accounts. Imports of services were almost as erratic but at a higher level of growth. The gap between imports and exports appeared to be closing in 1989. UK exports of goods and services rose at 2.9 per cent a year in volume in the 1980s, considerably more slowly than world markets, and imports at 5.2 per cent (see table 46), well over twice as fast as the UK economy, with a total terms-of-trade advantage of only 0.6 per cent a year. In previous decades the UK tended to

Figure 14. Trade balances as percentage of GDP, 1979–89

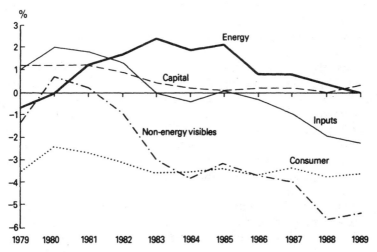

Source: Pink Book, 1990.

experience economic growth of about two-thirds of the industrial-country average, which held down import growth in line with export growth. When other countries slowed down to the same economic growth rate as the UK British export growth dropped to about two-thirds of the rate of import growth.

Britain's trade can be better understood from a supply-oriented examination of the highly diverse performance of its various categories. Export performance alone is a poor guide, since imports in the same industry may rise faster or more slowly. The balance between the two should therefore be examined but in the context of the growth of the economy rather than of current or price-adjusted money. Figure 14 shows how visible trade balances have moved as a percentage of GDP.

The energy balance comprises not only the surplus on oil but also the deficit on gas and coal, which was enough in 1989 to wipe out the modest oil surplus, affected as it was by supply interruptions in the North Sea. It rose from a small deficit in 1979 to a surplus of 2 per cent of GDP in 1984–6 (with a small dip in the two latter years on account of the coal strike). It was halved by the fall in oil prices in 1986.

The balance of goods other than energy deteriorated sharply from a surplus of 0.7 per cent of GDP in 1980 to a deficit of 3.8 per cent of GDP in 1984. This was masked by the rise in the energy surplus, so that the current account remained in surplus, though to a diminishing extent. From one point of view it was logical to argue that the UK should make its contribution to balancing world trade by allowing oil exports to displace other British exports, using the high exchange rate to effect the switch and at the same time to make imports cheaper and thus bring down inflation. With hindsight it is possible to say that the North Sea oil surplus was temporary, not permanent, income and should therefore have been channelled into a surplus of foreign investment to earn future income. This did happen to some extent but more by accident than by design.

During this time the UK managed to remain in surplus on capital goods, a traditionally strong sector. The surplus fell from 1.2 per cent of GDP in 1979–81 to 0.1 per cent in 1988 but then improved. While the 1987–9 boom may have sucked in imports of capital goods, UK exporters also benefited from the world-wide surge in capital-goods demand.

Consumer goods have for long been in deficit in the UK, and the slight worsening in the deficit in the 1980s appears to have been cyclical rather than structural. In the 1980 recession the deficit shrank from 3.5 to 2.5 per cent of GDP, but after the recovery began in 1983 it fluctuated, with no clear trend, around 3.5 per cent of GDP. Within consumer goods the normal deficit on food, beverages and tobacco was held at about 1.1 per cent of GDP after 1980 – a silver lining to the cloud of the EC common agricultural policy, which, at a cost to consumers, increased UK self-sufficiency. Manufactured consumer goods did less well, with a deficit running at over £11 billion a year after 1988, of which £5 billion was accounted for by cars.

The main weakness was in industrial inputs, such as semi-manufactures, and in intermediate manufactured goods. (Other inputs, such as raw materials and chemicals, did not do as badly.) Imports of these goods moved from a surplus of 2 per cent of GDP in 1980 to a deficit of 2.2 per cent in 1988. Because of the closure of large parts of manufacturing industry in the 1980-81 recession, in the 1987-9 boom the UK lacked the capacity to supply industrial demand for a wide range of materials and components of the kind provided by small and medium-sized engineering and contracting companies. As the OECD said in its 1989/90 *Economic Survey* of the UK on this point, 'industries switched supply lines to more cost-efficient producers abroad.'

There was a similar disparity in performance within the invisibles account, which comprises services; interest, profits and dividends (IPD) passing between the UK and other countries; and unrequited transfers to and from the government and the private sector. Services are 28 per cent of total invisible credits, divided equally between financial and business on the one hand and transport and travel on the other; IPD is 67 per cent and transfers 5 per cent.

Financial and business services, overlapping but not identical with the overseas earnings of the City of London, saw their traditional surplus rise from 1.9 per cent of GDP in 1980 to 2.8 per cent in 1986 and 1987, then fall to 2 per cent in 1989 because of a sharp fall in insurance-underwriting income and competition from other financial centres. Transport and travel earnings had a surplus of 0.7 per cent of GDP, worsening to a deficit of 0.8 per cent between 1979 and 1988, due mainly to rising net outflows of tourist income.

IPD rose from a deficit of 0.1 per cent of GDP in 1980 to a surplus of 1.8 per cent in 1984 and again in 1986, which fell to 1.2 per cent in 1989. They reflected, first, earnings on the rising accumulation of UK investment overseas after the abolition of exchange control in 1979, then the increase in the cost of servicing UK bank borrowing from abroad at high interest rates as the current account moved into deficit. The net outflows of bank interest rose to £5.4 billion in 1989. The earnings of overseas investment would be far higher if capital gains were included, since the UK still had a net asset surplus of £112 billion, or 25 per cent of GDP, at the end of 1989. Transfers, nearly all on the part of government, tend to be in deficit because of overseas defence commitments and contributions to EC institutions. The deficit, at 1.7 per cent of GDP, was no higher in 1979 than in 1989, although there was some improvement, followed by deterioration, in the meantime.

The invisibles balance rose from 0.7 per cent of GDP in 1980 to 2.9 per cent in 1986 but fell to 1.1 per cent in 1989. After the hope that the oil balance would rescue the current account was dashed in 1986 by the fall in oil prices, the other hope, that it would be rescued by invisibles, was eroded more gradually over the same period (see figure 12). After it peaked in the mid-1970s at a level similar to that of the mid-1980s, the invisibles surplus sank in the last few years of that decade. It was plagued by difficulties of measurement and tended to be revised upwards, but still it fluctuated even more unpredictably than visible trade. The visible balance fell from a surplus of 1.5 per cent of GDP in 1981 to a deficit of 5.5 per cent in 1989. While the invisibles balance increased the 1981 surplus to 3.1 per cent of GDP, it diminished the 1989 deficit only to 4.4 per cent of GDP.

The UK quickly became uncompetitive in manufactures as a result of the rise in the exchange rate in 1980, with an increase of 25 per cent in relative unit labour costs in a common currency in that one year. By 1989 the UK had regained its 1979 competitiveness, thanks to the gradual fall in the exchange rate and the improvement in relative productivity (see table 49). The rise in the exchange rate in 1990 and the increase in British unit labour costs relative to other countries reduced competitiveness but not to the same extent as in 1980. The relatively high exchange rate at which the UK joined the EMS ERM in October 1990 was an incentive to companies to bear down on unit labour costs. Pointing this out was about as far as the Government went to improve competitiveness; it was up to industry to be competitive through its own efforts.

Competitiveness and the balance of payments were two of the many issues about which the Government and the CBI seemed to be conducting a dialogue of the deaf. The CBI had been calling for entry into the EMS ERM since 1985, and, ministers argued, it had been given what it wanted and could now get on and make a success of it.

The Thatcher Government's relationship with industry was paradoxical. The Government was, in theory, devoted to the encouragement of business success, yet it cultivated a distant, arm's-length relationship with industry and commerce. The CBI and other bodies whose interest the Government purported to be promoting mistrusted ministers who seemed to be more familiar with the works of Adam Smith than with business realities. From the outset Mrs Thatcher's tough monetary policy antagonized industry because it provoked what seemed like an unnecessarily deep recession. Sir Terence Beckett, the Director-General of the CBI, told its annual conference in October 1980 that he might need to have a 'bare-knuckle fight' with ministers to make his point. In a more measured vein Sir Hector Laing, the Chairman of United Biscuits, told the House of Lords Select Committee in 1985: 'The present Government has in effect made a virtue of not having a vision of the future of British industry and a positive policy of distancing the state from the industrial sector. I think the Government should acknowledge that the nation does have an industrial problem in which it has a serious policy interest.'

Lord Young, writing after his resignation in 1988, saw the problem as arising from the lack of movement of senior people between government and business: 'We practise a doctrine of separation of experience which appears absolute. Then we wonder why it is that government has an imperfect understanding of the needs of commerce and industry – or even an enterprise society.'

The Thatcher Government was a *médecin malgré lui*,

continuing to dispense various nostrums to business by means of an industrial policy the existence of which it was barely willing to acknowledge. The frequent changes of ministers in charge of trade and industry was disruptive and coincided with bewildering shifts in the content of policy. The Government spent more on industrial subsidies when it could not avoid doing so but then undermined the effectiveness of those that remained by imposing public expenditure cuts on them.

Merger and takeover policy was permissive. Blocking interventions were decided somewhat arbitrarily in a small number of cases, but the results benefited the City more than industry. Policy to sharpen price competition was non-existent, since it took ten years to bring forward proposals that were then shelved. Deregulation was of major importance in financial services but relatively trivial in other areas. New legislation and regulation were greater in scale and scope than was deregulation.

There was a modest improvement in business income and rates of return, but this was most marked among the self-employed and in the financial-services sector. British business became over-indebted as a result of credit liberalization and the false optimism encouraged by the Government. The Government's exaggeration of business performance contributed to a new deterioration in it at the end of the 1980s. All the numbers were bigger, and the misery was more evenly spread, but the recession of 1990–91 looked as if it might have as severe an impact on British business as that of 1980–81. The balance-of-payments deficit, like the financial deficit that went with it, demonstrated that British industry was vulnerable as much in services as in manufacturing trade. The policy of benign neglect did not work.

7 Labour:
the market that didn't work

'We Conservatives hate unemployment.'
Mrs Thatcher, Blackpool, October 1975

Conservatives divided on policy

The Conservative Party has always been divided in its attitude to trade unions, between co-operation and confrontation and between incomes policy and free bargaining. The Heath Government carried out in the Industrial Relations Act of 1971 the most far-reaching measure ever of trade-union reform and then launched into a statutory incomes policy in 1972. Industrial relations were marred by the refusal of the unions to accept the implementation of many parts of the Act, and Heath lost the February 1974 election as the result of an ill-advised challenge to the National Union of Mineworkers.

When the Conservatives went into opposition they tried to devise a new and more workable trade-union policy. Among the authors of *The Right Approach to the Economy*, published in October 1977, were Geoffrey Howe, who had, as Solicitor-General, piloted the Industrial Relations Act through Parliament, Keith Joseph, the shadow industry secretary with overall policy responsibility, and James Prior, a leading representative of the Heath tendency who had become Mrs Thatcher's shadow employment secretary.

'Strict control of the money supply, firm cash limits on

public expenditure: these are the vital factors which can influence the pay climate,' they wrote in *RAE*. This was later to be expanded by the idea that monetary targets would influence pay bargaining by reducing them to levels consistent with the low inflation that would follow from them. Public-sector settlements, which were within the Government's control, were also held to influence those in the private sector. So they had to be held down, both to reduce public expenditure and to prevent private-sector pay inflation.

While opposed to a pay norm, the authors were in effect advocating a covert form of voluntary incomes policy.

In framing its monetary and other policies the Government must come to *some* conclusions about the likely scope for pay increases ... Some kind of forum is desirable, where the major participants in the economy can sit down calmly together to consider the implications – for prosperity as well as for unemployment and pay-bargaining – of the Government's fiscal and monetary policies. NEDC (National Economic Development Council) may well be the most appropriate for this purpose.

This approach, modelled on that of West Germany, was sometimes referred to as 'concerted action'.

Statutory incomes policy was excluded in favour of a return to free collective bargaining, with a reform of procedures to avoid strikes. Most of the Heath Government's trade-union reforms had been repealed by the Labour Government. Instead of setting out to retake all the lost territory, *RAE* held out an olive branch: 'We see the trade unions as a very important economic interest group whose co-operation and understanding we must work constantly to win and to keep, as we have done in the past. We see no need for confrontation and have no wish for it.'

It was hardly a surprise when, as Prior put it in his memoirs, 'Margaret absolutely refused to allow the document to be published as a shadow cabinet paper.' Mrs Thatcher's more radical advisers were planning confrontation with the unions – but this time they were going to win it by a quasi-military style of advance planning. Since the unions were strongest in the public sector, any policy to improve nationalized-industry performance had to tackle them. Nicholas Ridley circulated an unpublished plan to take on the National Union of Mineworkers again (see page 154), which was carried out almost to the letter in 1984. Another unpublished plan was *Stepping Stones*, written also in the autumn of 1977 by John Hoskyns, a businessman advising Mrs Thatcher who was later to become head of her policy unit: 'Any strategy which does not address the problem of the trades union role from the outset ensures failure in office,' it said.

Joseph, in a Bow Group lecture in 1978, was pointing to the connection between unions and unemployment. In his view, a free labour market required much more wage flexibility, down as well as up: 'It is in the interests of everyone to allow the supply of, and the demand for, skills or effort to be reflected in the price of labour. Workers can price themselves – or be priced by their negotiators – into as well as out of work.' His lecture was entitled significantly 'Conditions for Fuller Employment' and ended prophetically: 'Full employment is not in the gift of Governments. It should not be promised and it cannot be provided.'

The IEA published a series of conference papers and readings that influenced Mrs Thatcher. In *Trade Unions: Public Goods or Public Bads?* Charles Hanson argued, 'The balance of market advantage has moved in favour of the trade unions over the past few decades. But no trend is irreversible.' In the same booklet Brian Griffiths, who was to succeed Hoskyns as head of the policy unit at 10 Downing Street, summed up findings that were confirmed by subsequent research: 'Trade unions which control entry [a reference to the closed shop] . . . are able to raise their real wages but only at the expense of either trade-union members who are unemployed or other workers who receive lower wages.' David Metcalf of the London School of Economics reported some years later that the union mark-up in 1980 averaged 14 per cent in pre-entry closed shops but only about half that over the whole range of unionized firms.

The theme was developed by Fritz von Hayek, one of Mrs Thatcher's favourite economists, in a series of his essays published by the IEA, *1980s Unemployment and the Unions: The Distortion of Relative Prices by Monopoly in the Labour Market.* Hayek, not having to face the British electorate, had no reason to mince his words:

> The trade unions have become the biggest obstacle to raising the living standards of the working class as a whole; they are the chief cause of unemployment and the main reason for the decline of the British economy . . . Britain remains paralysed by the consequences of the coercive powers irresponsibly conferred on the unions by law; there can be no salvation for her until these special privileges are revoked.

Again Metcalf's subsequent findings confirmed Hayek's theories. He found that 'A third of non-union workplaces increased employment by more than 20 per cent between 1980 and 1984, while in the same period over a third of workplaces with a closed shop suffered a corresponding loss of jobs.'

Another IEA conference held in December 1978 condemned government intervention in the labour market, whether by job subsidies or by incomes policies, on the grounds that it interfered with the formation of wage levels that would clear the labour market. In *Job 'Creation' – or Destruction?* Malcolm Fisher argued, against the views of some moderate IEA supporters such as Lord Robbins, that 'incomes policies have added rigidity to the employment structure and so contributed to the growth of unemployment'.

The 1979 manifesto represented a compromise between Prior's co-operative approach and Mrs Thatcher's conviction that trade-union law reform was a high priority, as it had been for Heath in 1970. The four immediate measures were to be: a ban on secondary picketing; compensation for dismissal due to a closed shop, which would itself need to be ratified by a secret ballot by a large majority; public funds for postal ballots for union elections and other important issues (not specifically for strikes); and less favourable financial treatment for strikers.

There was a vestige of Prior's pay forum in the words 'There should be more open and informed discussion of the Government's economic objectives (as happens, for example, in Germany and other countries) so that there is wider understanding of the consequences of unrealistic bargaining and industrial action.' At the same time the free market carried the day against incomes policy. 'Pay bargaining in the private sector should be left to the companies and workers concerned. At the end of the day, no one should or could protect them from the results of the agreements they make.' As for pay bargaining in central and local government, 'we will reconcile these with the cash limits used to control public spending and seek to conclude no-strike agreements in a few essential services.'

The latter promise was undermined by the Conservatives' undertaking, during the election campaign, to implement the findings of the Clegg Commission appointed by the Labour Government to report on public-sector pay. As Hugo Young put it, 'Challenged to say where they stood on Clegg, as the election began, the leadership collapsed into fatal acquiescence. Although they knew it would be an albatross round all their plans, they did not dare to alienate public-sector workers by throwing it out. This was the leader's own decision ...'

The manifesto, following Joseph's lead, made no promise of full employment: 'Too much emphasis has been placed on attempts to preserve existing jobs. We need to concentrate more on the creation of conditions in which new, more modern, more secure, better-paid jobs come into existence. This is the best way of helping the unemployed ...' The campaign did, however, express the view that the unemployment rate, which had been over 5 per cent since 1976, was too high, with the slogan 'Labour isn't working' next to a picture of a dole queue. So while there was some doubt about how quickly unemployment, then seen as high, could be reduced, there was no suggestion that it might have to rise and no mention of anti-unemployment measures.

Although Prior had had the shadow job, it was something of a surprise when Mrs Thatcher made him Employment Secretary in 1979 in view of their known differences on trade-union law reform. Mrs Thatcher appeared to be steering an unsteady course between conciliation and confrontation. Prior made an apt comment in his memoirs:

'Where there is discord, may we bring harmony . . .' Margaret's choice of words on her arrival in Downing Street, quoting St Francis of Assisi, could scarcely have been less apt and from her lips were the most awful humbug: it was so totally at odds with Margaret's belief in conviction politics and the need to abandon the consensus style of government, which she blamed for Britain's relative economic decline . . .'

Trade-union law was reformed, but gradually; a new measure was put on the statute book every year or two (see figure 15). The pace and content of the reforms varied according to the preferences of Mrs Thatcher's six successive Employment Secretaries: James Prior, Norman Tebbit, Tom King, Lord Young, Norman Fowler and Michael Howard (see figure 10). As time went on, trade-union reform had to take its place alongside two policy objectives that had not appeared in the 1979 manifesto: first, special measures – featured in the 1983 manifesto – to reduce unemployment, which quickly became the Government's main electoral liability almost as soon as it took office; second, and linked with the first, a programme – featured in the 1987 manifesto – of education and training, which were recognized as essential to improve the supply side of the labour market. Never was there any question of incomes policy, which was dismissed as a cardinal error on the part of each of the two previous Governments. Monetary and fiscal policy were to influence the demand side of the labour market (see chapter 2) and tax and social security the supply side (see chapter 4). Official intervention operated on demand and on supply but not on the price of labour, which kept on rising at a disappointingly high rate.

Figure 15. Department of Employment activities 1980–90

	White Papers	Legislation	Special schemes
1980		Employment Act (secondary action, closed shop, postal ballots)	
1981	*Trade Union Immunities* (Green), Cmnd 8128 *A New Training Initiative*, Cmnd 8455		
1982		Employment Act (union damages, closed shop, trade disputes)	Community Programme Young Workers Scheme Enterprise Allowance
1983			Youth Training Scheme (16–18) Job Splitting Scheme
1984	*Training for Jobs*, Cmnd 9135	Trade Union Act (secret ballots)	Technical and Vocational Education Initiative (14–18)
1985	*Employment: The Challenge for the Nation*, Cmnd 9474. *Lifting the Burden*, Cmnd 9571 *		Job Clubs National Council for Vocational Qualifications
1986		Wages Act (Councils) Sex Discrimination Act (hours of work)	Restart Job Training Scheme Jobstart Allowance
1987	*Trade Unions and their Members* (Green), Cm 95		Compacts New Workers Scheme
1988	*Training for Employment*, Cm 316 *Employment for the 1990s*, Cm 540	Employment Act (closed shop, members' rights)	Employment Training (18–24) Career Development Loans
1989	*Removing Barriers to Employment* (Green), Cm 655	Employment Act (deregulation, training)	Business Growth Training Claimant Advisers
1990		Employment Act (job protection, unofficial action)	Training and Enterprise Councils Youth Training

Notes: White Papers announcing legislation are not listed separately from the legislation. * Published by the Minister without Portfolio.

Trade-union legislation – salami tactics

Prior's mission statement stood for his successors too. 'My purpose was to bring about a lasting change in attitude by changing the law gradually, with as little resistance, and therefore as much by stealth, as was possible. There were also dangers in having tougher legislation which employers might in practice be afraid to use. It would be wrong to pass legislation which the courts could not enforce, as had been the case with the 1971 Act.' It was to be salami tactics, not all-out assault.

Prior's 1980 Employment Act implemented the manifesto almost to the letter, yet during its passage he was harassed by pressure from Mrs Thatcher and her more radical advisers to take tougher measures, particularly after the 1980 steel strike. He was prepared to take further measures in good time but wanted to prepare the way by opening up issues for discussion in the January 1981 Green Paper, *Trade Union Immunities*. It covered all the main points in an impartial manner: trade-union funds, secondary action, picketing, the definition of trade disputes, collective agreements, secret ballots, closed shops and the protection of the community. It raised the fundamental question of whether workers should be given positive rights rather than unions negative immunities, and Prior inserted another reference to his idea of tripartite economic discussions in a forum such as the NEDC. The upshot was that he wanted to see how the 1980 Act worked before imposing further restrictions on union immunities. Mrs Thatcher became impatient. In September 1981 Prior was sent to Northern Ireland and replaced by Tebbit, one of Mrs Thatcher's 'trusties'.

Prior resented the move away from Employment but accepted the fate of 'wets' – to be sent to govern if not New South Wales then Northern Ireland (in his case), Scotland (Malcolm Rifkind, January 1986) or just plain Wales (Peter Walker, June 1987). Tebbit commented in his memoirs:

The Cabinet shuffle was rightly seen as a turning point in Margaret

Thatcher's premiership. She needed to strengthen the Government with colleagues who believed that the policy of the Government was right and that it could be carried through ... The change from Jim Prior to myself was widely seen as significant. To some it was a calculated insult to the unemployed, to others a welcome challenge at last to the abuses of trade-union power and the closed shop in particular.

Tebbit's Employment Act 1982 did no more than pick up some of the ideas in Prior's Green Paper. He resisted measures to ban the closed shop, on the grounds that they would not have worked, and confined himself to increasing protection against dismissal for individuals opting out of a closed shop by improving compensation for it that was binding on employers and unions. He restricted the definition of a trades dispute to industrial relations matters and lifted unions' immunity from damages if they took action on other, more political, kinds of dispute.

Tebbit shied away from removing immunity from strikes carried out without a secret ballot. It later turned out that this provision might have prevented the 1984 coal strike had it been in force. It was left to King, who succeeded him in October 1983, to bring in the Trade Union Act 1984, which introduced secret ballots for union elections, political activities and strikes. Secret ballots soon had an effect, preventing an Austin–Rover strike at the end of 1984 and a British Rail drivers' strike in the summer of 1985. In 1985 King also stretched to two years (from one year) the period after which an employee could claim unfair dismissal under Labour's Employment Protection Act 1975. (Prior had in 1980 lengthened the period from six months to a year.)

Lord Young, who took over as Employment Secretary in September 1985, was more concerned with freeing the supply side of the labour market than with trade-union law. Women's hours were derestricted by the Sex Discrimination Act 1986, and minimum wages set by Wages Councils covering just over a tenth of the labour force were abolished for under-21s by the Wages Act 1986. In February 1987 the

Green Paper *Trade Unions and their Members* covered the disposition of trade-union funds, the closed shop (yet again) and the extension of democracy in trade unions. It was left to Fowler, who took over in June 1987, to act on some of these proposals.

The Employment Act 1988 finally removed statutory support for the closed shop and protected employees against dismissal for non-union membership. It tightened up the secret ballot provisions and improved the rights of members *vis-à-vis* their unions – for example, against unlawful use of union funds – by setting up a Commissioner for the Rights of Trade-union Members. The Employment Act 1989 removed restrictions on the use of women for certain types of work and on the hours of work of youngsters.

In February 1989 Fowler published a Green Paper, *Removing Barriers to Employment*, that contained further proposals for dealing with the pre-entry closed shop and with industrial action. It was under Michael Howard, who succeeded Fowler in July 1990, that this was implemented largely as the Employment Act 1990. The Act gave industrial tribunals the capacity to protect anyone dismissed for either belonging or not belonging to a union but gave employers greater freedom to dismiss for unofficial industrial action, while removing the immunities of unions in support of such cases. It also removed immunity from union officials or shop stewards calling for unauthorized action.

Fewer strikes but little effect on pay rises

Mrs Thatcher was right to allow discretion to be the better part of valour. The gradual approach to trade-union law reform avoided the pitfall of trying to do too much at once and getting crucial details wrong. It also ensured a greater degree of acceptance from trade unions as the climate of opinion shifted during the 1980s. The effects were, however, less than was hoped at the outset and were in some ways perverse from the employers' point of view because the unions benefited by being forced to 'clean up their act'.

Trade-union membership fell by 3 million (a quarter) in the 1980s, from 57 to 46 per cent of all employees (see table 47). This was due partly to the fall in employment in manufacturing, where union density is higher, and the corresponding rise in services, where it is lower. There was also a similar fall in strike incidence between the 1970s and the 1980s, the result as much of the fall in union membership for reasons of industrial structure as of changes in union law. Working days lost in the first half of the 1980s were nearly as high as in the 1970s; the big change occurred in the second half of the 1980s, when they fell to just over a third of the level in the first half. This could be explained partly by the greater prosperity of the later period. There was a general decline in strike incidence in all countries between the 1970s and the 1980s, so the UK cannot claim exceptional merit. The decline in strikes has been more marked in the USA. The UK's strike record remains similar to that of Australia, another country with British-style unions, better than that of Italy, worse than that of France. Japan and Germany are not shown in the table because they lose so few days through stoppages.

There were a number of major strikes in the first half of the 1980s. They were affected only to a minor extent by trade-union reform, which tended to be influenced by the lessons of the most recent strikes and was therefore locking stable doors after horses had bolted. It was important for the Thatcher Government to win these strikes. The January 1980 steel strike was settled after some months, when the employers raised their offer from 2 to 16 per cent, and was followed by massive lay-offs resulting in spectacular productivity increases. Each side could thus claim victory but on different battlefields. The 1981 Civil Service strike went on for five months and could have been ended many weeks before had the Government agreed earlier to the 7½ per cent for which it eventually settled. Lord Soames, the minister responsible, was sacked by Mrs Thatcher soon afterwards for having pointed this out. This strike cost about £1.5 billion in uncollected taxes and in additional interest on public debt, thus undermining the Government's fiscal and monetary policy at a critical time. There were strikes on the railways and in the hospitals in 1982 and, in 1984, in the docks and in Government Communications HQ, where ministers tried to ban unions altogether.

Mrs Thatcher opted against a coal strike in February 1981, giving in to the NUM's demands, but lived to fight another day three years later. The 1984 coal strike, which went on for nearly a year, was the most spectacular confrontation of the decade. Like the News International strike at *The Times*'s new Wapping plant in 1985–6, it required massive use of police to protect non-strikers who were keeping production going and thus undermining the strike. Both strikes also resulted in the closure of antiquated production facilities and the elimination of overmanning, so that two more important industries were able to make large productivity gains.

The cost to the economy of the coal strike was about £2 billion, however, and it made a noticeable difference to the UK's rate of economic growth (see page 13). Nigel Lawson, then Chancellor of the Exchequer, regarded the £300 million extra public expenditure as 'even in narrow financial terms ... a worthwhile investment for the nation', presumably in terms of the benefits of a reduction in union power. Yet six years later, when Mrs Thatcher was forced to resign, Arthur Scargill was still – just – president of the NUM. The privatization of the coal industry, which might have yielded an even better return on the money invested in the strike, was still no more than a distant aspiration.

Employers' strike 'victories' characteristically involved a pattern familiar in the vastly greater number of cases where there were no strikes: higher pay, higher productivity, higher unemployment. No major strike was fought and won on the issue of a pay freeze accompanied by the maintenance of jobs. The change in the industrial climate was brought about more by high unemployment and the failure of a few highly visible strikes than by changes in trade-union law. While there was an undoubted shift in bargaining power away from the unions and towards the employers, it was far from having the effects that the reformers had hoped for.

The hope was that union reform would reduce unemployment by ending the power of the closed shop to keep out 'outsiders' prepared to undercut existing rates maintained by 'insiders'; bring inflation down by giving employers more flexibility in wage bargaining without fear of strikes; and improve productivity by agreements to end restrictive working practices.

The closed shop was unfortunately supported by some employers, who felt that it gave them more control over their workforce. The use of 'outsiders' to bid down pay rates, as in the News International dispute, could be disruptive to workplace relations. There was a reduction from 5.2 million to 3 million in the number of workers covered by closed shops during the 1980s, partly because of the loss of jobs in manufacturing, where they are more common. There was, however, little sign of a fall in the union mark-up.

Wage bargaining remained collective for over half the labour force in such a way that minimum increases above the rate of inflation were paid to all members of a group, and flexibility applied more to performance increases above the going rate, especially for top executives, rather than to the going rate itself. There was a shift from multi-employer to single-employer bargaining but not much from multi-union to single-union, apart from a few highly publicized cases involving the electricians' union EEPTU. Plant or single-employer bargaining made lay-offs easier to negotiate, but the presence of several unions made for higher settlements and fewer productivity improvements involving more flexible working practices. Where unions were not recognized, as in the North Sea, employers made sure that pay increases were high enough to convince employees that they would have nothing to gain from joining them.

Employers assumed that any pay increases they gave would be more or less matched by their competitors and could be passed through into prices after deducting something for productivity increases. Any employer in the home market who tried to increase market share by holding prices down through lower pay increases would, it was argued, lose his best employees to competitors. The possibility of being priced out of foreign markets could be averted by devaluation of the pound. Competition in the labour market was more active on the demand side than on the supply side, and competition in the product market was dominated by large price-leader firms with little more than a slap on the wrist to fear from laws on restrictive price-fixing agreements (see page 192).

As the OECD put it in its January 1986 *Economic Survey of the UK*: 'Companies seem to be willing to agree to higher wages where productivity improvements are being made, or in order to retain their skilled workforce. But there are also cases where employers concede wage claims, even without productivity improvements, rather than risk industrial action, with the hope that the cost increase can be passed on to consumers.' The idea that productivity improvements should be passed through into price cuts rather than pay increases was foreign to the culture of most UK employers and unions. Yet it could have produced lower prices all round, which would have meant that lower nominal pay increases could have resulted in the same real rises in earnings as occurred with higher nominal pay settlements.

Although strikes became more difficult for unions to organize and to win, the increasing capital intensity of businesses made them more damaging when they occurred. Often the mere possibility, if not the actual threat, of a strike was enough to make employers back down without waiting for it to happen. The CBI found that in 1980–86 6½ per cent of all settlements were accompanied by industrial action, while another 6½ per cent went with an effective threat of action. The strike-ballot legislation worked in the same direction. In 1987–9, 92 per cent of strike ballots were in favour of industrial action. This both gave strikes more democratic authority, if they occurred, and made it more difficult for union leaders to reach a compromise.

There was an improvement in employers' bargaining

power, but they used it almost entirely to increase productivity, not to lower nominal pay increases, although it would have been sensible to attempt both objectives. The former at least was a hope fulfilled. OECD commented in its January 1985 *Economic Survey of the UK*:

> The weakening of the unions has certainly contributed to greater flexibility in the labour market in changing working practices but has still not succeeded in imparting any downwards flexibility in real wages. In fact, higher productivity seems to have been the main result and this has itself contributed to holding up the real wage where earnings have been output-related. There may have been some collusion between management and unions whereby the introduction of high-productivity rationalization investment has been agreed at the cost of higher real wage levels but fewer jobs.

In many cases where management had been in fear of the unions there was a new mood of being 'free to manage' and imposing change whether the unions agreed to it or not. As one personnel manager told Michael Fogarty for his Policy Studies Institute survey: 'We have the bullets now.' Since the new management style went with the elimination of overmanning and the rise in unemployment that continued for most of the 1980s, it may be wondered whether it can survive periods of skill shortage and relatively low unemployment such as 1987–9.

Trade unions are known for the 'sword of justice' effect, acting to reduce inequality, particularly for groups with low bargaining power, such as women, children and immigrants. It is thus unsurprising that a reduction in union power went with an increase in the inequality of pay. As well as conceding real-wage increases averaging 2.4 per cent a year all through the 1980s (see table 14), employers increased pay differentials, as a result of more individually tailored contracts of employment, in an effort to provide performance incentives. The biggest increases of all went to directors and top executives, much to the Government's dismay, in spite of – or even because of – the big tax cuts on higher incomes. According to Incomes Data Services, quoted in the October

1989 *Employment Gazette* 'the latest rises of many chairmen or chief executives have generally outpaced any performance improvements based on indicators such as earnings per share. It has thus been difficult for them to refuse far more modest real increases lower down the scale.'

Real-pay increases have averaged 5.2 per cent a year for the top 10 per cent but only 1.7 per cent for the bottom 10 per cent, and the former now get 5.5 times as much as the latter rather than 3.9 times, as in 1979 (see table 48). The lowest-paid have done better than their counterparts in most other countries in terms of real wage increases, but the highest-paid have done a great deal better. The resulting income distribution is closer to the international norm and reflects greater flexibility in pay management. It has, however, been unnecessarily made even more unequal at the top end of the range by the 1987 tax changes (see table 27). This was always part of Mrs Thatcher's vision. Soon after her election to the leadership, she said in New York in September 1975: 'Opportunity means nothing unless it means the right to be unequal.' The following month she told the Conservative Party Conference at Blackpool: 'We believe that everyone has the right to be unequal.'

Given an apparent choice, lower nominal pay rises and static productivity or higher nominal pay rises and higher productivity, employers chose the latter. The former alternative would have meant lower inflation and lower real growth, while the latter brought higher real growth at the cost of higher inflation. This was a false dilemma, but both employers and unions behaved as if it were genuine. Government intervention to educate both sides through a forum such as the National Economic Development Council (NEDC) might, as Prior claimed, have been helpful. NEDC was allowed to survive on sufferance, and little was achieved by its meetings, even though the Government did sit at the same table as the unions and the employers.

The partial improvement in the relative performance of the UK labour market can be judged from table 49. The UK's nominal hourly earnings increase in manufacturing averaged 10.3 per cent in the 1980s, compared with 16.6 per cent in 1974-9, but this was 58 per cent higher than the OECD average, compared with 54 per cent in the earlier period. The UK's pay inflation was better than Italy's, slightly worse than France's and about double that of the USA or Germany in both periods.

UK real earnings rose by less than 1 per cent a year in 1974-9 but were at least in line with low productivity growth; only the USA had lower figures, while in other major countries both real earnings and productivity rose faster, with Japan showing a surplus of productivity over earnings and Italy the opposite. In 1980-88 UK real earnings rose by 2.8 per cent, with a corresponding productivity rise of 4.2 per cent (5.5 per cent, counting only the best years 1982-8). This was comparable with Italy (with, again, an excess of real-wage increases over productivity rises). Productivity rose faster in the UK and Italy than in other industrial countries save Japan, where real wages also rose only half as fast as in the UK. The USA had a productivity increase of 3.3 per cent, while real wages fell by 0.8 per cent a year.

Productivity levels are still lower in the UK than in the other main industrial countries, with the exception of Japan (due to the large and inefficient farming sector), and it will take many years of more rapid growth before they catch up. On a per-employee basis whole-economy productivity in 1986 was 41 per cent higher in the USA than in the UK, 19 per cent higher in France, 13 per cent higher in Germany and 6 per cent lower in Japan; by 1990 Japan may have caught up with the UK. The UK's immediate prospect of catching up has been delayed by the slow-down in output in 1989-90, which caused productivity to become negative for the whole economy in 1989 and for manufacturing by the third quarter of 1990.

Unit labour costs (ULC) in manufacturing are nominal earnings and other labour costs divided by productivity and are an indicator of international competitiveness. The UK had the worst record on ULC in 1974-9, double the average and worse than Italy. ULC increases in the UK fell from 18 per cent then to under 5 per cent in 1980–88. This was better than Italy and France but well above the average and the US and German figures, all 2–3 per cent. Japan's ULC fell by 1 per cent a year. The figures for relative ULC in a common currency show that, thanks to devaluation, the UK, France and Italy remained competitive on ULC in the 1980s, but the UK had a relatively high cost base in 1979 because of the rise in the pound, causing loss of competitiveness, in 1976–9. The USA became more competitive because of the fall in the dollar before 1979 and after 1984. Japan and Germany became less competitive because of the rise in their currencies but were able to overcome the handicap by moving up-market in their mix of traded products.

William Brown and Sushil Wadwhani conclude their survey of the effects of trade-union legislation: 'The impact of the legislation on British trade unions is undeniable; its impact upon Britain's economic performance is far less obvious.' Another verdict on pay inflation was that of Samuel Brittan in the *Financial Times* survey of the Thatcher years: 'An incomes policy does not work; but not having an incomes policy doesn't work either.' While trade-union reform was worth undertaking to limit the irresponsible use of power by union leaders and to increase the responsible exercise of democracy by their members, it was never likely that it would replace incomes policy as a way of keeping nominal wage increases down.

Nicholas Oulton reported that a quarter to a half of the 4 per cent improvement in labour productivity between the 1970s and the 1980s was due to 'a decline in the disadvantages of unionization: that is, when all other effects are taken into account, unionization still seems to reduce productivity growth, but to a lesser extent than it used to. If so, the Thatcher Government's programme of trade-union reform should receive a share of the credit.' Mrs Thatcher's reasons for trade-union reform were as much political as economic, and by this standard it was more successful. As she told Kenneth Harris in an interview: 'I don't think the unions should be considered a sort of Fourth Estate of the realm.'

There is still a school of thought close to the IEA that believes that Mrs Thatcher's trade-union reforms were not nearly radical enough and that union power remains much stronger than in Japan, Germany or France. In their 1988 IEA pamphlet *Striking out Strikes* Charles Hanson and Graham Mather wrote: 'The abolition of all trade-union immunities would be simple, it would be effective, and the benefits to the British economy would be immense.' The Government view was by then very different: 'If the trade unions do not modernize themselves, they will see their members continue to drift away,' said Norman Fowler, then Employment Secretary, in a speech on 14 June 1988. The unions may become weaker just by losing members, as in the USA, but if they do modernize, with the help of some of the Government's reforms, they could retain and even regain their influence in bargaining on pay and a wide range of other matters. The Government never decided whether it wanted to eliminate unions or improve them and ended up doing a bit of both.

Unemployment – first the solution, then the problem

The unemployment of the 1980s can be attributed to many causes: the world recession of 1980–82, the Thatcher Government's unusually deflationary monetary policy, the trade unions' preference for real-wage increases rather than job preservation, the increase in the population of working age, the high benefit/post-tax income ratio for some family men, the lack of pressure on benefit claimants to take a job and the high costs of dismissing new employees. The best attempt to measure the respective contribution of each factor was made by Richard Layard and Stephen Nickell at the LSE Centre for Labour Economics, who attributed about three-quarters of the increase to the Thatcher Government's distinctive policies.

The unemployment caused partly by the trade unions had

two consequences. It reduced the unions' bargaining power more quickly and effectively than the reform of trade-union law and thus made it easier for employers to increase productivity by means of still more lay-offs rather than by increases in production. It also reduced wage inflation, though not the union mark-up, in a way that trade-union reform could not – by making employees afraid of losing their jobs altogether, either by dismissal or by the bankruptcy of the employer due to excessive pay awards.

Although the Government had originally hoped to reduce unemployment, the increase became an unintentional but essential part of its mechanism for the reduction of both inflation and trade-union power. The MTFS announced in March 1980 was supposed to have an effect on pay bargaining such as to limit the amount of unemployment temporarily required to bring inflation down. Referring to the loss of output and jobs, the MTFS said: 'The size and duration of these initial effects will depend in large measure on how quickly behaviour, particularly in pay bargaining, takes account of the new monetary environment.' Just over ten years later the Government made the same point when unemployment accelerated as a result of the interest- and exchange-rate discipline of the ERM.

The UK stood out from other countries for its real-wage rigidity, which was generally ascribed to trade-union influence. The OECD (*Economic Outlook*, July 1985) defines real-wage rigidity or flexibility as the short-run elasticity of money wages with respect to inflation divided by the elasticity of money wages with regard to unemployment. If money wages are flexible and go up and down with inflation, this means that real wages are rigid. If money wages are flexible and go up and down as unemployment goes down and up, then real wages are flexible too. Real-wage rigidity occurs when the first elasticity is high and/or the second is low. The UK in the early 1980s had the highest wage rigidity, Japan and the USA the highest flexibility, with the continental European countries in between. David Coe of OECD found in 1985 that British wages changed to fully the same extent as prices after a lag of two and a half years – not so different from other countries – but the UK was peculiar in that wages fell by only 0.17 per cent for each 1 per cent rise in the unemployment rate.

The inverse relationship between inflation and unemployment, known as the Phillips Curve, gives the UK a relatively unfavourable trade-off, the more so as unemployment gets higher. It took a doubling of the numbers unemployed between 1979 and 1981, to 2 million, to cut the rate of increase of average real earnings from 2¼ per cent to ¾ per cent. Unemployment then went on rising by another 50 per cent to well over 3 million during the next five years to 1986, but average nominal earnings stuck at about 8 per cent a year, even though price inflation fell to an average of 5 per cent, giving real increases of 3 per cent (see table 14). (The 1984 figures are lower because of the effect of the coal strike on miners' earnings.) The UK's problem appears to be that wages are quicker to follow prices up than to chase them down.

The change rather than the level of unemployment appeared to lower wage settlements, so that a high, but only slowly rising, unemployment total brought diminishing returns in the fight against inflation. A rising proportion of the unemployed – three-fifths by 1987 – had been out of work for six months or more. They had relatively little effect in bringing wage settlements down because they had been discouraged in their search for jobs.

From being the solution to inflation, unemployment became a problem in its own right, particularly by 1983, when inflation was no longer such an issue. The Government refused to deploy macro-economic policy against unemployment during the recession because it believed that premature fiscal or monetary reflation would bring back inflation and that the labour market would work better if left to itself. Both views were gradually abandoned as it became clear that unemployment was a major election issue. By its last term the Government was embarked on twin policies of monetary expansion and labour-market activism that brought unemployment down, contrary to all expectations, as fast as it had risen in the recession.

Francis Pym, Defence and then Foreign Secretary in Mrs Thatcher's first term, wrote in 1984:

There is one fallacy held about life after the recession, which is that when it ends and when sustained growth returns to the economy, there will be a steady if slow return to full employment. This will not happen. Indeed, it is feasible that unemployment could actually rise as the economy recovers. If gains in productivity outstrip economic growth, without a commensurate reduction in working hours, unemployment will be bound to rise.

For giving such prophetic warnings while in government Pym was sacked after the 1983 election by Mrs Thatcher, to whom the 'wets' saw him as a rival.

To begin with, the Government used a package of indirect weapons, based on the analysis of free-market economists such as Patrick Minford of Liverpool University. The causes of unemployment, he argued, were high union density, an excessive ratio of benefits to wages and too much taxation of both employers and employees. Trade-union reform, the reduction of earnings-related benefits, the abolition of the National Insurance Surcharge on employers and income-tax cuts, though they were all being pursued for reasons that originally had nothing to do with unemployment, thus became a ready-made supply-side package for reducing it. The only problem was that it seemed to be ineffective. Critics argued that such supply-side factors had been swamped by the massive fall in demand in the labour and product markets, which needed to be reversed if unemployment was to be brought down.

The one part of the Minford package that affected the demand side was employer taxation. The Government gradually reduced it so as to bring down the real cost of labour to employers. Treasury economists found that a 1 per cent fall in real wages would increase employment by about $\frac{3}{4}$ per cent, or 165,000. This would not reduce unemployment by more than about 100,000 because some of the employees would be women not counted as unemployed, but it would still mean ½ per cent off the unemployment percentage.

The Government cut payroll taxes for employers first by gradually abolishing the National Insurance Surcharge then, in the March 1985 Budget, by reducing contribution rates for lower-paid employees (see figure 7). It also worked on the supply side of the labour market by cuts in income tax and employee contributions, whose main incentive effect was on married women. The 'tax wedge' between the gross of tax cost of labour to the employer and the net of tax take-home pay of the employee was reduced. The tax changes were one of the main proposals of the Department of Employment White Paper accompanying the 1985 Budget, *Employment: The Challenge for the Nation*, which also emphasized special job-creation measures of the kind that went against pure free-market principles.

Special job-creation measures

More direct intervention was needed, both to improve the supply and stimulate the demand for workers and to remove some of the excess supply from the market. The key role in this policy was played by David Young, a successful property developer who had entered Whitehall as a friend and personal adviser of Mrs Thatcher. Young differed from his colleagues in that he lacked experience of politics, but he was also free of ideological baggage such as might have restrained him from interfering in the free play of the labour market. His fertile imagination spawned a whole series of special employment measures (SEMs), which built upon those that had been inherited from the Labour Government. He became Chairman of the Manpower Services Commission in 1982. He was given a life peerage in September 1984 so that he could become Minister without Portfolio (dubbed 'Minister for Unemployment') and was then Employment Secretary from September 1985 to June 1987.

By 1982 there was a feeling of national outrage at the sudden rise in unemployment, combined with a sense of helplessness in the search for solutions. A House of Lords Select Committee reported in May 1982: 'We believe unemployment to be among the causes of ill-health, mortality, crime and civil disorder.' The Committee recommended a programme of special training and job-creation measures, 'good value for money' at a cost of £5 billion. The Employment Institute was set up in 1985 with support from all political parties to put forward alternative policies. (The Institute held a meeting in Canterbury Cathedral, addressed by three MPs, Andrew Rowe (Conservative), Frank Field (Labour) and Shirley Williams (SDP).) The Archbishop of Canterbury set up a study group on the problems of the inner cities, including unemployment, whose report, *Faith in the City*, irked Mrs Thatcher as yet another example of the Church meddling in politics. (Its chairman, Sir Richard O'Brien, had been displaced by Young from the chair of the Manpower Services Commission (MSC).)

The SEMs went hand in glove with a series of changes in the definitions of unemployment that served the same purpose of reducing the published unemployment totals (for details see the author's *Measuring the Economy*). The relationship between benefit offices and Jobcentres has always been important to both unemployment and the unemployment statistics. Benefits were paid and the unemployed registered for jobs at the same offices until 1972, when the two functions were given to separate offices. This improved the profile of the Jobcentres but reduced pressure on the unemployed to seek work, causing some rise in unemployment. In 1982 registration at Jobcentres became voluntary, not obligatory, for benefit recipients, who had to sign on for benefit only once a fortnight as part of the Government's economy programme. (It was a false economy because it made it easier for fraudsters to claim benefit and to avoid official job offers without detection.) Jobcentre registrations no longer covered all the unemployed, so the count switched to recipients of benefit. This reduced 'unemployment' by 190,000.

The following year another 162,000 were removed from

the unemployment figures because, being over 60, they were regarded as entitled to benefit without looking for work. However, by 1985 the benefit count was actually giving higher readings than labour-force surveys showing who was actively seeking work. Some benefit claimants were long-term unemployed discouraged from seeking work; others were doing part-time or even full-time jobs in the black economy.

Young had the brainwave of calling in all the long-term unemployed for six-monthly Restart interviews, starting in 1986. The purpose was to offer them training courses or help them to find jobs, with rather little success, but the effect was that about ¾ million 'unemployed' ceased to claim benefit – according to Bank of England research – as a result either of attending their interviews or not attending them. There were 2.2–2.3 million Restart interviews a year in the three years 1987–9, and about 10 per cent of those called did not come. The next move, not made until 1989, was the obvious one of bringing the benefit offices and Jobcentres back under the same roof, which will take until 1992–4.

There were relatively few schemes involving subsidies to the employer – such as the Temporary Short-time Working Compensation Scheme, ended in 1984 – because they fell foul of an EC ban on this kind of subsidy and did not bring wages down. Many schemes involved the use of cheap labour by employers that the trade unions were powerless to block. The Community Programme, which replaced a similar scheme from 1982, was attractive to young single workers because of its flat-rate pay; from 1988 it was replaced by Employment Training, on a 'benefit-plus' basis, which made it less attractive to young single workers but more attractive to family men.

The Community Programme did little to improve the supply side of the labour market, apart from getting some of it out of the long-term unemployment figures. (One reason why those unemployed for over six months fell to half the total in 1990 is that a short spell of work or training, even if not followed by a permanent job, turns a long-term into a short-term unemployed person.) Young made more serious efforts to improve the quality of the labour force with the Youth Training Scheme (YTS) for school leavers and the Technical and Vocational Education Initiative for 14–18 year olds, starting in 1983 and 1984. The idea of these schemes was first put forward in the 1981 White Paper *A New Training Initiative* (see figure 15). This was followed by *Training for Jobs* in 1984, by which the MSC was given further powers to purchase more work-related, non-advanced further education from local authorities.

The House of Commons Employment Committee reported in January 1986 that the SEMs were not extensive enough. It called for an extra 750,000 jobs to be created over three years, over half in the building industry and health and social services and the others by means of a subsidy to employers specific to the long-term unemployed. It backed the idea of a job guarantee for the long-term unemployed that had been pioneered by the Employment Institute and its sister organization, Charter for Jobs. Young turned the report down on the grounds that it would cost £4 billion, which would be better spent on tax cuts, and that Restart was a better idea.

Young discovered a key text in the Beveridge Report that was common to his own approach and the practice already adopted for many years in Sweden. 'Young people should not get unconditional unemployment benefit at all,' Beveridge had written: 'Their unemployment should be made the occasion for further training.' Young's problem was the Treasury's refusal to fund two-year YTS courses so as to keep school-leavers out of unemployment altogether between 16 and 18. The low quality of some YTS courses also made the refusal of benefit to under-18s, which became official policy in 1988, insufficient as an incentive to make them attend.

Government expenditure on employment and training rose from £2.4 billion in 1979–80 to £4 billion in 1986–7 (in 1988–9 prices) as unemployment rose but was then cut back to £3.2 billion in 1989–90, with further cuts planned, even though unemployment was expected to rise again. The Government's linkage of training with unemployment, originally motivated by the need to reduce the unemployment statistics, was short-sighted because it ignored the need to improve skills among the employed as well. It was only after the 1987 election, in Mrs Thatcher's third term, that the Government began to get to the roots of the skills deficit by means of extensive reforms of the education system, with a national curriculum and performance checks on the teachers as well as the taught.

In February 1988 the next White Paper, *Training for Employment*, had to confess that the rise in unemployment had created problems for training and work:

First, many job seekers – particularly those who have been unemployed for six months or more – lack the skills needed to fill the jobs our economy is generating. Second, many longer-term unemployed people have lost touch with the jobs market, and lack the motivation to take up a job, training, or other opportunities. Third, there is evidence, particularly in the most prosperous parts of the country, that significant numbers of benefits claimants are not available for work.

The MSC, now redesignated the Training Commission, was given the responsibility for running a single unified programme, Employment Training (ET), which took the place of the Community Programme and the YTS. The Restart scheme, and more searching fraud inquiries, were designed to get the fraudulently employed out of unemployment benefit and the genuinely unemployed into employment.

The new policy was elaborated by the December 1988 White Paper, *Employment for the 1990s*, which set up a Task Force to establish a new locally based system of Training and Enterprise Councils (TECs), in which employers would play a central part. The TECs, due to be functioning by mid-1991, were in danger of failing to live up to expectations because of the paucity of official funding, based on the view that employers were prepared to find the money in view of the advantages to them. While employers as a whole may benefit from training, the employer who pays the cost may find that his skilled employees are bid away by rivals. Training is a public, but not always a private, good.

Young had set up the National Council for Vocational Qualifications in 1984. The official inspectors of YTS, found 'a high and growing proportion of schemes offering nationally recognized qualifications', but against this they found that 'many trainers lacked the levels of knowledge and skill needed to guide trainees towards recognized qualifications or credits towards them' (*Employment Gazette*, July 1990). Similarly, Paul Gregg criticized Employment Training on the grounds that 'a mismatch of training to skills required means little raising of future employment prospects of participants' and that 'the growing compulsion to participate may reduce the status of participants in employers' eyes as participation no longer indicates self-motivation'.

The Government was slow off the mark in developing the skills of the labour force in order to narrow the productivity gap between the UK and its competitors. According to Hilary Steedman, the proportion of the labour force with intermediate vocational qualifications rose between 1979 and 1988 from 23 per cent to 26 per cent in the UK but from 32 per cent to 40 per cent in France. The two main reasons for the UK's relative backwardness were, first, the persistent under-funding of salaries and equipment throughout the education and training system and, second, the constant upheaval of the institutions responsible in the entourage of the Department of Employment. In 1988 the Manpower Services Commission was replaced by the Training Commission, which was replaced by the Training Agency, whose functions are now exercised through the Training and Enterprise Councils. There are still a few Industrial Training Boards left over from the perfectly workable system of the 1970s that the Government short-sightedly swept away when it came into office.

The Government's policy to reduce unemployment went in tandem with its more positive policy of creating employment. 'New jobs' were expected to come about as a result of tax cuts, deregulation and other supply-side incentives to business enterprise. Most of the 'old jobs' lost were in manufacturing, and the new jobs were mainly in services. Full-time male manual workers in the north were replaced by part-time female clerical workers in the south. There was thus a mismatch in the labour market that could have been rectified only to a limited extent by more active regional policy, greater housing mobility and improved training, however desirable in their own right.

Young was responsible, as Minister without Portfolio, for small firms and tourism, both believed to be good sources of job creation and in line with the Government's wish to increase economic freedom. The Training Agency operated a Small Firms Service to give advice. The Small Firm Loan Guarantee Scheme, operated by the clearing banks, brought into being a modest amount of lending that they would not have carried out on an unguaranteed basis. The evidence that small firms created more jobs than large was open to question, however, since one new entrant in three fell by the wayside within three years.

Working on the statistics

There are at least three ways of presenting the UK unemployment statistics. The first (see table 50), is to show what they were at the time of publication, since these are the figures as they were perceived and acted on by policymakers. The second is the Orwellian revision now used that rewrites history by showing what the last two decades would have looked like if we had measured unemployment then as we do now. The third is the OECD standard basis, using labour-force surveys, which is more accurate – if less frequently published – and makes international comparisons easier.

On all three measures UK unemployment was on average six percentage points higher in the 1980s than in the 1970s. While the UK revised figures show the lowest average of 9 per cent in the 1980s, they also show that unemployment would have been as low as 3¼ per cent in the 1970s on the same basis – something of an 'own goal'. In spite of having banished nearly half a million from the official count, the UK's contemporaneous figure exceeded 13 per cent in 1985. It was then cut by 1.4 per cent by being expressed as a proportion of the total of employees and self-employed instead of only the former, although on the revised definition, and in terms of numbers, it reached its peak of over 3 million in 1986. On the labour-force definition it peaked at 12.4 per cent as early as 1983. Had the Government done then what it later proposed – to publish a labour-force total with interpolations from other sources – the pressure to reflate in 1986 and later years might have been less and the excessive expansion of demand might have been avoided.

UK unemployment, on any definition, fell below 6 per cent in 1990. While the Government claimed this as a policy success, it was clearly below the non-accelerating inflation rate of unemployment (NAIRU). Even though some of the Government's trade-union and labour-market measures may have lowered the NAIRU, it was probably still at least 7 per cent. This meant that unemployment had to rise temporarily above that level if inflation were to decelerate.

Although the UK rate was above that of the EC as a whole for most of the 1980s, it fell below in 1987–9. France and Italy had to let their unemployment rise to double figures for most of the second half of the 1980s as the cost of converging towards lower German price inflation through the ERM. The German rate averaged only 6 per cent, however, and only Japan among major countries has done better, with a 2½ per cent average. The US rate was below that of the UK after 1980, thanks to the strong recovery of 1983–4, and the workforce also expanded by 19 per cent in the 1980s compared with 6 per cent in the UK.

Since unemployment and inflation often move in opposite directions, one measure of total welfare can be taken by adding them into a 'misery index' (see table 50). Misery averaged just under 15 per cent in the 1970s, just over in the

1980s, but in the latter period unemployment was a higher, inflation a lower, proportion. The Labour Government brought misery down from a peak of 27 per cent in 1975 to 12½ per cent in 1978, while the Conservatives reduced it from 23 per cent in 1980 to 15 per cent in 1983. It rose again to 17 per cent in 1985, then fell to 13 per cent in 1988 before rising again. The UK's misery index is higher than that of most major countries because both inflation and unemployment are higher on average.

The UK's record on employment creation is mixed (see table 51). In 1980–83 2.1 million jobs were lost, 0.4 million more than the rise of 1.7 million in unemployment because of people leaving the active workforce. In 1984–6 both employment and unemployment slowly increased, by just over 0.3 million in each case, as the population of working age rose by 0.6 million and more people became active, many of them becoming self-employed. At last in 1987–90, 1.9 million new jobs were created, reducing unemployment by 1.5 million and drawing large numbers into activity, although the demographic increase slowed down.

The 2.1 million jobs lost were won back but with hardly any net increase between 1979 and 1990. There was a huge rise of 1.5 million in the number of self-employed, from 1.9 million to 3.4 million. As Mrs Thatcher told Peter Jay in an interview in 1986: 'We'll only get more people employed by the creation of more small businesses and more self-employment.' This was a success for the policy of letting more people run their own lives. A survey in the June 1989 *Employment Gazette* showed that only a quarter of them had become self-employed because they were unemployed. Over half had done so because they wanted more independence and just under a third for the greater financial rewards.

Up to half a million people at any one time were in work-related training, although the number who went through government schemes is several times that. There was a net increase of 0.5 million in the number of unemployed between 1979 and 1990. There was thus a 2.5 million increase in the total workforce, about 1.5 million because of demography and about 1 million because of higher activity rates. At the same time the number of people with two jobs, or a combination of self-employment and a job, trebled to well over 1 million.

The composition of employment shifted towards part-timers (see table 52) and towards women. The proportion of part-timers among employees rose from a fifth in 1979 to a quarter in 1990, a rise of 1 million; there was almost as large a fall in the number of full-time employees. 'Part-time' does not usually mean second-best: only 7 per cent of part-timers accept such jobs because they cannot find a full-time job; two-thirds work part-time because they do not want to work full-time – understandably, since 83 per cent of part-timers are women, many with home responsibilities. There was an increase of 1.5 million in women employees, equally split between full-time and part-time, and a similar fall in the number of men, all full-time. Women were 48 per cent of all employees, but 42 per cent of all women employees worked part-time.

In spite of its high unemployment, the UK managed to provide jobs or self-employment for a higher proportion of its population than did most continental countries. Labour participation rose almost as much as in the USA, though to levels still somewhat below those in Scandinavia. The participation rate rose from 74 to 76 per cent, while in France it fell from 68 to 66 per cent. Women's participation rose from 58 to 65 per cent in the UK, while in France it went up from 54 to only 56 per cent, with a much bigger drop in male participation than in the UK, mainly because of early retirement.

The Government's labour-market policies brought about enormous changes in the pattern of employment. The increases in women employees, part-time jobs and service activities satisfied the demand for work in one part of the labour market, but the fall in manufacturing jobs for men in the traditional industrial areas left a trail of urban, social and environmental problems in its wake. Few of these were foreseen or intended. The Government gradually succeeded in limiting the power of the trade unions, but wages are still too rigid and have become more unequal without corresponding performance pay-offs. The Government was no more successful in tackling wage–cost inflation than in restraining demand inflation. Attempts to improve the quality of the labour supply were too little, too late, and even the foundations for future improvements still await completion.

8 Conclusions: the curate's egg

> 'Thatcherism is not for a decade. It is for centuries.'
> Mrs Thatcher, *Newsweek*, 15 October 1990

> 'Only a true star could survive a show as ill-conceived as this.'
> Adam Sweeting on Cher's concert, *Guardian*, 18 October 1990

Defects and qualities of Mrs Thatcher's style

Mrs Thatcher, like previous leaders of the Opposition new to 10 Downing Street, came to office with some radical policies that had not been properly worked out or even fully revealed to the public. Some of her early problems, like those of Wilson, Heath and again Wilson, arose from the difficulties of putting theory into practice. Other new Prime Ministers had the strength of mind to change policies when they thought that they were wrong. Mrs Thatcher had the strength of mind not to change policies when she thought that she was right. There was no U-turn into incomes policy, only a change in the mix of monetary and fiscal policy in 1981. There was no entry into the EMS ERM until the death-bed repentance of her last month in office. There was no retreat from the poll tax. There was some softening under strong pressure from her ministers: on trade-union reform, on the welfare state, on industrial subsidies.

Some of the major mistakes were therefore difficult to undo because of the peculiar mixture of rebelliousness and sycophancy that typified the relationships between Mrs Thatcher and members of her cabinet – sometimes in both directions. Ministers were too loyal, or too afraid of the sack, to question mistaken policies fundamentally, but they and their civil servants were sometimes able to make changes of detail that resulted only in muddled implementation and impaired effectiveness. Mrs Thatcher, on her side, boosted her favourites of the moment in what they were doing but was on other issues, notably European policy, a rebel against her own Government.

Collective responsibility became a fiction because important policies were announced to, rather than discussed in, cabinet. Mrs Thatcher became, by the 'elective dictatorship' of the British constitution, personally responsible for everything. Even her formidable intellectual grasp was not sufficient to replace the powers of judgement and action of which capable ministers were deprived by the quasi-presidential rule of 10 Downing Street. The whole Government was weakened because the captain would not give enough of the game to other members of the team but wanted to hog both the batting and the bowling, to use one of Mrs Thatcher's favourite metaphors. When the game was going well she took most of the credit, but when it was going badly the offending player was dropped from the team.

Mrs Thatcher's relations with her Chancellors were crucial to economic policy. Howe was a lawyer and not an economist, but this was an advantage when he was carrying out some of the iconoclastic aspects of Thatcherism that he could claim to have invented before Mrs Thatcher appeared on the scene, such as the reform of trade unions, taxation and the public sector. He was nevertheless pushed further than he wanted to go at some points. Lawson was an economist and thought he knew better than Mrs Thatcher how to run the Treasury of which she was First Lord. Lawson allowed Mrs Thatcher to overrule him on crucial issues such as the ERM and the poll tax, where his threatened or actual resignation at an earlier stage might have better served the country's economy and his own reputation. Yet she failed to overrule him where she should have done, notably on the abandonment of monetary controls and the fuelling of demand by tax cuts.

Mrs Thatcher, and Lawson himself, relied too much on the advice of the policy unit – the 10 Downing Street 'kitchen cabinet' – and the various think tanks with which it was in touch. Not only did they fail to heed the advice of ministerial colleagues and experienced civil servants, but they stifled discussion and consultation with interest groups outside Whitehall, such as the CBI and the TUC, that they nevertheless expected to comply with and implement their policies. Mrs Thatcher and Lawson relied too much on their own intuitions and not enough on the country's institutions; some, such as local government, were badly weakened, while others, such as the House of Lords, gave as good as they got.

Mrs Thatcher and her ministers, aided by the Downing Street Press Office, were against open government when it came to policy-making, unless it consisted of flying their own policy kites. They were too conscious of their own rectitude and the errors of others – including most of the economics profession – to have much time for argument. Yet they were also fearful of their own ability to stand up to pressure groups in open debate if a policy were prematurely released before being announced as a *fait accompli* (witness the climb-down on tax privileges of pension funds in the run-up to the 1985 Budget).

Policies were thought up and implemented on the hoof after the initial execution of some of the radical thoughts from Opposition days. They were thus not well designed at the moment of implementation and had to be changed or even abandoned as they buckled under pressure, as in the cases of monetary targets and training measures. As John MacGregor, then Minister of Education, put it (referring to vouchers): 'There is not much point in trying to invent a radical idea every minute if you have not actually carried through the one before' (*Guardian*, 18 October 1990).

Conclusions 253

Even when policies were successful, as in the case of the control of inflation in the first term, it was as much by accident as by design, and the success was not consolidated or built into an institutional framework, such as an independent Bank of England or a fully functioning National Economic Development Council. Mrs Thatcher and her closest associates came in with a Utopian vision of a free-market society that they could neither implement nor abandon. They were reduced to piecemeal engineering, which might sometimes be a case of half a loaf being better than no bread, but it was well below their own aspirations and the expectations of their supporters.

The paradox was that Mrs Thatcher came to office promising to get the Government off people's backs, yet used her complete command of the apparatus of power to intervene in the economy as much as any of her predecessors had, only in different ways. Her interventionist temperament was at odds with her philosophical libertarianism. As she said about others, many of her own interventions may have caused matters to get worse and not better – for example, the imposition of high interest rates in 1980–81 on an economy already experiencing a high exchange rate and recession.

Mrs Thatcher had the strengths of her defects. She knew how to take risks, even if she was luckier in the outcome of the Falklands campaign than in the fight against unemployment and more successful on the political than on the economic battlefield. Mrs Thatcher knew how to take decisions, right or wrong, though she impressed foreigners more by the style of her leadership than she impressed the British people by its substance. She was able to inspire confidence in her policies – an advantage of a kind even when they were mistaken – among both ordinary people and financial markets. She was a superb saleswoman for herself, the Conservative Government and the United Kingdom; it was a pity she applied this talent against, rather than in favour of, the European Community. She thus made some people feel good about her and Britain, though the objective basis of her achievement was at many points lacking.

Mrs Thatcher's disagreements with her colleagues were played down as differences of style rather than substance. Yet her style was the basis of her achievement, influencing the substance and often taking its place. *Le style, c'est la femme.* In this respect, as in many others, she resembled Général de Gaulle, who restored France's sense of national pride, though it was hard to measure how much difference his presence made to the country's performance. It was *le gouvernement par la parole*, government by public pronouncement. De Gaulle used his press conferences at the Élysée Palace to make policy; Mrs Thatcher used *The Jimmy Young Show*.

Mrs Thatcher was like the new wife coming into the stately home. She sent some of the aristocratic relatives packing because they wouldn't do things her way. She turned the house upside down and redecorated it at considerable expense, throwing many priceless relics into the rubbish. Rather than opening it to the public, she held occasional open days when everything looked grand, but the dust had been swept under the carpet. Essential repairs were skimped because her grocery-store childhood made her mean with the housekeeping money. Yet she saw nothing wrong with borrowing huge sums from the bank manager to pay the entertainment bills. When the oil boiler began to malfunction no one bothered at first, but after some time the house began to feel chilly. The family didn't know how to go about it, but they were profoundly relieved when she was persuaded to move into one of the lodges – even though she chose one with a view of the house rather than her original choice well beyond the ha-ha.

In assessing Mrs Thatcher's influence on the economy we need some idea of what would have happened in her absence. Comparisons with other industrial countries, or with previous British Governments, can give only a rough indication. In saying 'There Is No Alternative' Mrs Thatcher was fighting for her own survival. Had the Conservative Party or the country believed that there was an alternative to her policies in 1979–83, they would surely have taken it and ditched her. Yet it is obvious that no other Prime Minister, of either party, would have acted exactly as she did. The question is whether the alternatives would have produced better or worse results.

By the end of Mrs Thatcher's reign it looked as if the UK had learned nothing from its own recent economic history and seemed condemned to repeat it. The 1990s show opened just as the 1980s show had opened: the gloomy recession act took up most of the time before the first interval; seat prices had doubled; and everyone was 25 per cent better off than they had been ten years before but fearful of finding they had no job when they came out. The disappointment was all the greater because expectations had been pitched so much higher. It was like a game of chess in which one player sacrifices the queen to gain a commanding positional advantage, then fails to win the endgame because of an elementary howler.

The Government was too ambitious and did not understand the extent to which its different policy objectives cut across each other. All Governments face trade-offs between different objectives; Mrs Thatcher's was different in often refusing to recognize that fact. She wanted both monetary control and financial market freedom and blamed the banks when she found she could not have both. Some of the Government's policy objectives were achieved for some of the time, but they could not all be carried out simultaneously. Some of the objectives were controversial, and attempts to carry them out interfered with more widely accepted objectives. For example, some of the tax cuts could be afforded only by starving some public services of funds. The reduction of inflation began as the Government's top priority but was later subordinated to other objectives, such as employment, tax cuts, financial deregulation, profit maximization and economic growth. *Newsweek* asked Mrs Thatcher in October 1990 what she thought of the charge by a former Labour minister that she had failed because inflation was once again in double figures. She replied:

Absolute poppycock. Is he not having any regard for the total industrial and commercial transformation that has taken place in this country, the colossal increase of production, the colossal increase in efficiency in our manufacturing industries, the freeing up of the whole financial services and London being the freest sector? Is he not considering the far fewer strikes we have now because we got trade-union law right? Is he not considering the extra investment we are now getting in industry because people know that under the new framework there is a prospect, there is a future, that people are no longer afraid of the word 'profit'? Is he suggesting that his way of running Britain would have got this strength of the economy, would have rebuilt Britain's reputation? Poppycock. Codswallop. Bunkum and balderdash. They could not have done it. They may wish they could have done it. It took someone with real spine to do it.

Successes and failures

Let us take each main policy objective in turn and examine how far it was achieved and to what extent it interfered with, and was interfered with by, others.

1 Economic growth

The priority that the Government gave to the reduction of inflation caused an unnecessary loss of economic growth. The new radical policies designed to stem relative decline by means of higher growth resulted at first not just in relative but in absolute decline. The 1980–81 recession was deeper than expected; the 1987–9 boom was stronger than forecast; and another recession began just before Mrs Thatcher left office. The recession of 1980–81 caused cumulative deviations of output below the long-term rate of growth amounting to nearly six months' GDP. The Government began with excessive pessimism over growth prospects but ended with excessive optimism.

The decline in the UK's economic growth relative to that of the EC was halted, but the growth rate was the same in the 1980s as in the 1970s, though not as good as in the 1960s. It was achieved by slower growth in inputs of both labour and capital and faster growth in the productivity of both factors. The share of non-oil profits in the national income fell sharply in 1980–81 before recovering. The share of non-energy labour incomes rose in 1980–81 before returning to its previous level. There was a big rise in self-employment incomes, which the Government intended, and in net bank interest.

The Government welcomed faster growth in services than in manufacturing, but its supply-side policies of tax-cutting and deregulation were not sufficient to stimulate the British economy to supply as much as they stimulated it to demand. It achieved its aim of faster growth in the private than in the public sector and faster growth of private investment than of private consumption. While investment rose, saving fell as a proportion of GDP. Demand increased by a third but output by only a quarter. The result was a huge balance-of-payments deficit. Imports rose nearly twice as fast as exports. The cost of the seven good years of the Thatcher recovery was not only the stop–go of the early 1980s that preceded it but also the stop–go of the early 1990s that followed it.

2 Money and inflation

In 1979 the Government mistakenly renounced the options of joining the EMS ERM, and making the Bank of England independent. It did not adopt monetary base control and failed to check the rise in money supply by means of interest rates. The increase in interest rates caused a rise in the exchange rate and a deep recession, with rising unemployment. The Government also failed at first to control public borrowing but then succeeded by means of an unusual increase in taxation in its 1981 Budget. It was all this together with the fall in commodity prices, rather than monetary control, that reduced inflation more sharply in the UK than elsewhere during the Government's first term.

During its second term the Government again missed a

good opportunity to join the ERM in 1985 and then failed to make use of the fall in oil prices to achieve its aim of zero inflation, allowing the pound to be devalued and profit margins to rise. In its third term it eventually achieved a Budget surplus in spite of cuts in tax rates. This was still not sufficient to reduce the supply of money and credit because private-sector borrowing expanded faster than public-sector borrowing contracted. The Government threw away its achievements by allowing domestic demand to expand too quickly, letting inflation rise again to the double-figure level it had inherited.

The use of high interest rates rather than fiscal policy to control inflation slowed the growth of the economy and bore heavily on home-owners in spite of massive mortgage subsidies. The Government's performance over the 1980s as a whole was better than that of the previous decade but only average by the standards of other industrial countries. The battle against inflation was a Pyrrhic victory, at an unacceptable cost in unemployment, followed by a self-inflicted defeat that could have been avoided by a more cautious management of demand.

3 Public expenditure

Mrs Thatcher, Sir Keith Joseph and some of their advisers saw the public sector as an enemy country, to be conquered, deprived of much of its territory and put under the yoke of the Treasury. They wanted to reduce public expenditure so as to control the money supply while cutting taxes and to provide the private sector with more room to grow. They tried to give priority to some public services, such as social security, health and education. The cuts therefore fell heavily on housing, trade and industry and transport, as well as on most capital expenditure. In its early years the Government failed in its aim of cutting real public expenditure, which increased because of the recession and the Clegg pay awards. It then set out to freeze real spending but abandoned this aim too in favour of public expenditure falling as a percentage of GDP – in other words, rising but at a slower rate than GDP. This aim was achieved in the second half of the 1980s, and in some years public expenditure even fell in real terms. It was a mistaken objective because it could not be achieved when unemployment was rising except by cutbacks even in priority public services.

The system of cash planning acted as a curb on public expenditure. The Treasury's refusal to take relative price effects into account was partly successful in holding back inflation in public spending, especially pay. It led to an exaggeration of 'real-terms' spending, as measured by the general GDP deflator, because this left out higher relative inflation in parts of the public sector where pay is a large proportion of costs. The Government claimed to have spent 14 per cent more on education and 32 per cent more on health in real terms during the 1980s, but this was a new kind of 'funny money'. The increases in input volumes were zero and 12 per cent. The volume of outputs may have been higher than that of inputs in so far as there were increases in efficiency, but these are hard to measure. The curbs on public expenditure made the UK a country of private affluence and public squalor.

4 Taxation

Taxes were switched from direct to indirect, but this made the control of money and inflation more difficult, particularly with the rise in VAT in 1979. The main benefits from income-tax cuts and independent taxation went to higher-income households. Smaller income-tax cuts for the rest of the population were offset partly by the rise in National Insurance Contributions, which were reduced only in 1989. In theory, the income-tax changes should have had incentive effects, particularly for high earners, but these are difficult to establish and were in any case counteracted by high unemployment until the second half of the 1980s. Tax incentives to save influenced the channels rather than the total flow of savings, which became inadequate to finance investment.

The reform of corporate taxation shifted the balance

against manufacturing and in favour of services investment. It improved incentives for short-term profits and capital expenditure and increased tax revenue. It failed to allow for inflation and so became a burden on business when inflation rose again. The poll tax had worse disadvantages than the rates that it replaced and departed from the intentions of its inventors. It resulted in an increase in local taxation and expenditure instead of keeping them down and left the UK without a tax on property. It was unnecessarily allowed to increase the published rate of inflation, and it was a reverse switch from indirect to direct taxation.

The UK's total tax burden rose sharply in the early 1980s; although it then fell, it was higher at the end of the decade than when Mrs Thatcher took office. It was similar to Germany's and lower than France's. Too many tax privileges for special-interest groups still distort the free market. Tax reform was piecemeal and incoherent rather than being based on a long-term blueprint.

5 Privatization

The right to buy for council tenants, together with the liberalization of mortgages and the maintenance of tax relief on them, increased owner-occupation to two-thirds of all households, in line with the Government's ideal of a property-owning democracy. However, it combined with cutbacks in public-sector housebuilding and delays in rent decontrol to reduce public and private rental accommodation, which aggravated homelessness.

The Government succeeded in privatizing about half the public corporations, thus dealing with the problem of managing the nationalized industries, but could have moved more decisively on coal, the railways and the Post Office. Its need to raise funds by means of public-asset sales inhibited it from breaking up the monopolies so as to increase competition for British Telecom and British Gas. It had to go against its policy of business deregulation by setting up new regulatory bodies. The break-up of the electricity industry was limited by the (in the event) unsuccessful attempt to privatize nuclear power. Any improvement in the performance of privatized corporations cannot be attributed to privatization because a similar improvement took place in the performance of public corporations and of British industry in general. Economic freedom was increased by privatization, particularly that of industrial companies in competitive markets.

Privatization and demutualization trebled the number of shareholders to 9 million, or 21 per cent of the over-16 population, but most of the new holdings were small, and many were short-lived. The Government subsidized share ownership by means of large discounts and high banking fees, but profits were small and many applicants were disappointed. Employee shareholding, encouraged by tax incentives, was on a small scale but made a contribution to business performance.

6 Industry and the balance of payments

The Government cut subsidies to industry by a quarter after an initial rise. The large sums that it spent were none the less rendered less effective by its lack of belief in industrial policy. The frequent ministerial changes at the Department of Trade and Industry also made for short-termism in an area requiring long-term continuity. Mergers and takeovers were left mostly to the market, but in the second half of the 1980s the Government could not prevent an excessive boom in them, which overstrained the financial system with few corresponding economic advantages. The Government failed to impose a stricter regime to ensure price competition, publishing weak legislation against restrictive pricing agreements between firms only in 1989 and then not implementing it. It thus allowed inflation to rise faster and ignored its own free-market principles. Deregulation played an important part in foreign exchange and financial services but had to be controlled by a costly new structure of regulation.

Business income from self-employment, financial services and construction rose rapidly in real terms, but manufacturing profits only just recovered at the end of the decade to where they had been at the beginning before the recession, and oil profits fell heavily after 1985. Industrial management improved, but financial control was shaky, with an excessive increase in borrowing in the late 1980s based on an over-optimistic view of the future encouraged by the Government.

The sharp deterioration of the balance of payments from 1987 onwards showed that industry was still deficient on the supply side, particularly in intermediate goods. The visible trade balance was less worrying than the invisibles balance, whose rising surplus disappeared at the end of the 1980s. The Government's policy of non-intervention in industry and its balance-of-payments problems were inconsistent with its attempts to control the rate of interest and the growth of money and credit.

7 *The labour market and the unions*

Trade-union reform was worth undertaking to limit the irresponsible use of power by union leaders and to increase the responsible exercise of democracy by their members. It was never likely that it would replace incomes policy as a way of keeping nominal wage increases down. The reforms, together with higher unemployment and the failure of some big strikes, helped employers to raise the productivity of labour by reducing restrictive practices. The Government won some major public-sector strikes in the first half of the 1980s, and there were fewer strikes in the second half. Higher productivity in manufacturing was achieved at the cost of job losses and excessive wage rises. Pay awards were greater for those on higher than for those on lower incomes, increasing the degree of inequality and restoring differentials, but in many cases these turned out not to be related to performance. Pay bargaining became more flexible upwards rather than downwards. The Government could do little to counteract the rigidity of both real and nominal wages, which made it difficult to reduce inflation.

The rise in unemployment was not intended. It helped to reduce pay inflation but caused an overshoot in public expenditure. Unemployment rose faster in the UK than elsewhere, partly because of the severity of the UK's monetary policy, partly because of the increase in the population of working age. The Government's special job-creation measures and its manipulation of the statistics reduced the rise in unemployment, but their training element was too little and too late to bring about the improvement in the supply of skills needed in the recovery. The increase in employment, which began well before unemployment began to fall, was mainly in self-employment, in part-time jobs for women, in the service industries and in the southern regions. There was a big net loss of jobs for men in the northern regions and in manufacturing. Unemployment fell rapidly in the boom of the late 1980s, but the Government had to tighten policy, so that it began to rise again in 1990.

The Government's record was thus, like the curate's egg, good only in parts. It was nothing like the brilliant success that Mrs Thatcher and her entourage persuaded many voters she had achieved. There were seven clearly successful policy outcomes: labour productivity, business profitability, economic independence for the individual, trade-union reform, home ownership, public debt management and tax cuts. There were seven clearly unsuccessful ones: savings, monopoly control, price competition, pay restraint, unemployment, homes for rent and monetary targets. There were seven mixed outcomes, with elements of good and bad: economic growth, capital investment, inflation, public expenditure, privatization, business regulation and EC matters.

Mrs Thatcher is likely to go down in history more for her political and military than for her economic and social record. She won one hot war, one cold war and three elections. She raised the morale of the Conservative Party and left a capable team of ministers to carry out a big agenda of unfinished business. She forced the Labour Party to abandon doctrinaire socialism for a moderate policy similar to that of the once heroic, now defunct, Social Democratic Party. As she told *Newsweek*: 'We were able to roll back the frontiers of socialism.' Yet, as Neil Kinnock might have retorted, 'Socialism is dead. Long live the Labour Party.' If the Conservatives remain in power, they will thank Mrs Thatcher both for her political inheritance and for departing when she did. If the Labour Party takes power, it too will have her to thank for dragging it back to the centre ground.

Appendix: Tables

Table 1. Economic growth trends, 1950–89

Percentage changes in GDP (factor cost, average estimate, 1985 prices)

1950	3.6	1960	5.6	1970	2.0	1980	−2.0
1951	1.9	1961	2.7	1971	1.7	1981	−1.2
1952	0.8	1962	1.4	1972	2.8	1982	1.7
1953	3.9	1963	4.0	1973	7.4	1983	3.8
1954	4.2	1964	5.6	1974	−1.5	1984	1.8
1955	3.6	1965	2.9	1975	−0.8	1985	3.8
1956	1.4	1966	1.9	1976	2.6	1986	3.6
1957	1.7	1967	2.2	1977	2.6	1987	4.4
1958	−0.2	1968	4.4	1978	2.9	1988	4.7
1959	4.0	1969	2.5	1979	2.8	1989	2.1

Compound mean annual rates of increase and standard deviations

By decades		By 4–6 year cycles (peak to peak)		By political party	
1950–59	2.5	1951–54	2.7	Con	
SD	1.5			1952–64	3.0
SD/mean	0.59	1955–60	2.7		
1960–69	3.3	1961–64	3.4	Lab	
SD	1.4			1965–70	2.7
SD/mean	0.43	1965–68	2.9		
1970–79	2.2	1969–73	3.3	Con	
SD	2.3			1971–74	2.6
SD/mean	1.03	1974–79	1.4		
1980–89	2.2	1980–83	0.6	Lab	
SD	2.2			1975–79	2.0
SD/mean	0.99	1984–88	3.7		
1950–89	2.6			Con	
SD	1.8			1980–89	2.2
SD/mean	0.69				

Source: Blue Book, 1990, tables 1.1, 16.9.

Table 2. The UK and the Big Five: growth comparisons in the 1980s

Annual percentage changes in real GDP

	UK	France	Germany	Italy	Japan	USA	EEC	OECD
1980	−2.0	1.6	1.5	4.2	4.3	−0.2	1.5	1.5
1981	−1.2	1.2	0.0	1.0	3.7	1.9	0.1	1.7
1982	1.7	2.5	−1.0	0.3	3.1	−2.5	0.8	−0.1
1983	3.8	0.7	1.9	1.1	3.2	3.6	1.6	2.7
1984	1.8	1.3	3.3	3.0	5.1	6.8	2.5	4.8
1985	3.8	1.9	1.9	2.6	4.8	3.4	2.4	3.4
1986	3.6	2.3	2.3	2.5	2.6	2.7	2.6	2.7
1987	4.4	2.4	1.7	3.0	4.6	3.7	2.8	3.5
1988	4.7	3.8	3.6	4.2	5.7	4.4	3.9	4.4
1989	2.1	3.7	4.0	3.2	4.9	3.0	3.5	3.6
Mean	2.2	2.1	2.0	2.5	4.2	2.6	2.2	2.8
SD	2.2	1.0	1.5	1.3	1.0	2.4	1.1	1.4
SD/mean	0.99	0.45	0.74	0.50	0.23	0.93	0.51	0.49

GDP at purchasing-power parities 1989

	UK	France	Germany	Italy
Total ($bn)	818.4	817.4	941.7	801.9
Per head ($)	14,308	14,570	15,213	13,922
UK = 100	100	102	106	97

Sources: Blue Book, 1990, table 16.9; OECD, *Economic Outlook*, June 1990, table R.1. GDP at PPP, Hansard, 26 July 1990, col. 235.

Table 3. Labour and capital contributions to economic growth (annual percentage changes)

	Employees in employment		Gross capital stock		Total factor inputs		GDP growth
	Numbers	Productivity	Volume	Productivity	Volume	Productivity	
Whole economy							
1980	−0.8	−1.3	2.5	−4.5	0.4	−2.4	−2.0
1981	−4.8	3.8	1.9	−3.0	−2.4	1.4	−1.2
1982	−2.2	4.0	1.9	−0.2	−0.7	2.5	1.7
1983	−1.6	5.5	2.0	1.7	−0.4	4.2	3.8
1984	0.8	1.0	2.2	−0.4	1.3	0.5	1.8
1985	0.9	2.9	2.2	1.5	1.4	2.4	3.8
1986	−0.2	3.8	2.1	1.5	0.6	3.0	3.6
1987	0.9	3.5	2.4	2.0	1.4	2.9	4.4
1988	3.2	1.5	2.9	1.8	3.1	1.6	4.7
1989	2.2	−0.1	3.0	−0.9	2.4	−0.4	2.1
Mean							
1970–79	0.2	2.0	3.3	−1.1	1.3	0.9	2.2
1980–89	−0.2	2.5	2.2	0.1	0.6	1.6	2.2
Manufacturing							Manufactures growth
1980	−4.4	−4.5	1.5	−10.1	−2.3	−6.5	−8.7
1981	−10.3	4.8	0.5	−6.4	−6.5	0.9	−6.0
1982	−5.8	6.4	0.4	−0.1	−3.6	4.1	0.2
1983	−5.8	9.1	0.3	2.6	−3.7	6.8	2.9
1984	−2.1	6.1	0.6	3.2	−1.2	5.1	3.8
1985	−0.9	3.6	0.8	1.8	−0.3	3.0	2.7
1986	−2.5	3.8	0.7	0.5	−1.4	2.7	1.2
1987	−1.5	6.8	0.7	4.5	−0.7	6.0	5.2
1988	1.4	5.9	1.0	6.2	1.2	6.0	7.3
1989	0.2	4.0	1.2	3.1	0.6	3.7	4.3
Mean							
1973–79	−1.0	1.5	1.6	−1.1	−0.1	0.6	0.5
1980–89	−3.2	4.5	0.8	0.4	−1.8	3.2	1.2
Non-manufacturing							
Mean							
1980–89	1.0	1.6	2.6	0.0	1.6	1.0	2.6

Note: Total factors are a weighted average of labour (65%) and capital (35%). Figures for employees in manufacturing before 1972 are unavailable.
Source: Blue Book, 1990, tables 2.4, 14.8, 16.3, 17.1.

Table 4. GDP growth by industry (value added, percentages)

	Annual output change at 1985 prices			Share of GDP at current prices		
	1980–84	1985–89	1980–89	1979	1984	1989
North Sea oil and gas	8.3	−5.5	1.2	3.3	7.0	1.7
Other energy, water	−3.8	5.9	0.9	4.8	3.6	3.5
Agriculture	7.0	−1.3	2.7	2.1	2.2	1.5
Manufacturing	−1.7	4.1	1.2	28.4	23.8	22.2
Construction	0.9	4.8	2.8	6.2	6.1	6.9
Financial and business:	5.8	8.9	7.3	11.6	14.0	19.8
adjustment for net interest				−3.8	−4.6	−5.8
Other private services	1.2	4.2	2.7	32.5	31.9	33.6
Education and health	1.0	1.7	1.4	8.2	8.8	9.7
Administration and defence	−0.2	0.4	0.1	6.7	7.2	6.8
Total services	1.7	4.2	2.9	55.2	57.3	64.1
Total ex-North Sea	0.5	4.3	2.4	96.7	93.0	98.3
Total	0.8	3.8	2.3	100.0	100.0	100.0

Source: Blue Book, 1990, tables 2.4, 16.4.

Table 5. GDP by type of income (percentage shares in total domestic income at factor cost)

	Self-employment income	Rent, etc.	Non-energy economy		Energy sector	
			Gross trading profit	Employment income	Gross trading profit	Employment income
1979	8.8	7.5	14.1	61.4	5.4	2.8
1980	8.7	7.9	10.2	63.5	6.5	3.2
1981	8.9	8.3	8.4	63.6	7.6	3.2
1982	9.1	8.3	9.2	62.5	7.8	3.1
1983	9.3	8.0	10.3	61.2	8.4	2.8
1984	9.7	7.9	10.3	61.5	8.5	2.2
1985	9.6	7.9	11.3	60.8	7.9	2.5
1986	10.4	8.2	12.2	62.0	4.6	2.5
1987	10.8	7.9	13.4	61.1	4.5	2.2
1988	11.2	7.9	14.6	60.9	3.5	2.0
1989	11.9	8.0	13.1	61.9	3.2	2.0
Mean 1979–89	9.9	8.0	11.6	61.9	6.2	2.6

Note: Gross trading profits include those of industrial, commercial and financial companies, and gross trading surpluses of public corporations and general government enterprises. They are given before deducting stock appreciation. Rent, etc. includes about 1 per cent non-trading capital consumption.
Source: Blue Book, 1990, tables 2.1, 16.3.

Table 6. GDP growth by type of expenditure (annual percentage increases at constant 1985 prices)

	Consumers' expenditure	General government final consumption	Gross domestic fixed capital formation	Stocks and work in progress (change as % of GDP)	Domestic demand	Exports of goods and services	Total final expenditure	Imports of goods and services	Gross domestic product	Domestic demand minus GDP	Real national disposable income
1980	0.1	1.6	-5.4	-2.1	-2.8	0.0	-2.2	-3.4	-2.0	-0.8	-1.5
1981	0.1	0.3	-9.6	0.0	-1.6	-0.7	-1.4	-2.8	-1.2	-0.4	-0.3
1982	1.0	0.8	5.4	0.6	2.4	0.8	2.0	4.9	1.7	0.7	1.7
1983	4.6	2.0	5.0	0.8	5.0	2.0	4.4	6.5	3.8	1.1	4.4
1984	1.6	0.9	8.5	-0.1	2.4	6.6	3.4	9.9	1.8	0.6	2.2
1985	3.5	0.0	4.0	0.1	2.8	5.9	3.5	2.6	3.8	1.0	2.9
1986	6.3	1.9	1.9	0.0	4.6	4.6	4.6	6.9	3.6	1.0	3.7
1987	5.3	1.3	9.5	0.1	5.3	5.7	5.4	7.9	4.4	0.9	4.1
1988	7.2	0.5	14.8	0.7	7.9	0.2	6.2	12.8	4.7	3.0	5.4
1989	3.9	0.8	4.8	-0.4	3.1	4.3	3.4	7.0	2.1	1.0	2.5
Mean	3.3	1.0	3.7	0.0	2.9	2.9	2.9	5.1	2.3	0.6	2.5
SD	2.4	0.6	6.7	0.8	3.0	2.6	2.6	4.9	2.2	1.0	2.0
SD/mean	0.7	0.6	1.8	-26.0	1.0	0.9	0.9	1.0	1.0	1.6	0.8
1989/1979	38.9	10.5	43.4		32.7	33.3	32.9	64.5	24.9		27.9
Contribution to GDP growth (mean times 1979 share)											
	2.0	0.2	0.6	0.0	2.8	0.8	3.6	-1.3	2.3		
Percentage shares in GDP at current prices											
1979	60.4	19.6	18.6	1.1	99.7	27.7	127.4	-27.4	100.0	0.3	
1989	64.1	19.4	19.6	0.6	103.7	24.1	127.8	-27.8	100.0	-3.7	
Change	3.7	-0.2	1.0	-0.5	4.0	-3.6	0.4	0.4	0.0	-4.0	

Saving by sector as percentage of GDP

	Personal	Public	ICCs	FCIs	Total
1979	8.3	1.4	8.0	2.3	20.0
1989	4.5	3.7	4.7	3.6	16.5
Change	-3.8	2.3	-3.3	1.3	-3.5

Note: ICCs = industrial and commercial companies. FCIs = financial companies and institutions. Stock appreciation is deducted from saving and from GDP.
Source: Blue Book, 1990, tables 1.6, 3.5, 16.6.

Table 7. Money GDP, output and prices

Years projected	Year of publication in FSBR (March), percentage increases projected						Outcome	Difference from latest projection
	1985	1986	1987	1988	1989	1990		
Money GDP								
1985–86	8½						9.3	0.7
1986–87	6½	6¾					7.1	0.3
1987–88	5¾	6½	7½				10.8	3.1
1988–89	5	6	6½	7½			10.8	3.1
1989–90		5½	6	6½	7¾		8.6	0.8
1990–91			5½	6	6	5¾	46.6	8.0
1991–92				5½	6	6¾		
1992–93					5½	6¼		
1993–94						5¾		
GDP deflator								
1985–86	5						5.4	0.4
1986–87	4½	3¾					3.3	−0.4
1987–88	3½	3¾	4½				5.3	0.8
1988–89	3	3½	4	4½			7.3	2.7
1989–90		3	3½	4	5½		7.4[2]	1.6
1990–91			3	3½	4	4½[2]	28.3	5.9[1]
1991–92				3	3	4¾		
1992–93					2½	3½		
1993–94						3		
Real GDP								
1985–86	3½						3.7	0.2
1986–87	2	3					3.7	0.7
1987–88	2	2½	3				5.2	2.2
1988–89	2	2½	2½	3			3.3	0.3
1989–90		2½	2½	2½	2¼		1.5	−0.7
1990–91			2½	2½	2	1	17.4	4.1[1]
1991–92				2½	2¾	2		
1992–93					2¾	2¾		
1993–94						2¾		

Notes: [1] The sum of absolute differences. [2] Adjusted for abolition of domestic rates, both these figures would have been 6½ per cent.
Source: Financial Statement and Budget Report; Blue Book, 1990.

Table 8. Fiscal and monetary stance of budgets (+ = tighter, − = looser)

	Budget measured against indexed base		Changes in PSBR from:		Bank base rates after Budget	
	(£bn)	(% of GDP)	Previous year (% of GDP)	Previous figure for same year (% of GDP)	Change (%)	Level (%)
1979	−1.1	−½	+1	n.a.	+2	14
1980	+1.0	+½	+1	−¼	0	17
1981	+4.3	+1¾	+1¾	−1¼	−2	12
1982	−1.5	−½	+¾	−¼	−½	13
1983	−1.7	−½	0	0	−½	10½
1984	0	0	+1	+¼	−½	8¾–9
1985	−0.7	−¼	+1¼	0	−½	13
1986	−1.0	−¼	+¼	+¼	−1	11½
1987	−2.9	−¾	0	+¾	−½	10½
1988	−4.3	−1	0	+1¾	−½	8½
1989	−1.9	−¼	−¼	+2¾	0	13
1990	+0.4	0	0	−½	0	15

Source: Financial Statement and Budget Report, various years.

Table 9. The results of monetary targetry (successful outcomes are underlined)

Year targeted	\multicolumn{8}{c}{Year of publication of FSBR (March), percentage increases}	Outcome		Overshoot over top end of range	
	1979	1980	1981	1982	1983	1984	1985	1986				
£M3[1]												
1978–79	8–12								16.2		5.2	
1979–80	7–11								18.4		7.4	
1980–81		7–11							12.8		2.8	
1981–82		6–10	6–10						<u>11.1</u>		0.0	
1982–83		5–9	5–9	8–12					<u>9.5</u>		0.0	
1983–84		4–8	4–8	7–11	7–11				11.9		1.9	
1984–85				6–10	6–10	6–10			16.3		7.3	
1985–86					5–9	5–9	5–9		18.7		<u>3.7</u>	
1986–87						4–8	4–8				28.3	
1987–88						3–7	3–7				=31.1%	
1988–89						2–6	2–6	11–15				

M1 and PSL2[2]									M1	PSL2	M1	PSL2
1982–83				8–12					12.3	<u>11.5</u>	0.3	0.0
1983–84				7–11	7–11				14.0	12.4	<u>3.0</u>	<u>1.4</u>
1984–85				6–10	6–10						3.3	1.4
1985–86					5–9						=14.3%	=6.1%

M0	1984	1985	1986	1987	1988	1989	1990	
1984-85	4-8							5.4
1985-86	3-7	3-7						4.1
1986-87	2-6	2-6	2-6					3.5
1987-88	1-5	1-5	2-6	2-6				6.4
1988-89	0-4	0-4	1-5	1-5	1-5			6.8
1989-90			1-5	1-5	1-5	1-5		5.0
1990-91				0-4	0-4	0-4	1-5	
1991-92					0-4	0-4	0-4	
1992-93						-1-3	0-4	
1993-94							-1-3	

	0.0
	0.0
	0.0
	0.4
	1.8
	0.0
	2.2
	= 5.2%

Notes: [1] Renamed M3 in May 1987; no longer published from June 1989. [2] Renamed M5 in May 1987. From 1982 onwards only the next year's figure was a target; those for subsequent years became 'illustrative ranges'.
Sources: *Financial Statement and Budget Report*; *Financial Statistics*, Bank of England.

Table 10. The public-sector borrowing requirement, forecasts and outcomes (successful outcomes are underlined)

Years projected PSBR	Year of publication in FSBR (March), percentage of GDP												Outcome[1]	Overshoot
	1979	1980	1981	1982	1983	1984	1985	1986	1987	1988	1989	1990		
1978–79	$5\frac{1}{2}$													
1979–80	$4\frac{1}{2}$	$4\frac{3}{4}$											5.0	0.5
1980–81		$3\frac{3}{4}$	6										5.7	2.0
1981–82		3	$4\frac{1}{4}$	$4\frac{1}{4}$									$\underline{3.5}$	
1982–83		$2\frac{1}{4}$	$3\frac{1}{4}$	$3\frac{1}{2}$	$2\frac{3}{4}$								$\underline{3.3}$	
1983–84		$1\frac{1}{2}$	2	$2\frac{3}{4}$	$2\frac{3}{4}$	$3\frac{1}{4}$							3.2	0.4
1984–85				2	$2\frac{1}{2}$	$2\frac{1}{4}$	$3\frac{1}{4}$						3.1	0.8
1985–86					2	2	2	2					$\underline{1.6}$	
1986–87						2	2	$1\frac{3}{4}$	1				$\underline{0.9}$	
1987–88						$1\frac{3}{4}$	$1\frac{3}{4}$	$1\frac{3}{4}$	1	$-\frac{3}{4}$			$\underline{-\frac{3}{4}}$	
1988–89						$1\frac{3}{4}$	$1\frac{3}{4}$	$1\frac{1}{2}$	1	$-\frac{3}{4}$	-3		$\underline{-3}$	
1989–90								$1\frac{1}{2}$	1	0	$-2\frac{3}{4}$	$-1\frac{1}{4}$	$-1\frac{1}{4}$	$\underline{1.0}$
1990–91									1	0	$-1\frac{3}{4}$	$-1\frac{1}{4}$		$\underline{4.7}$
1991–92										0	-1	$-\frac{1}{2}$		
1992–93											$-\frac{1}{2}$	0		
1993–94												0		

Notes: [1] Final outcomes, which may differ from provisional outcomes at Budget time, given for financial years just ending at head of columns. A negative PSBR is a positive public-sector debt repayment (PSDR) and has in recent years been published in this form. We treat it as a negative PSBR for consistency with earlier years.
Source: Financial Statement and Budget Report.

Table 11. Money GDP: the split between prices and output

	Money GDP (% change)	Volume GDP (% change)	GDP deflator (% change)	Changes as percent of money GDP	
				Volume	Deflator
1970	9.8	2.3	7.4	24	76
1971	11.7	1.9	9.7	16	84
1972	11.7	3.5	7.9	31	69
1973	14.9	7.3	7.1	51	49
1974	13.0	−1.8	15.0	−13	113
1975	26.4	−0.7	27.3	−3	103
1976	18.5	2.8	15.3	15	85
1977	16.5	2.4	13.8	15	85
1978	15.4	3.6	11.4	24	76
1979	17.8	2.9	14.5	17	83
1980	16.9	−2.2	19.5	−12	112
1981	10.0	−1.3	11.5	−13	113
1982	9.4	1.8	7.4	19	81
1983	9.2	3.6	5.4	40	60
1984	6.8	2.2	4.5	33	67
1985	9.5	3.5	5.8	38	62
1986	7.6	3.9	3.6	52	48
1987	9.9	4.6	5.0	48	52
1988	11.7	4.7	6.7	41	59
1989	9.2	2.1	6.9	23	77
Means					
1970–79	15.6	2.4	12.9	18	82
1980–89	10.0	2.3	7.6	27	73
1970–89	12.8	2.4	10.3	22	78

Source: Blue Book, 1990, table 1.7.

Table 12. Taxation, public expenditure and borrowing (percentages of GDP at market prices, rounded to nearest 0.25)

	Tax revenue				Other revenue[2]		Total revenue		Public expenditure exc. privatization		PSBR		Privati- zation proceeds	PSBR + privatization proceeds	
	Non-North Sea		Total												
	Level[1]	Change	Level	Change	Level	Change	Level	Change	Level	Change	Level	Change	Level	Level	Change
1979-80	35.00		35.00		3.50		38.50		43.50		5.00		0.25	5.25	
1980-81	36.00	1.00	36.75	1.75	3.25	-0.25	40.00	1.50	45.75	2.25	5.75	-0.75	0.00	5.75	-0.50
1981-82	38.50	2.50	39.50	2.75	3.50	0.25	43.00	3.00	46.50	0.75	3.50	2.25	0.25	3.75	2.00
1982-83	38.00	-0.50	39.00	-0.50	4.50	1.00	43.50	0.50	46.75	0.25	3.25	0.25	0.25	3.50	0.25
1983-84	37.50	-0.50	38.50	-0.50	4.00	-0.50	42.50	-1.00	45.75	-1.00	3.25	0.00	0.25	3.50	0.00
1984-85	37.75	0.25	39.00	0.50	4.00	0.00	43.00	0.50	46.00	0.25	3.00	0.25	0.50	3.50	0.00
1985-86	37.00	-0.75	38.50	-0.50	4.50	0.50	43.00	0.00	44.50	-1.50	1.50	1.50	0.75	2.25	1.25
1986-87	37.50	0.50	38.00	-0.50	4.50	0.00	42.50	-0.50	43.50	-1.00	1.00	0.50	1.00	2.00	0.25
1987-88	37.75	0.25	38.00	0.00	4.00	-0.50	42.00	-0.50	41.25	-2.25	-0.75	1.75	1.00	0.25	1.75
1988-89	37.00	-0.75	37.25	-0.75	3.00	-1.00	40.25	-1.75	37.25	-4.00	-3.00	2.25	1.50	-1.50	1.75
1989-90	36.75	-0.25	36.75	-0.50	2.75	-0.25	39.50	-0.75	38.25	1.00	-1.25	-1.75	0.75	-0.50	-1.00
Mean	37.25	0.25	37.75	0.25	3.75	0.00	41.50	0.00	43.50	-0.50	2.00	0.75	0.50	2.50	0.50
Change '89-'79	1.75		1.75		-0.75		1.00		-5.25		-6.25		0.50	-5.75	

Notes: [1] Non-North Sea taxes as percentage of non-North Sea GDP. [2] Debt interest, national accounts adjustment and repayment of public-corporation borrowings.
Sources: Financial Statement and Budget Report 1990, table 2.5; The Government's Expenditure Plans 1990–91 to 1992–93, Cm 1021, table 21.2.1.

Table 13. Monetary indicators (annual average percentages)

	Bank base rates			Mortgage rates	Sterling effective exchange rate		Monetary aggregates		Monetary conditions
	Level nominal	Change nominal	Level real	Level	Level	Change	M0 Change	M4 Change	Change
1979	13.7			11.9	107.0		8.3	15.3	
1980	16.3	2.6	-1.9	14.9	117.6	9.9	4.4	17.6	5.1
1981	13.3	-3.0	2.9	14.1	119.0	1.2	1.0	17.8	-2.7
1982	11.9	-1.4	4.5	13.3	113.7	-4.5	5.9	13.4	-2.5
1983	9.8	-2.1	4.1	11.0	105.3	-7.4	5.5	12.8	-4.0
1984	9.7	-0.1	4.0	11.8	100.6	-4.4	4.6	13.6	-1.2
1985	12.2	2.5	6.4	13.5	100.0	-0.6	4.0	15.2	2.4
1986	10.9	-1.3	8.0	12.1	91.6	-8.4	4.5	15.3	-3.4
1987	9.7	-1.2	4.4	11.6	90.1	-1.6	4.5	15.3	-1.6
1988	10.1	0.4	3.2	11.1	95.5	6.0	6.9	17.3	1.9
1989	13.9	3.8	6.1	13.7	92.6	-3.0	5.7	18.1	3.0
1989/1979 multiple					0.87		1.6	4.3	
Mean	11.8		4.1	12.7	102.6	-1.3	5.1	15.6	
SD	2.1		2.5	1.3	10.3	5.4	1.8	1.9	
SD/mean	0.18		0.61	0.10	0.10	-4.2	0.36	0.12	

Note: Monetary conditions: change in base rate plus 0.25 change in exchange rate. Real base rates are nominal rates divided by GDP deflator.
Source: Financial Statistics, tables 11.1, 13.1, 13.15.

Table 14. Inflation indicators (annual percentage increases)

	Retail prices index		Retail prices index	RPI exc. mortgage	Consumer expendit. deflator	Sterling import prices	GDP deflator (output)	Unit profit costs	Unit labour costs	Average earnings Nominal	Average earnings Deflated by RPI
	6.5	1970	18.0	16.8	16.3	10.0	18.5	13.7	20.8	20.8	2.3
	9.2	1971	11.9	12.2	11.2	7.9	10.1	10.6	9.9	12.8	0.8
	7.5	1972	8.6	8.6	8.7	7.0	7.0	13.5	4.2	9.4	0.7
	9.1	1973	4.5	5.1	4.8	7.4	5.5	11.2	2.7	8.5	3.8
	15.9	1974	5.0	4.5	5.1	8.7	5.5	6.3	5.0	6.0	0.9
	24.1	1975	6.0	5.1	5.4	4.1	5.5	8.0	4.1	8.5	2.3
	16.6	1976	3.4	3.7	4.4	−4.4	2.7	−0.1	4.2	7.9	4.4
	15.9	1977	4.2	3.7	4.3	2.6	5.1	7.1	4.0	7.8	3.5
	8.2	1978	4.9	4.6	4.9	−1.0	6.7	7.6	6.1	8.7	3.6
	13.4	1979	7.8	5.9	5.9	6.5	7.4	4.2	9.4	9.3	1.4
1989/1979 multiple	3.30		2.03	1.95	1.97	1.60	2.02	2.18	1.95	2.57	1.15
Mean	12.5		7.3	6.9	7.0	4.8	7.3	8.1	6.9	9.9	2.4
SD	5.3		4.3	4.1	3.7	4.4	4.1	4.0	5.1	4.0	1.3
SD/mean	0.42		0.58	0.59	0.53	0.91	0.56	0.50	0.74	0.40	0.55

Sources: Blue Book, 1990, table 1.7; *Economic Trends*, table 24.

Table 15. The UK and the Big Five: inflation comparisons (annual percentage changes in consumers' expenditure deflators)

	UK	France	Germany	Italy	Japan	USA	EEC	OECD
1980	16.3	13.3	5.8	20.5	7.1	10.8	12.9	11.3
1981	11.2	13.0	6.2	18.1	4.4	9.2	11.6	9.5
1982	8.7	11.5	4.8	16.9	2.6	5.7	10.2	7.2
1983	4.8	9.7	3.2	15.2	1.9	4.1	8.1	5.5
1984	5.1	7.7	2.5	11.8	2.1	3.8	6.8	4.9
1985	5.4	5.8	2.1	9.0	2.2	3.3	5.5	4.3
1986	4.4	2.7	−0.5	5.8	0.6	2.4	3.2	2.7
1987	4.3	3.1	0.6	4.9	−0.2	4.7	3.1	3.4
1988	4.9	2.7	1.2	5.3	−0.1	3.9	3.3	3.3
1989	5.9	3.3	3.1	6.0	1.7	4.4	4.4	4.3
1989/1979 multiple	1.97	2.00	1.33	2.89	1.24	1.66	1.94	1.73
Mean	7.0	7.2	2.9	11.2	2.2	5.2	6.9	5.6
SD	3.7	4.1	2.1	5.6	2.1	2.5	3.5	2.7
SD/mean	0.53	0.57	0.73	0.50	0.94	0.49	0.50	0.48

Source: Blue Book, 1990, table 1.7; OECD, *Economic Outlook*, June 1990, table R.11.

Table 16. Public expenditure, 1970–89 (percentages)

	Planning totals change		GDP (exp.) deflator	Real GGE	Real GGE as percentage of GDP		Real GDP	GGE as percentage of GDP	Transfer payments
	Cash	Real	Change	Change	Level	Change	Change	Goods and services	
1970–71				3.3	40.6	0.4	2.3	22.4	18.2
1971–72				3.2	41.1	0.5	2.3	22.6	18.5
1972–73				5.1	40.8	−0.3	5.4	22.5	18.3
1973–74				7.9	42.7	1.9	3.5	23.9	18.8
1974–75	34.1	12.4	19.3	12.4	48.0	5.3	−0.1	25.6	22.4
1975–76	24.2	−1.2	25.7	−0.2	48.5	0.4	−1.1	26.5	22.0
1976–77	11.5	−1.8	13.5	−2.3	46.0	−2.5	2.9	25.4	20.6
1977–78	4.4	−8.3	13.9	−5.0	42.6	−3.3	2.3	23.3	19.3
1978–79	15.7	4.5	10.7	5.1	43.3	0.6	3.7	22.5	20.8
1979–80	18.1	1.2	16.7	3.2	43.4	0.1	2.8	22.3	21.0
1980–81	19.5	0.8	18.5	1.8	45.9	2.5	−3.8	23.9	22.0
1981–82	12.2	2.3	9.7	1.3	46.5	0.6	0.0	23.5	23.0
1982–83	9.2	1.9	7.2	2.5	46.7	0.2	2.1	23.7	23.1
1983–84	6.0	1.3	4.6	1.7	45.8	−0.9	3.8	23.6	22.2
1984–85	8.0	2.8	5.0	2.7	46.1	0.3	1.9	23.7	22.4
1985–86	2.8	−2.4	5.4	0.0	44.4	−1.7	3.7	22.8	21.6
1986–87	4.2	0.9	3.3	1.6	43.5	−0.9	3.7	22.5	21.1
1987–88	4.7	−0.6	5.3	−0.1	41.4	−2.2	5.2	21.9	19.5
1988–89	2.6	−4.4	7.3	−2.5	39.0	−2.3	3.3	20.8	18.2
1989–90	12.6	5.2	7.0	0.9	38.8	−0.2	1.5		

Mean							
1970–79	18.0	1.1	16.6	3.3	43.7	0.3	2.4	23.7	20.0
1980–89	8.2	0.8	7.3	1.0	43.8	−0.5	2.1	22.9	21.5

Notes: Planning totals are on the old pre-1990 basis. Planning totals and GGE are deflated by the GDP deflator to give real-terms changes. GGE is equal to planning totals plus debt interest and national accounts and public corporation adjustments. Changes in GGE minus changes in GDP times previous year's GGE/GDP ratio equal differences in current year ratio.

Source: Derived from *The Government's Expenditure Plans 1990–91 to 1992–93*, Cm 1021, table 21.2.1.

Table 17. Public expenditure, cash plans and outcomes

Years projected	Year of publication (Jan. or Feb.) (percentage increases in planning totals)										Outcome	Difference[1]
	1982	1983	1984	1985	1986	1987	1988	1989	1990			
1982–83	8.5										9.2	0.7
1983–84	5.1	5.8									6.0	0.2
1984–85	6.0	5.7	6.1								8.0	3.0
1985–86		4.7	5.0	6.5							2.8	−0.3
1986–87			4.5	3.1	3.5						4.2	0.6
1987–88			3.5	3.5	3.6	5.1					4.7	−1.1
1988–89				3.5	3.5	5.8	5.8				2.6	−3.8
1989–90					3.3	3.8	6.4	5.3			12.6	3.7
1990–91						4.7	6.6	8.9	11.3			3.0
1991–92							5.4	7.4	10.5			
1992–93								6.8	7.4			
									5.8			

Note: [1] Outcome minus plan published at end of financial year before that projected.
Source: The Government's Expenditure Plans, various years, and January 1990 issue, Cm 1021, chapter 21, table 21.2.1.

Table 18. Public expenditure, 'real-terms' plans and outcomes

Years projected	Year of publication (Jan. or Feb.) ('real-terms' percentage increases in planning totals)											Outcome	Difference[1]
	1980	1981	1982	1983	1984	1985	1986	1987	1988	1989	1990		
1980–81	−0.8											0.8	1.6
1981–82	−2.3	3.7										2.3	3.3
1982–83	−2.3	−1.0	1.4									1.9	0.7
1983–84	0.0	−1.7	1.1	0.3								1.3	−0.4
1984–85		−3.1	−1.1	1.7	1.0							2.8	2.8
1985–86			−1.1	0.5	0.0	1.7						−2.4	−1.1
1986–87				0.4	0.3	−1.3	−1.4					0.9	1.8
1987–88					−0.3	−0.5	−0.9	2.2				−0.6	−2.9
1988–89						0.2	0.0	2.3	1.5			−4.4	−6.2
1989–90							0.3	0.3	1.8	−0.9		5.2	1.5
1990–91								1.7	3.0	3.7	4.0		1.1
1991–92									2.3	3.8	5.3		
1992–93										3.7	3.8		
											2.7		

Notes: 'Real terms', formerly called 'cost terms', means cash terms deflated by the GDP deflator. 'Real terms' deflated by the relative price effect are volume terms, not shown in Treasury plans. [1] Outcome minus plan published at end of financial year before that projected.

Source: The Government's Expenditure Plans, various years, and January 1990 issue, Cm 1021, chapter 21, table 21.2.1.

Table 19. General government expenditure as percentage of GDP, plans and outcomes

Years projected	Year of publication (Jan. or Feb.) (GGE plus privatization proceeds as a percentage of GDP)				Outcome	Difference [1]
	1987	1988	1989	1990		
1986–87	$44\frac{1}{2}$				$43\frac{1}{2}$	-1
1987–88	44	$42\frac{1}{2}$			$41\frac{1}{4}$	$-2\frac{3}{4}$
1988–89	$42\frac{3}{4}$	42	$39\frac{3}{4}$		39	-3
1989–90	$42\frac{1}{4}$	$41\frac{3}{4}$	$39\frac{1}{4}$	$38\frac{3}{4}$	$38\frac{3}{4}$	$-\frac{1}{2}$
1990–91		$41\frac{1}{4}$	39	39		$-7\frac{1}{4}$
1991–92			$38\frac{3}{4}$	$38\frac{3}{4}$		
1992–93				$38\frac{1}{2}$		

Note: [1] Outcome minus plan published at end of financial year before that projected.
Source: The Government's Expenditure Plans, various years, and January 1990 issue, Cm 1021, chapter 21, table 21.2.1.

Table 20. Changing priorities in public expenditure

	Shares of total (%)			'Real-terms' changes (%)		
	1979-80	1984-85	1989-90	1979-80/1984-85	1984-85/1989-90	1979-80/1989-90
Social security	25.9	30.3	30.3	29.7(30.0)	1.6(3.9)	31.8(35.0)
Defence	12.0	13.0	11.6	21.3(15.7)	−9.9(−7.1)	9.2(7.5)
Education	14.1	12.9	14.2	1.9(−2.7)	11.5(2.3)	13.7(−0.5)
Health	12.1	12.7	14.1	16.5(6.1)	13.2(5.2)	31.8(11.6)
Housing	7.1	3.4	2.1	−47.6	−37.0	−67.0
Transport	4.8	4.3	3.9	1.4	−7.1	−5.8
Environment	4.3	3.4	4.1	−11.1	21.4	7.9
Law and order	4.1	4.7	5.6	28.3	19.5	53.3
Trade and industry	3.7	4.0	2.1	16.4	−48.5	−38.2
Employment and training	1.7	2.2	1.9	50.0	−11.1	33.3
Other	10.2	9.1	10.1	0.7	11.6	12.3
Total expenditure	100.0	100.0	100.0	11.4	1.4	12.9
Real GDP				3.9	18.6	23.3
Memorandum item: debt interest	12.2	12.2	10.1	10.7	−15.7	−6.7

Note: The changes in brackets are volume changes derived from the Blue Book for the equivalent calendar years (see table 22).

Sources: *The Government's Expenditure Plans 1990-91 to 1992-93*, Cm 1021, chapter 21, tables 21.2.11 and 12.

Table 21. Social security expenditure by groups of beneficiaries

	Expenditure (£bn)	Percentage	Real increase since 1978–79 (%)	Numbers (m)
Elderly	25.6	51	24	9.8
Sick and disabled	9.5	19	63	2.0
Family	9.2	18	52	n.a.
Unemployed	4.7	9	46[1]	1.5
Widows and orphans	1.2	2	−23	0.4
	50.2	100	34	n.a.

Note: [1] Expenditure on the unemployed rose 171%, from £3.2 bn to £8.8 bn between 1978–79 and 1986–87, then fell 46% to £4.7 bn in 1989–90, all at 1989–90 prices.

Source: The Government's Expenditure Plans 1990–91 to 1992–93, Cm 1041, tables 14.7–14.12.

Table 22. The volume of general government expenditure (percentage changes at 1985 constant prices)

	Central government						Local authorities						General government			
	Final consumption				Fixed capital	Total	Final consumption			Fixed capital	Total	Goods and services		Personal	
	Defence	NHS	Other	Total			Education	Other	Total				Final consumption	Fixed capital	Total	Transfers

Mean annual volume changes

| 1970-79 | -0.6 | 4.2 | 3.2 | 1.9 | -1.3 | 1.7 | 3.4 | 3.0 | 3.2 | | | | 2.4 | -4.7 | 1.2 | |
| 1980-89 | 0.7 | 1.1 | 1.6 | 1.1 | 6.0 | 1.4 | 0.0 | 1.8 | 0.9 | 0.5 | 0.2 | | 1.0 | 0.6 | 0.9 | |

Period volume changes

1970-74	-7.3	26.1	26.7	10.7	8.0	10.6	31.1	16.4	24.4				15.9	-1.8	12.1	
1975-79	1.9	19.4	8.0	9.7	-18.5	7.0	6.5	15.0	10.2				9.9	-37.2	0.8	
1970-79	-5.6	50.6	36.9	21.4	-12.0	18.3	39.7	33.9	37.1				27.4	-38.3	13.1	
1980-84	15.7	6.1	-0.9	7.8	24.5	9.8	-2.7	8.3	2.6	-7.9	-3.0		5.7	-10.0	4.3	
1985-89	-7.1	5.2	17.9	3.4	44.5	4.8	2.3	10.3	6.4	13.8	5.6		4.5	18.6	5.1	
1980-89	7.5	11.6	16.8	11.4	79.9	15.1	-0.5	19.5	9.2	4.8	2.4		10.5	6.7	9.6	

Mean annual relative price changes relative to GDP deflator

1970-79	2.3	1.5	1.1	1.7	0.7	1.6	0.6	1.2	0.9				1.4	1.1	1.3	-0.9
1980-89	0.4	2.0	1.2	1.3	-1.3	1.0	1.1	1.0	1.0	-0.2	0.5		1.1	-2.2	0.8	-0.3
1970-89	1.4	1.8	1.2	1.5	-0.3	1.3	0.9	1.1	1.0	-0.2	0.5		1.3	-0.6	1.1	-0.6

Note: The volume changes shown differ from 'real-terms' changes, since they are based on specific deflators, including relative price effects, and not on the GDP deflator used by the Treasury to calcuate 'real terms'.

Source: Derived from Blue Book, 1990, tables 1.7, 9.2, 9.3.

Table 23. Public-sector job cuts

	Headcount '000s 1979	Headcount '000s 1989	% change 1980–89
National Health Service	1,152	1,221	6.0
Other central government	1,235	1,082	−12.4
Central government total	2,387	2,303	−3.5
Education	1,539	1,440	−6.4
Other local authorities	1,458	1,494	2.5
Local authorities total	2,997	2,934	−2.1
General government total	5,384	5,237	−2.7
% of workforce in employment	21.2	19.9	−1.3
Public corporations	2,065	844	−59.1
% of workforce in employment	8.1	3.2	−4.9
Public-sector total	7,449	6,081	−18.4
% of workforce in employment	29.3	23.1	−6.2
Memo: Civil Service	738	585	−20.7

Source: Economic Trends, December 1989.

Table 24. Public-sector capital expenditure, 1989–90

Public-sector asset creation	£m	Percentage of GGE	GDP
Central government:			
Defence	5,764	2.9	1.1
Transport	1,599	0.8	0.3
Health and social services	1,539	0.8	0.3
Housing	1,101	0.6	0.2
Other	3,257	1.7	0.6
Total CG	13,260	6.8	2.6
Local authorities:			
Housing	4,247	2.2	0.8
Other environmental	1,972	1.0	0.4
Transport	952	0.5	0.2
Education	924	0.5	0.2
Other	695	0.4	0.1
Total LA	8,790	4.5	1.7
CG + LA = General govt	22,050	11.2	4.3
Public corporations	5,280	2.7	1.0
CG + LA + PC = Public sector	27,330	13.9	5.3
Public-sector asset creation within the planning total			
Deductions:			
Defence current expenditure	−5,169	−2.6	−1.0
Local authorities	−8,790	−4.5	−1.7
Public corporations	−5,077	−2.6	−1.0
Planning total	8,294	4.2	1.6
Memorandum item:			
Asset sales			
LA housing	−3,100	−1.6	−0.6
Other GG receipts	−2,500	−1.3	−0.5
GG purchases	800	0.4	0.2
Net GG receipts	−4,800	−2.4	−0.9
Privatizations	−4,250	−2.2	−0.8
Total asset sales	−9,050	−4.6	−1.8
Asset creation − sales	18,280	9.3	3.5

Source: Derived from *The Government's Expenditure Plans 1990–91 to 1992–93*, Cm 1021, tables 21.2.14–17.

Table 25. Tax revenue as percentage of GDP: international comparisons, 1970–89

	USA	Japan	Germany	France	UK	EEC
1970	29.2	19.7	32.9	35.1	37.0	30.8
1971	27.8	20.0	33.4	34.5	34.8	31.5
1972	28.7	20.7	34.7	34.9	33.3	31.5
1973	28.7	22.5	36.3	35.0	31.4	31.4
1974	29.2	23.0	36.5	35.5	35.0	32.3
1975	29.0	20.9	35.7	36.9	35.7	33.4
1976	28.3	21.8	36.8	38.7	35.5	34.4
1977	29.1	22.3	38.1	38.7	34.8	35.0
1978	29.0	24.0	37.9	38.6	33.1	35.1
1979	29.0	24.4	37.7	40.2	32.7	35.2
1980	29.5	25.5	38.0	41.7	35.4	36.4
1981	30.0	26.2	37.6	41.9	36.7	37.0
1982	29.9	26.7	37.4	42.8	39.2	38.0
1983	28.4	27.2	37.3	43.6	37.5	39.2
1984	28.4	27.4	37.5	44.6	38.0	39.4
1985	29.2	28.0	38.0	44.5	38.0	39.4
1986	28.9	28.9	37.6	44.1	37.8	40.1
1987	30.1	30.1	37.7	44.8	37.2	40.6
1988	29.8	31.3	37.4	44.4	37.3	40.8
1989			38.1	43.9	36.5	
1970–79	28.8	21.9	36.0	36.8	34.3	33.1
1980–89	29.4	27.9	37.7	43.6	37.4	39.0

Source: OECD, *Revenue Statistics,* 1965–1989.

Table 26. Tax allowance systems and costs: the effects of each system on single, one-earner, and two-earner households

	Pre-1990 system	Transferable allowances 1980 GP	Independent taxation 1986 GP	1990 system
Single	1	1	$1\frac{1}{2}$	1
1E	$1\frac{1}{2} + 0 = 1\frac{1}{2}$	$1 + \frac{1}{2} = 1\frac{1}{2}$	$1\frac{1}{2} + 1\frac{1}{2} = \underline{2\frac{1}{2}}$	$1 + \frac{1}{2} = 1\frac{1}{2}$
2E	$1\frac{1}{2} + 1 = 2\frac{1}{2}$	$1 + 1 = 2$	$1\frac{1}{2} + 1\frac{1}{2} = 2\frac{1}{2}$	$1 + \frac{1}{2} + 1 = 2\frac{1}{2}$
Total cost	5	$4\frac{1}{2}$	$6\frac{1}{2}$	5

Notes: 1E = one-earner couples. 2E = two-earner couples. 0 = no allowance. $\frac{1}{2}$ = partially transferable non-earning wife's or married couple's allowance. 1 or $1\frac{1}{2}$ = single or wife's earned-income allowance. $1\frac{1}{2}$ = married man's allowance. Changes from pre-1990 system underlined. The extra costs of the 1990 system cannot be shown in this matrix; see text for details.

Table 27. Gains from income-tax and NIC changes, 1978–79 to 1990–91

	Married man, multiples of average earnings				
	⅔	1	2	5	10
Tax + NIC (% of gross earnings)					
1978–79	21.9	27.8	31.4	50.5	66.5
1990–91	21.2	25.5	28.8	35.5	37.8
Change (%)	−0.7	−2.3	−2.6	−15.0	−28.7
Real net earnings (% rise)	34.7	37.8	38.5	73.8	148.1
Gross earnings (£ a week) in 1990–91	202.53	303.80	607.60	1,519.00	3,038.00
Tax + NIC cut in £	1.42	6.99	15.80	227.85	871.91

	Taxpayers (m)	Reductions in tax	
		Total (£m)	£ a head
Range of individual's income in 1990–91 (£)			
Under 5,000	2.9	480	110
5,000–10,000	8.6	2,840	320
10,000–15,000	6.4	4,390	690
15,000–20,000	3.8	3,860	1,030
20,000–30,000	2.6	4,190	1,590
30,000–50,000	1.0	3,300	3,270
50,000–70,000	0.2	2,160	9,390
Over 70,000	0.2	5,770	36,060
Total	25.7	26,990	980

Source: Hansard, 3 April 1990, cols. 524–8.

Table 28. Tax burden by income range, 1987

| | Quintile group of households by equivalized disposable income ||||||
	Bottom	Second	Third	Fourth	Top	All
Percentages of gross income						
Original income	27.8	58.1	83.5	93.1	97.4	85.1
plus cash benefits	72.2	41.9	16.5	6.9	2.6	14.9
Gross income	100.0	100.0	100.0	100.0	100.0	100.0
less income tax and NICs	13.2	16.0	19.8	22.0	24.5	21.4
Disposable income	86.8	84.0	80.2	78.0	75.5	78.6
less indirect taxes	23.7	19.6	18.7	16.6	12.2	16.0
Post-tax income	63.1	64.4	61.6	61.4	63.4	62.6
Total taxes	36.9	35.6	38.4	38.6	36.6	37.4

Source: 'The effects of taxes and benefits on household income, 1987', *Economic Trends*, May 1990.

Table 29. UK taxes as percentage of total taxation

	1 Personal income taxes	2 Corporate income taxes	3 Employee social security	4 Employer social security	5 National insurance surcharge	6 Personal property taxes	7 Corporate property taxes	8 Value added tax	9 Excise & specific duties	1+3+6 Personal taxes	2+4+5+7 Corporate taxes	8+9 Indirect taxes
1978	33.0	7.5	7.7	10.3	2.9	5.9	6.1	9.1	17.5	46.6	26.8	26.6
1979	30.9	8.0	7.5	9.8	4.4	6.0	6.3	10.5	16.6	44.4	28.5	27.1
1980	29.8	8.3	7.1	9.5	4.2	5.8	6.2	14.4	14.7	42.7	28.2	29.1
1981	29.5	9.5	7.3	8.8	3.8	6.1	6.7	12.4	15.9	42.9	28.8	28.3
1982	28.0	9.9	8.2	8.9	3.4	6.0	6.6	13.4	15.6	42.2	28.8	29.0
1983	27.6	10.9	8.7	9.2	1.4	6.0	6.3	14.0	15.9	42.3	27.8	29.9
1984	26.8	11.8	8.7	9.1	1.0	5.7	6.2	14.8	15.9	41.2	28.1	30.7
1985	26.5	12.6	8.6	9.0	0.1	5.9	6.0	15.7	15.6	41.0	27.7	31.3
1986	27.1	10.5	8.9	9.3	0.0	6.5	6.5	15.7	15.5	42.5	26.3	31.2
1987	26.7	10.5	8.8	9.4	0.0	6.9	6.3	16.0	15.4	42.4	26.2	31.4
1988	26.6	10.8	9.0	9.5	0.0	6.7	6.0	16.5	14.9	42.3	26.3	31.4
1989	26.5	12.3	7.7	9.8	0.0	6.6	6.0	16.9	14.2	40.8	28.1	31.1
1980–89	27.5	10.7	8.3	9.3	1.4	6.2	6.3	15.0	15.4	42.0	27.6	30.3

Source: OECD, Revenue Statistics, 1965-89.

Table 30. Public-sector housing sales to owner-occupiers

	Local authorities Great Britain ('000)	England (£ bn f. year)	New towns Great Britain ('000)	Housing assns Great Britain ('000)	Total Great Britain ('000)	Gen. govt sales of land and buildings (£ bn f. year)	Mortgage-interest relief (£ bn f. year)
1980	86	0.9	6	0	92	1.2	1.96
1981	112	1.5	6	7	125	1.9	2.05
1982	215	1.9	7	17	239	2.6	2.15
1983	154	1.4	7	16	177	2.2	2.78
1984	117	1.3	6	13	136	2.2	3.58
1985	106	1.2	5	9	120	2.3	4.75
1986	101	1.4	4	8	113	2.8	4.67
1987	116	1.9	5	7	128	3.9	4.90
1988	176	2.9	7	9	192	5.9	5.40
1989	192	3.1	9	7	208	5.6	6.90
Total	1,375	17.5	62	93	1,530	30.6	39.14

Notes: £ bn figures include some sales other than to owner-occupiers.
New-town sales of land and buildings were £0.6 bn in 1989–90.
Sources: Housing and Construction Statistics, 1979–89, table 9.6; *The Government's Expenditure Plans 1990–91 to 1992–93,* Cm 1021, table 21.2; *Inland Revenue Statistics,* 1990, table 5.1.

Table 31. Changes in housing tenure

	December 1979 ('000)	December 1979 (%)	December 1989 ('000)	December 1989 (%)	Change ('000)	Change (%)
Housing stock						
Owner-occupied	11,605	54.7	15,413	66.5	3,808	11.8
Rented:						
Privately	2,496	11.7	1,686	7.3	−810	−4.4
Housing associations	419	2.0	642	2.8	223	0.8
Council or new town	6,713	31.6	5,438	23.5	−1,275	−8.1
Total	21,233	100.0	23,178	100.0	1,945	0.0
	1979		1989			
Completions						
Private sector	118	56.5	148	86.6	30	30.1
Public sector:						
Local authorities	67	31.8	13	7.6	−54	−24.2
Housing associations	16	7.8	9	5.4	−7	−2.4
New towns	7	3.4	0	0.0	−7	−3.4
Government departments	1	0.4	1	0.4	neg.	0.0
Total	209	100.0	171	100.0	−38	0.0

Source: Housing and Construction Statistics, 1979–89, tables 6.1, 9.3.

Table 32. Privatization and the public finances

	Privatization proceeds (£bn)	General government sales of land and buildings (£bn)	Total sales of public assets (£bn)	PSBR (£bn)	PSBR plus privatization proceeds (£bn)	Public-sector financial deficit (£bn)	PSBR plus total public-asset sales (£bn)	Percentages of general government expenditure Privatization proceeds (%)	Percentages of general government expenditure Total public-asset sales (%)
1979–80	0.4	0.8	1.2	10.0	10.4	8.1	11.2	0.4	1.3
1980–81	0.2	1.2	1.4	12.7	12.9	11.6	14.1	0.2	1.3
1981–82	0.5	1.9	2.4	8.6	9.1	5.0	11.0	0.4	2.0
1982–83	0.5	2.6	3.1	8.9	9.4	8.4	12.0	0.4	2.3
1983–84	1.1	2.2	3.3	9.7	10.8	12.1	13.0	0.8	2.3
1984–85	2.5	2.2	4.7	10.1	12.6	13.5	14.8	1.7	3.1
1985–86	2.8	2.3	5.1	5.6	8.4	7.9	10.7	1.8	3.2
1986–87	4.5	2.8	7.3	3.6	8.1	8.2	10.9	2.7	4.4
1987–88	5.2	3.9	9.1	−3.4	1.8	1.2	5.7	3.0	5.3
1988–89	7.1	5.9	13.0	−14.5	−7.4	−9.0	−1.5	4.0	7.2
1989–90	4.3	5.6	9.8	−7.9	−3.7	−4.6	1.9	2.1	4.9
Total	29.2	31.4	60.6	43.4	72.6	62.4	104.0	17.5	37.5

Note: Privatization proceeds and other asset sales have been subtracted from GGE.
Sources: Other tables; *Financial Statistics*.

Table 33. Main corporations privatized

	Energy sector	(£bn)	Major industrial	(£bn)	Other (£bn)	Total (£bn)
1979–80	BP	276			101	377
1980–81			BAerospace	43	167	210
1981–82			Cable & Wireless	181	312	493
1982–83	Britoil	334			211	545
1983–84	BP	543				
	Britoil	293			277	1,113
1984–85	Enterprise Oil	384	Telecom	1,402		
	Wytch Farm	82	Jaguar	297	304	2,469
1985–86	Britoil	426	Telecom	1,307		
			Cable & Wireless	577		
			BAerospace	347	130	2,787
1986–87	British Gas	2,570	Telecom	1,384		
			BAirways	435	142	4,531
1987–88	British Gas	1,758	Rolls-Royce	1,028		
	BP	863	BAA (airports)	534		
			BAirways	419		
			Telecom	273	353	5,228
1988–89	British Gas	1,805	British Steel	1,138		
	BP	3,030	BAA (airports)	689		
			Telecom	335	112	7,109
1989–90	BP	1,370	British Steel	1,280		
	British Gas	850	Water plcs	500		
			Rover	150	198	4,348
	Energy	14,584	Industrial	12,319	2,307	29,210
Totals for multiple offerings						
	BP	6,082	Telecom	4,701		
	Britoil	1,053	(loan/preference	996)		
	British Gas	6,983	Water plcs	3,480		
	(debt	1,850)	BAA	1,223		
			BAirways	854		
			BAerospace	390		
			Cable & Wireless	758		

Source: The Government's Expenditure Plans 1990–91 to 1992–93, Cm 1021, January 1990, table 21.2.1, updated.

Table 34. Performance of public corporations

	Privatized			Not privatized			Manufacturing industry
	B. Gas	B. Steel	Telecom	B. Coal	B. Rail	PO	
Return on capital employed (%)							
1979	20.3	negative	4.8	7.9	negative	7.6	8.8
At privatization	16.9	13.0	16.7				
1989	5.8	16.8	21.8	8.6	5.2	4.7	9.2
Total factor productivity change (% p.a.)							
1980–83	−0.2	7.5	1.9	0.6	−0.4	3.4	1.2
1984–89	4.4	8.2	3.2	5.6	4.2	3.0	4.4

Source: London Business School.

Table 35. Personal-sector wealth

	Housing	Other non-financial	Shares and unit trusts	Life assurance and pension funds	Other financial	Total
1979 (£bn)	270.6	162.6	36.2	81.6	132.7	683.7
(%)	39.6	23.8	5.3	11.9	19.4	100.0
1989 (£bn)	1,025	293	186.6	511.6	430.3	2,446.5
(%)	41.9	12.0	7.6	20.9	17.6	100.0
Real change (%)[1]	92	−8	162	218	65	82

Note: [1] Deflated by consumer price deflator, which rose 97%.
Source: Blue Book, table 12.2, updated.

Table 36. The public sector in the economy (percentage shares)

	Public corporations	Central government	Local authorities	Public sector
Net capital stock at current replacement cost			
1979	17.7	6.6	19.8	44.1
1989	7.7	6.7	16.2	30.6
Gross domestic fixed-capital formation at current prices			
1979	15.3	4.2	9.7	29.2
1989	4.8	5.0	4.0	13.8
Gross domestic product (income) at current factor cost			
1979	10.5	7.3	9.4	27.2
1989	4.7	7.2	8.4	20.3
Employment (millions)			
1979	8.1	9.4	11.8	29.3
1989	3.2	8.7	11.2	23.1

Source: Blue Book, tables 2.5, 13.3, 14.7; *Economic Trends*, December 1989.

Table 37. Government expenditure on trade and industry (at 1989–90 prices)

	1979–80 (£m)	(% of total)	1989–90 (£m)	(% of total)	Percentage real change
Regional and general	1,074	46	372	22	−65
Scientific and technological assistance	564	24	297	17	−47
Aerospace, shipbuilding, steel and vehicles	404	17	173	10	−57
International trade	44	2	44	3	0
Statutory and regulatory	102	4	217	13	+113
Central and miscellaneous	204	9	271	16	+33
ECGD	56	2	341	20	+509
Central Government[1]	2,322	100	1,714	100	−26

Note: [1] Excluding Scottish and Welsh Development Agencies and NEB and including the Export Credit Guarantee Department.
Sources: The Government's Expenditure Plans 1980–81 to 1983–84, Cmnd 7841, table 2.4, and *The Government's Expenditure Plans 1990–91 to 1992–93*, Cm 1004, Chapter 4, 'Trade and Industry'.

Table 38. *Takeovers and mergers, overseas investment and capital spending: industrial and commercial companies (£bn at 1985 prices)*

	Number of cos. acquired	Takeovers and mergers Total spending (£bn) (% change)	Cash outlay	(% cash)	Domestic fixed-capital spending (£bn) (% change)		Overseas investment (£bn) (% change)		Total investment (£bn) (% change)		Percentage of total investment Takeover and merger	Fixed-capital spending	Overseas investment
1979	534	2,534		1,428	56.4	21,544		5,502		29,580		8.6	72.8	18.6
1980	459	1,896	−25.2	977	51.5	19,527	−9.4	3,815	−30.7	25,238	−14.7	7.5	77.4	15.1
1981	452	1,338	−29.4	906	67.7	17,577	−10.0	4,510	18.2	23,425	−7.2	5.7	75.0	19.3
1982	463	2,507	87.4	1,458	58.2	17,766	1.1	3,075	−31.8	23,348	−0.3	10.7	76.1	13.2
1983	447	2,578	2.8	1,129	43.8	17,481	−1.6	2,586	−15.9	22,645	−3.0	11.4	77.2	11.4
1984	568	5,781	124.3	3,111	53.8	20,712	18.5	3,169	22.5	29,662	31.0	19.5	69.8	10.7
1985	474	7,090	22.6	2,837	40.0	24,800	19.7	3,489	10.1	35,379	19.3	20.0	70.1	9.9
1986	842	14,722	107.6	3,891	26.4	25,415	2.5	5,553	59.1	45,690	29.1	32.2	55.6	12.2
1987	1,527	15,081	2.4	5,205	34.5	29,337	15.4	13,125	136.4	57,543	25.9	26.2	51.0	22.8
1988	1,499	19,583	29.9	13,714	70.0	34,610	18.0	11,933	−9.1	66,126	14.9	29.6	52.3	18.0
1989	1,330	21,975	12.2	18,394	83.7	37,069	7.1	13,253	11.1	72,298	9.3	30.4	51.3	18.3
Mean	781		24.1		53.3		5.6		9.2		9.3	18.4	66.2	15.4

Note: The gross domestic fixed-capital formation deflator has been used to convert nominal to real amounts.
Source: Financial Statistics, tables 8.2, 8.8.

Table 39. UK acquisitions for over £500 million, 1985–90: industrial and commercial companies

Acquiring company	Acquired company	Value of transaction (£m)	Year
Hanson	Consolidated Gold Fields	3,275	1989
Nestlé	Rowntree	2,666	1988
Hanson Trust	Imperial Group	2,564	1986
Guinness	Distillers	2,531	1986
British Petroleum	Britoil	2,323	1988
Isosceles	Gateway Corporation	2,043	1989
GEC Siemens	Plessey	2,030	1989
Ford Motor	Jaguar	1,500	1989
Cilva Holdings	Avis Europe	900	1989
Boots Company	Ward White Group	873	1989
Vantona Viyella	Coats Patons	738	1986
William Hill	Mecca Bookmakers	685	1989
Argyll Group	Safeway Food Stores	681	1987
BAT	Hambro Assurance	662	1985
Mount Charlotte Hotels	Thistle Hotels	645	1989
British & Commonwealth Holdings	Exco International	641	1987
Management buy-out	Magnet	631	1989
Burton	Debenhams	579	1985
Associated Dairies	MFI	571	1985
Carlton Communications	UEI	508	1989

Note: Cross-border mergers are not listed, but mergers involving UK subsidiaries of foreign parent companies are.
Source: Bank of England.

Table 40. Gross trading profits and other business income by sector: 'real-terms' changes and shares of total (%)

	Energy and water		Manufacturing		Construction		Distribution		Transport and communication		Financial services		Other services		Total business income change			
	Change	Share	Change	Share	Change	Share	Change	Share	Change	Share	Change	Share	Change	Share	Gross trading profits	GTP net of stock appreciation	Rent	Total GTP net + rent
1979		14.1		21.1		6.5		14.3		5.7		14.7		3.9				
1980	14.9	17.9	−27.6	16.9	−3.6	7.0	−20.8	12.5	−19.8	5.0	−4.1	15.6	−3.4	4.2	−11.2	−4.9	−0.3	−4.2
1981	13.6	21.0	−13.9	14.9	−2.4	7.0	−15.6	10.9	5.5	5.5	−11.4	14.2	0.7	4.3	−4.3	−1.7	3.2	−0.8
1982	3.5	20.8	10.8	15.9	6.0	7.1	2.2	10.7	10.3	5.8	4.3	14.2	−3.7	4.0	5.2	7.3	0.5	6.0
1983	11.7	21.4	6.2	15.5	11.6	7.3	11.4	10.9	0.1	5.3	20.4	15.8	13.7	4.2	10.5	9.4	1.2	8.1
1984	2.5	21.1	9.3	16.3	−6.0	7.4	4.2	11.0	5.1	5.4	1.2	15.4	4.0	4.2	4.7	4.0	0.5	3.4
1985	−2.7	19.7	4.1	16.3	2.1	7.3	7.3	11.3	6.5	5.5	19.0	17.5	9.3	4.4	4.5	6.3	3.5	5.8
1986	−40.4	11.7	5.7	17.1	17.6	8.5	13.6	12.8	12.0	6.2	15.4	20.1	8.7	4.7	−0.9	1.2	6.2	2.0
1987	3.8	11.3	5.2	16.8	16.2	9.3	7.5	12.8	6.8	6.1	9.9	20.6	11.8	4.9	8.4	5.1	1.9	4.6
1988	−18.8	8.6	10.9	17.5	15.8	10.0	9.8	13.2	5.9	6.1	15.3	22.3	9.7	5.1	6.8	6.0	5.3	5.9
1989	−6.7	7.8	−2.5	16.7	5.8	10.4	1.7	13.1	−0.3	5.9	9.2	23.8	5.6	5.2	2.4	2.1	3.0	2.2
Mean	−3.4	15.9	0.0	16.8	7.3	8.0	1.5	12.1	2.8	5.7	7.4	17.7	5.5	4.5	2.4	3.4	2.5	3.2

Notes: Gross trading profits include self-employed income. Shares do not add to 100 because imputed rent from owner-occupation is not shown. The GDP deflator has been used to convert nominal to real changes. Profits for each sector are gross of stock appreciation, and those for financial services include net interest.
Source: Derived from Blue Book, table 2.1.

Table 41. Contributions to increase in business income

	Self-employment income	Gross trading profits			Rent	Net bank interest	Total business income
		Private sector	Public sector	Both sectors			
1979 (% share)	22.8	42.3	8.3	50.8	17.2	9.3	100.0
1989 (% share)	29.1	36.0	3.7	39.7	17.3	13.8	100.0
Real changes:							
1980–89 total	65.3	10.2	−42.1	1.6	30.4	91.9	29.5
Annual mean	5.2	1.0	−5.3	0.2	2.7	6.7	2.6
Contribution to annual mean change of business income	1.2	0.4	−0.4	0.1	0.5	0.6	2.6

Note: The GDP deflator has been used to calculate real changes.
Source: Blue Book, 1990, tables 2.1, 2.5.

Table 42. Gross domestic fixed-capital formation by sector (annual changes, 1985 prices, %)

	Agri-culture	Oil and gas	Energy & water	Manu-facturing	Con-struction	Distri-bution & hotels	Trans-port	Post and telecom.	Fin. leasing	Fin. services	Other services	Housing	Land & building	Total GDFCF
1980	-10.7	-5.0	7.7	-13.6	-30.6	-10.0	-13.0	9.5	11.4	4.7	-2.3	-7.4	-5.8	-5.4
1981	-14.0	11.7	0.3	-24.9	-11.5	-8.1	-29.1	-8.7	-3.4	13.0	-6.6	-17.2	5.8	-9.6
1982	17.8	2.7	-0.7	-3.3	13.0	6.9	-11.7	-4.5	14.2	8.5	16.0	6.4	9.8	5.4
1983	8.9	-6.0	4.5	1.0	8.6	3.3	17.0	12.4	-10.5	5.4	3.8	12.4	10.0	5.0
1984	-6.0	5.6	-15.3	21.5	-16.2	15.7	25.4	5.3	38.2	8.3	9.1	2.5	7.3	8.5
1985	-21.6	-13.5	4.6	11.9	-3.8	7.8	-3.6	16.4	34.6	8.5	4.6	-5.5	-0.1	4.0
1986	-9.4	-11.9	3.3	-2.2	-1.3	5.4	-12.1	7.7	-17.1	15.1	5.8	8.0	3.2	1.9
1987	3.4	-22.5	-3.0	7.4	8.6	19.5	9.2	7.3	19.4	34.4	2.4	7.0	7.1	9.5
1988	-3.7	-2.9	-2.5	11.9	55.9	14.5	21.9	38.7	29.0	25.9	6.8	5.7	9.4	14.8
1989	20.0	12.3	12.4	5.0								-3.0	-28.0	4.8
Mean	-2.4	-3.5	0.9	0.6	0.2	5.7	-1.1	8.6	11.2	13.4	4.2	0.5	1.2	3.7
Output[1]	2.7	1.2		1.2	2.8	2.8	2.3	4.9		7.3		1.1		2.3

Source: Blue Book, 1990, tables 2.4, 13.7. [1] Mean of real output changes 1980-89.

Table 43. Industrial and commercial companies 1989 account (£bn)

Gross trading profits	70.6
Other income	13.3
Overseas income	18.6
Total company income	102.5
Less UK taxes	18.8
Net company income	83.7
Less interest, etc.	24.0
Net income after interest	59.7
Less overseas outgoings	9.0
Net income in UK	50.7
Less depreciation (replacement cost)	25.5
Less stock appreciation	6.6
UK income net of depreciation and stock appreciation	18.6
Less dividends	19.2
Net saving	−0.6
Net capital formation	−20.5
Net stockbuilding	−3.5
Company security purchases	−18.1
Financial asset purchases	−12.7
Overseas investment	−21.6
Total funding required:	77.0
Bank borrowing	33.3
Other capital issues	31.9
Unidentified items	11.8
Memo: Net income in UK	50.7
Less dividends	19.2
Undistributed income	31.5
Less depreciation	25.5
Less net capital formation	20.5
Less stock appreciation	6.6
Less stockbuilding	3.5
Financial deficit	24.6
Memo: Total funding	77.0
Less unidentified	11.8
Less financial asset purchases	12.7
Net borrowing requirement	52.5

Sources: Blue Book, tables 5.1–5.4; *Financial Statistics*, tables 8.1–8.3.

Table 44. Industrial and commercial companies: changes in assets, liabilities and ratios (real changes, %, using GDP deflator)

	Assets				Liabilities				Ratios					
	Tangible	Overseas	Financial	Total	Bank loans	UK equity	Overseas	Total	Bank loans/ deposits	Liab./ financial assets	Liab./ total assets	Equity/ net wealth	Equity/ tangible assets	Bank loans/ equity
1979	−7.3	−9.2	−6.8	−7.2	0.3	−1.3	−4.9	−3.9	1.96	1.67	0.54	0.46	0.31	0.38
1980	−1.5	22.3	7.6	1.5	13.0	−2.8	2.9	1.5	1.98	1.72	0.56	0.51	0.33	0.39
1981	−0.8	8.6	5.4	1.4	−1.2	26.7	−0.4	10.0	1.82	1.62	0.56	0.48	0.33	0.45
1982	1.6	5.2	8.9	4.2	3.0	18.4	6.5	11.1	1.75	1.69	0.60	0.68	0.42	0.35
1983	9.5	31.0	16.1	12.0	12.9	18.9	0.3	12.3	1.52	1.73	0.65	0.86	0.49	0.31
1984	0.5	−9.4	−1.4	−0.2	−0.5	12.3	0.9	6.3	1.62	1.67	0.65	0.92	0.53	0.29
1985	4.2	10.9	9.8	6.3	10.4	30.6	11.8	19.2	1.59	1.80	0.69	1.17	0.59	0.26
1986	6.3	2.2	5.0	5.8	9.0	9.6	3.0	7.5	1.50	1.95	0.77	1.96	0.74	0.22
1987	15.2	15.9	5.4	11.4	29.1	3.6	8.4	7.0	1.49	2.00	0.78	2.15	0.76	0.22
1988	5.9	29.2	15.8	9.5	25.7	20.3	32.5	19.1	1.82	2.03	0.75	1.75	0.68	0.27
1989									1.99	2.09	0.82	2.62	0.78	0.28
Mean	3.2	9.8	6.4	4.3	9.7	13.1	5.7	8.8	1.73	1.81	0.67	1.23	0.54	0.31

Note: Equity includes about 5 per cent loan capital.
Source: Derived from Blue Book, 1990, table 12.3 (tangible assets for 1988 and 1989 estimated).

Table 45. The rise in the external deficit, 1984–90: forecast and actual

	Net oil exports (m) (tonnes)[1]		Oil trade balance (£bn)		Non-oil trade balance (£bn)		Invisibles net (£bn)		Current account (£bn)	
	A	B	A	B	A	B	A	B	A	B
1983	45.6	45.5	7.0	7.0	−7.5	−8.5	3.4	5.3	2.9	3.8
1984	50	50.9	8.8	6.9	−10.7	−12.3	3.1	7.2	1.2	1.8
1985	54	52.7	9.5	8.1	−11.8	−11.4	3.4	6.1	1.1	2.7
1986	46	49.4	8.1	4.1	−13.0	−13.5	3.7	9.4	−1.2	0.0
1987	35	47.6	6.2	4.2	−14.4	−15.4	4.1	6.9	−4.1	−4.3
1988	23	37.8	4.2	2.8	−15.9	−23.9	4.5	5.5	−7.2	−15.5
1989	13	12.5	2.5	1.3	−17.5	−25.3	5.0	4.1	−10.0	−19.9
1990	0	10.7	0.2	1.6	−19.3	−19.5	5.5	4.1	−13.6	−13.8

Note: [1]Since the UK's oil exports are higher in unit value than oil imports, a small surplus on oil trade still results from zero net oil exports.

Sources: A = Lloyds Bank, *Economic Bulletin*, September 1984.

B = Actual from *Monthly Digest of External Trade Statistics*, April 1991, and CSO press release, June 1991.

Table 46. Export and import trends 1980–89 (average % changes)

	Volume	Price	Value
Exports			
All goods	3.5	5.0	8.7
Non-oil goods	3.7	5.2	9.1
Services	1.2	6.6	7.8
Goods and services	2.9	5.4	8.4
Imports			
All goods	5.4	4.6	10.3
Non-oil goods	6.4	4.4	11.2
Services	3.9	5.5	9.4
Goods and services	5.1	4.8	10.1
GDP factor cost	2.2	7.3	9.7

Source: Pink Book, 1990, table 4.1.

Table 47. Trade-union membership and stoppages

	Total membership		Working days lost through stoppages (per thousand employees)				
	(m)	(Percentage of employees)	UK	USA	France	Italy	Australia
1979	13.3	57.4	1,270	230	180	1,920	780
1980	12.9	56.4	520	230	90	1,140	630
1981	12.1	55.3	190	190	80	730	780
1982	11.6	54.2	250	100	130	1,280	370
1983	11.2	53.4	180	190	70	980	310
1984	11.0	51.8	1,280	90	70	610	240
1985	10.8	50.5	300	70	40	270	230
1986	10.5	49.3	90	120	30	390	240
1987	10.5	48.5	160	40	30	320	220
1988	10.2	46.0	166				
1989			182				
Means							
1969–78			472[1]	533	205	1,625	638
1980–87			371	129	68	715	378
1980–84			484	160	88	948	466
1985–89			180				

Note: [1] The UK average for 1969–79 was 544.
Source: Employment Gazette, November 1980, June 1989, May 1990.

Table 48. The rise in income inequality (gross employment earnings, full-time adults)

	Share of decile (%)		£ a week			Decile multiples			Gini coefficient
	Top	Bottom	Top decile	Bottom decile	Average	Top/bottom	Top/average	Bottom/average	
1979	18.1	4.6	162.00	41.50	89.60	3.90	1.81	0.46	22.9
1989	22.7	4.1	544.60	98.50	239.70	5.53	2.27	0.41	27.4
Real change[1]									
Annual			5.2	1.7	2.9				
Total	4.8	−0.5	66.7	17.8	32.7	1.63	0.48	−0.15	4.5

Note: [1] Adjusted for the RPI increase.
Source: Income and Wealth in the 1980s, Thomas Stark, Fabian Society.

Table 49. International competitiveness comparisons (annual averages, %, manufacturing industry)

	OECD	USA	Japan	Germany	France	Italy	UK
Nominal hourly earnings							
1974–79	10.8	8.6	11.8	7.2	14.9	26.0	16.6
1980–88	6.5	4.8	3.9	4.3	8.8	17.9	10.3
Real hourly earnings							
1974–79	2.2	0.0	1.6	2.4	3.7	8.5	0.9
1980–88	1.0	−0.8	1.4	1.3	1.0	5.6	2.8
Labour productivity per employee							
1974–79	2.6	0.9	5.0	3.1	3.7	5.3	0.6
1980–88	3.3	3.3	5.8	2.9	2.2	4.0	4.2
Unit labour costs							
1974–79	8.6	8.0	6.8	4.9	11.2	15.9	18.0
1980–88	2.9	2.2	−1.0	2.7	6.7	8.5	4.8
Relative unit labour costs in a common currency							
1976–79		−1.7	0.6	2.7	−1.5	−4.7	3.9
1980–80		−1.1	2.2	1.4	0.0	0.6	0.0
Relative productivity – whole economy, 1986							
Per employee		141	94	113	119	n.a.	100
Per hour		132	67	105	117	n.a.	100

Sources: OECD, *Main Economic Indicators, Historical Statistics*; OECD, *Economic Outlook Historical Statistics*; IMF, *International Financial Statistics*; *Economic Progress Report*, April 1989.

Table 50. International unemployment comparisons

Year	United Kingdom				Year	United Kingdom			OECD standard basis						
	Original	Revised	Misery index	OECD		Original	Revised	Misery index	UK	USA	Japan	Germany	France	Italy	EEC
1970	2.6	2.6	9.1	3.0	1980	6.8	4.8	22.8	6.4	7.0	2.0	3.0	6.3	7.5	6.4
1971	3.4	2.5	11.7	3.6	1981	10.5	7.9	19.8	9.8	7.5	2.2	4.4	7.4	7.8	8.2
1972	3.7	2.9	10.4	4.0	1982	12.0	9.5	18.1	11.3	9.5	2.4	6.1	8.1	8.4	9.5
1973	2.6	2.1	11.2	3.0	1983	12.4	10.5	15.0	12.4	9.5	2.6	8.0	8.3	8.8	10.4
1974	2.6	2.0	17.9	2.9	1984	12.6	10.7	15.7	11.7	7.4	2.7	7.1	9.7	9.4	10.7
1975	4.0	3.0	27.1	4.3	1985	13.1	10.9	16.9	11.2	7.1	2.6	7.2	10.2	9.6	10.8
1976	5.4	4.1	20.7	5.6	1986	11.5	11.8	15.2	11.2	6.9	2.8	6.4	10.4	10.5	10.8
1977	5.8	4.4	20.3	6.0	1987	10.3	10.3	14.5	10.3	6.1	2.8	6.2	10.5	10.9	10.5
1978	5.8	4.4	12.6	5.9	1988	8.1	8.3	13.2	8.5	5.4	2.5	6.2	10.0	11.0	9.8
1979	5.4	4.0	17.4	5.0	1989	6.4	6.4	14.2	6.9	5.2	2.3	5.5	9.6	10.9	8.9
Mean	4.1	3.2	15.8	4.3		10.4	9.1	16.5	10.0	7.2	2.5	6.0	9.1	9.5	9.6

Notes: Original UK figures are those published three months after the end of each year. Revised UK figures are based on benefit count as percentage of total workforce. OECD figures are based on labour-force surveys. Misery index = sum of RPI increase and revised unemployment rate.
Sources: *Economic Trends*; OECD, *Economic Outlook*.

Table 51. Employment creation ('000s, seasonally adjusted)

June	Employees in employment	Self-employed	HM forces	Govt training programmes	Workforce in employment	Unemployed, 2nd quarter	Workforce	Non-working population	Working-age population
1979	23,145	1,906	314		25,365	1,089	26,454	6,514	32,905
1980	22,965	2,013	323		25,301	1,186	26,487	6,684	33,051
1981	21,870	2,119	334		24,323	2,068	26,391	6,918	33,300
1982	21,395	2,170	324		23,889	2,478	26,367	6,488	33,563
1983	21,054	2,221	322	16	23,613	2,769	26,382	6,178	33,741
1984	21,229	2,496	326	175	24,226	2,849	27,075	6,222	33,891
1985	21,414	2,610	326	176	24,526	3,037	27,563	6,045	34,064
1986	21,379	2,627	322	226	24,554	3,115	27,669	5,872	34,189
1987	21,575	2,860	319	311	25,065	2,954	28,019	5,654	34,279
1988	22,269	2,986	316	343	25,914	2,403	28,317	5,360	34,317
1989	22,757	3,240	308	462	26,767	1,858	28,625		
1990	23,238	3,380	303	424	27,345	1,612	28,957		
1990–79 change	93	1,474	−11	424	1,980	523	2,503	−1,154	1,412
Percentage changes									
1980	−0.8	5.6	2.9		−0.3	8.9	0.1		
1981	−4.8	5.3	3.4		−3.9	74.4	−0.4		
1982	−2.2	2.4	−3.0		−1.8	19.8	−0.1	2.6	0.4
1983	−1.6	2.4	−0.6		−1.2	11.7	0.1	3.5	0.8
1984	0.8	12.4	1.2	993.8	2.6	2.9	2.6	−6.2	0.8
1985	0.9	4.6	0.0	0.6	1.2	6.6	1.8	−4.8	0.5
1986	−0.2	0.7	−1.2	28.4	0.1	2.6	0.4	0.7	0.4

1987	0.9	8.9	−0.9	37.6	2.1	−5.2	1.3	−2.8	0.5
1988	3.2	4.4	−0.9	10.3	3.4	−18.7	1.1	−2.9	0.4
1989	2.2	8.5	−2.5	34.7	3.3	−22.7	1.1	−3.7	0.3
1990	2.1	4.3	−1.6	−8.2	2.2	−13.2	1.2	−5.2	0.1
Mean	0.0	5.9	−0.4	4.0	0.8	4.0	0.9	−1.9	0.4

Sources: Economic Trends Annual Supplement; Employment Gazette, April 1990; *Labour-market Statistics*; Department of Employment press release.

Table 52. Changing employment patterns (employees in employment, Great Britain, '000s)

	Male employees			Female employees				All employees		
	Full-time	Part-time	All	Full-time	Part-time	All		Full-time	Part-time	All
June 1979	12,432	751	13,183	5,598	3,837	9,435		18,030	4,588	22,618
June 1990	10,767	953	11,720	6,346	4,640	10,986		17,113	5,593	22,706
Percentages										
June 1979	94.3	5.7	58.3	59.3	40.7	41.7		79.7	20.3	100.0
June 1990	91.9	8.1	51.6	57.8	42.2	48.4		75.4	24.6	100.0
Changes June 1979–1990										
'000	−1,665	202	−1,463	748	803	1,551		−917	1,005	88
%	−13.4	26.9	−11.1	13.4	20.9	16.4		−5.1	21.9	0.4

Participation rates (%)

	UK	USA	France	UK	USA	France	UK	USA	France
1981	90	86	83	58	59	54	74	72	68
1989	87	86	75	65	68	56	76	77	66
Change	−3	0	−8	7	9	2	2	5	−2

Source: *Employment Gazette*; OECD, *Employment Outlook*, July 1990, tables G, H.

References

1 *Economic growth: can one succeed without really trying?*

CRAFTS, N. (1988). *British Economic Growth Before and After 1979: a Review of the Evidence*. Centre for Economic Policy Research.

EASTON, W. W. (1990). 'The interest rate transmission mechanism in the UK', *Bank of England Quarterly Bulletin*, May 1990.

FEINSTEIN, C., and MATTHEWS, R. (1990). 'The growth of output and productivity in the UK: the 1980s as a phase of the post-war period', *National Institute Economic Review*, August 1990.

HIBBERD, J. (1990). 'Official statistics in the late 1980s', *Treasury Bulletin*, Summer 1990.

JOHNSON, C. (1985). *The Financial and Economic Consequences of UK Membership of the European Community*, pp. 159-74. Treasury and Civil Service Committee, HC 57-II. HMSO.

LAYARD. R., and NICKELL, S. (1989). *The Thatcher Miracle?*. Centre for Economic Policy Research.

OECD (1988). *UK Economic Survey 1987/88*, pp. 48-64.

PATTERSON, P. (1990), 'The Treasury's forecasting performance', *Treasury Bulletin*, Autumn 1990.

WALTERS, A. (1983). *The British Renaissance 1979-?*, pp. 11-12. American Enterprise Institute for Public Policy Research.

2 *Inflation: the monetarist experiment that was never tried*

BECKERMAN, W., and JENKINSON, T. (1986). 'What stopped the inflation? Unemployment or commodity prices?', *Economic Journal*, March 1986.

BRITTAN, S. (1981). *How to End the 'Monetarist' Controversy*. Institute of Economic Affairs.

CONGDON, T. (1989). *Monetarism Lost and Why it must be Regained*. Centre for Policy Studies.

DOW, C., and SAVILLE, I. (1988). *A Critique of Monetary Policy*. Clarendon Press.

FFORDE, J. (1983). 'Setting monetary objectives', *Bank of England Quarterly Bulletin*, June 1983.

GOODHART, C. (1975). *Money, Information and Uncertainty*. Macmillan.

GOODHART, C. (1984). *Monetary Theory and Practice: The UK Experience*. Macmillan. (Goodhart's Law, p. 96.)

GOODHART, C. (1986). 'Financial innovation and monetary policy', *Oxford Review of Economic Policy*, Winter 1986.

GOODHART, C. (1989). 'The conduct of monetary policy', *Economic Journal*, June 1989.

GRICE, J., and BENNETT, A. (1981). *The Demand for £M3 and other Aggregates in the UK*. Treasury Working Paper 20.

HALL, S. G., HENRY, S. G. B., and WILCOX, J. B. (1989). *The Long-run Determination of the UK Monetary Aggregates*. Bank of England.

JOHNSON, C. (ed.) (1991). *Monetarists and Keynesians*. Pinter.

JOHNSTON, R. B. (1984). *M0: the Demand for Non-interest-bearing Money in the UK*. Treasury Working Paper 28.

LAWSON, N. (1980). *The New Conservatism*. Centre for Policy Studies.

LAWSON, N. (1984). 'What are we going to do when the oil runs out?'. Press release, 9 April 1984. HM Treasury.

LEIGH-PEMBERTON, R. (1984). 'Some aspects of monetary policy', *Bank of England Quarterly Bulletin*, December 1984.

LEIGH-PEMBERTON, R. (1986). 'Financial change and broad money', *Bank of England Quarterly Bulletin*, December 1986.

LEIGH-PEMBERTON, R. (1987). 'The instruments of monetary policy', *Bank of England Quarterly Bulletin*, August 1987.

LEIGH-PEMBERTON, R. (1990). 'Monetary policy in the second half of the 1980s', *Bank of England Quarterly Bulletin*, May 1990.

MIDDLETON, P. (1978). 'The relationships between monetary and fiscal policy', Institute for Fiscal Studies (mimeo.).

PEPPER, G. (1990). *Money, Credit and Inflation*. Institute of Economic Affairs.

PICKFORD, S., et al. (1989). *Government Economic Statistics*. A Scrutiny Report. Cabinet Office. HMSO.

ROWLATT, P. A. (1987). *Analysis of the Inflation Process*. Treasury Working Paper 50.

SENTANCE, A., and MCWILLIAMS, D. (1990). *The UK's Inflation Performance*. Confederation of British Industry.

SMITH, D. (1987). *The Rise and Fall of Monetarism*. Penguin.

TREASURY AND CIVIL SERVICE COMMITTEE (1980). *Monetary Control*. HC 713. HMSO.

TREASURY AND CIVIL SERVICE COMMITTEE (1980). *Memoranda on Monetary Policy*. HC 720. HMSO.

TREASURY AND CIVIL SERVICE COMMITTEE (1981). *Monetary Policy*; Vol. I Report, Vol. II Minutes of Evidence, Vol. III Appendices. HC 163. HMSO.

TREASURY, HM (1980). *Monetary Control*. Cmnd 7858. HMSO.

VINES, D., MACIEJOWSKI, J. M., and MEADE, J. E. (1983). *Demand Management*. Allen and Unwin.

WALTERS, A. (1971). *Money in Boom and Slump*. Institute of Economic Affairs.

WESTAWAY, P., and WREN-LEWIS, S. (1989). *Is there a Case for the MTFS?*.

National Institute of Economic and Social Research Discussion Paper 170.

WREN-LEWIS, S. (1981). *The Role of Money in Determining Prices: A Reduced-form Approach.* Treasury Working Paper 18.

Treasury and Civil Service Committee

Reports on Budgets and Autumn Statements

References are tabulated by the years in which Budgets and Autumn Statements fell, giving dates of publication and House of Commons (HC) numbers. Reports are published with transcripts of oral evidence and memoranda submitted by specialist advisers and others. All reports are published by HMSO.

	Budget report		Autumn Statement report	
	Date	HC no.	Date	HC no.
1980	30 Apr.	584	15 Dec.	79
1981	6 Apr.	232	16 Dec.	28
1982	31 Mar.	270	14 Dec.	49
1983	11 Apr.	286	6 Feb. ('84)	170
1984	10 Apr.	341	3 Dec.	44
1985	22 Apr.	306	2 Dec.	57
1986	21 Apr.	313	3 Dec.	27
1987	6 Apr.	293	14 Dec	197
1988	20 Apr.	400	14 Dec.	89
1989	19 Apr.	288	13 Dec.	20
1990	3 Apr.	314	17 Dec.	41

3 Public expenditure: the enemy country

ASHWORTH, M., HILLS, J., and MORRIS, N. (1984). *Public Finances in Perspective.* Institute for Fiscal Studies.

BACON, R., and ELTIS, W. (1976). *Britain's Economic Problem: Too Few Producers.* Macmillan.

BURTON, J. (1985). *Why No Cuts?* Institute of Economic Affairs.

HEALD, D. (1983). *Public Expenditure.* Martin Robertson.

HENNESSY, P. (1989). *Whitehall.* Secker and Warburg.

LEVITT, M. S. (ed.) (1987). *New Priorities in Public Spending.* Gower.

LEVITT, M. S., and JOYCE, M. A. S. (1987). *The Growth and Efficiency of Public Spending.* Cambridge University Press.

LIKIERMAN, A. (1988). *Public Expenditure.* Penguin.

LITTLECHILD, S., et al. (1979). *The Taming of Government.* Institute of Economic Affairs.

PLIATZKY, L. (1982). *Getting and Spending.* Blackwell.

PLIATZKY, L. (1985). *Paying and Choosing*. Blackwell.

TREASURY, HM (1984). *The Next Ten Years: Public Expenditure and Taxation in the 1990s*. Cmnd 9189. HMSO.

TRINDER, C. (1990). *Trends and Cycles in Public Sector Pay*. Public Finance Foundation.

Treasury and Treasury and Civil Service Committee papers

Public-expenditure White Papers (PEWPs), entitled *The Government's Expenditure Plans* (followed by the years covered), are published in January of each year. Publication moved forward from March, then February, over the 1980s. The new Conservative Government's 1979 White Paper appeared, exceptionally, in November. The Command numbers are given. Autumn Statements have been published each November since 1982, and have no reference number.

Treasury Committee reports appear about a month after the Autumn Statement each year and a month after the PEWP each year from 1981 to 1988. (After 1988 the Committee ceased to publish reports on the PEWP, making its comments on public expenditure in its reports on the Autumn Statement.) The House of Commons numbers are given. Numbers of Treasury and Civil Service Committee reports on Autumn Statements are given in the references to Chapter 2.

	PEWP Command no.	Treasury Committee report on PEWP	
		Date	HC no.
1979	7746		
1980	7841	30 Apr.	584
1981	8175	6 Apr.	232
1982	8494	5 Apr.	316
1983	8789	28 Feb.	204
1984	9143	1 Mar.	285
1985	9428	25 Feb.	213
1986	9702	10 Feb.	192
1987	56	9 Feb.	153
1988	288	17 Feb.	292
1989	601–621		
1990	1001–1021		

4 Taxation: piecemeal reform of the system

BLUNDELL, R., and WALKER, I. (1988). *Labour Supply Incentives and the Taxation of Family Income*. Institute for Fiscal Studies.

BROWN, C., et al. (1986). *Taxation and Family Labour Supply in Great Britain*. University of Stirling.

References

CHANCELLOR OF THE EXCHEQUER (1972). *Proposals for a Tax-Credit System.* Cmnd 5116. HMSO.
CHANCELLOR OF THE EXCHEQUER (1980). *The Taxation of Husband and Wife.* Cmnd 8093. HMSO.
CHANCELLOR OF THE EXCHEQUER (1982). *Corporation Tax.* Cmnd 8456. HMSO.
CHANCELLOR OF THE EXCHEQUER (1986). *Reform of Personal Taxation.* Cmnd 9756. HMSO.
COMPTROLLER AND AUDITOR GENERAL (1990). *The Elderly: Information Requirements for Supporting the Elderly and Implications of Personal Pensions for the National Insurance Fund.* National Audit Office. HMSO.
DEVEREUX, M., and MAYER, C. (1984). *Corporation Tax.* Institute for Fiscal Studies.
DILNOT, A., and WALKER, I. (eds.) (1989). *The Economics of Social Security.* Oxford University Press.
ENVIRONMENT, SECRETARY OF STATE (1981). *Alternatives to Domestic Rates.* Cmnd 3449. HMSO.
ENVIRONMENT, SECRETARY OF STATE (1983). *Rates.* Cmnd 9008. HMSO.
ENVIRONMENT, SECRETARY OF STATE (1986). *Paying for Local Government.* Cmnd 9714. HMSO.
EUROPEAN COMMUNITIES SELECT COMMITTEE (1985). *Income Taxation and Equal Treatment for Men and Women.* HL 15. HMSO.
FISCAL STUDIES (1979–90). *Passim.* Institute for Fiscal Studies.
GAMMIE, M. (Chairman) (1988). *Reforming Capital Gains Tax.* Institute for Fiscal Studies.
HILLS, J. (1984). *Savings and Fiscal Privilege.* Institute for Fiscal Studies.
HILLS, J. (1988). *Changing Tax.* Child Poverty Action Group.
JOHNSON, P., and STARK, G. (1989). *Taxation and Social Security 1979–1989: The Impact on Household Incomes.* Institute for Fiscal Studies.
KAY, J., and KING, M. (1986). *The British Tax System.* Oxford University Press.
KAY, J. (1990). 'Tax policy: a survey', *Economic Journal*, March 1990.
KING, J., and WOOKEY, C. (1987). *Inflation: The Achilles' Heel of Corporation Tax.* Institute for Fiscal Studies.
LAWSON, N. (1988). *Tax Reform: The Government's Record.* Conservative Political Centre.
LONDON ECONOMICS (1990). *Corporation Tax and Investment in UK Manufacturing.* London Economics.
MASON, D. (1985). *Revising the Rating System.* Adam Smith Institute.
MEADE, J. (Chairman) (1978). *The Structure and Reform of Direct Taxation.* Institute for Fiscal Studies.
PREST, A., et al. (1977). *The State of Taxation.* Institute of Economic Affairs.
TREASURY AND CIVIL SERVICE COMMITTEE (1983). *The Structure of Personal Income Taxation and Income Support.* HC 386, HC20-I and II. HMSO.

5 Privatization: progress on some fronts

BEESLEY, M., and LITTLECHILD, S. (1983). 'Privatization: principles, problems and priorities', *Lloyds Bank Review*, July 1983. (Reprinted in JOHNSON (1988).)

BISHOP, M., and KAY, J. (1988). *Does Privatization Work? Lessons from the UK*. London Business School.

BOLEAT, M. (1989). *Housing in Britain*. Building Societies Association.

BRITTAN, S. (1986). 'Privatisation: a comment on Kay and Thompson', *Economic Journal*, March 1986.

CBI (1984). *A Share in the Action*. Confederation of British Industry.

ENVIRONMENT, DEPARTMENT OF (1990). *Housing and Construction Statistics 1979–1989*. HMSO.

EDINBURGH, DUKE of (1985). *Inquiry into British Housing: Report, Supplement, the Evidence*. National Federation of Housing Associations.

ERMISCH, J. (ed.) (1990). *Housing and the National Economy*. Avebury.

FOSTER, K., WILMOT, A., and DOBBS, J. (1990). *General Household Survey 1988*, chapter 8. Office of Population Censuses and Surveys. HMSO.

GOODISON, N. (1986). *Shares for All: Steps towards a Share-owning Society*. Centre for Policy Studies.

GRETTON, J., and HARRISON, A. (1987). 'How far have the frontiers of the state been rolled back between 1979 and 1987?' *Public Money*, December 1987.

GREVE, J., and CURRIE, E. (1990). 'Homelessness in Britain', *Findings*, February 1990. Joseph Rowntree Memorial Trust.

HEALD, D., et al. (1984). 'A symposium on privatisation and after', *Fiscal Studies*, February 1984.

HOWE, G., and JONES, C. (1956). *Houses to Let*. Bow Group.

HUNDRED GROUP (1989). *Public Utilities – the Financing of State-owned Industries and the Regulation of Public Utilities*. The Hundred Group.

JOHNSON, C. (ed.) (1988). *Privatization and Ownership: Lloyds Bank Annual Review*. Pinter.

KAY, J. (1987). *The State and the Market: The UK Experience of Privatisation*. Group of Thirty.

KAY, J., MAYER, C., and THOMPSON, D. (1986) (eds.). *Privatisation and Regulation – the UK Experience*. Clarendon Press.

KAY, J., and THOMPSON, D. (1986). 'Privatisation: a policy in search of a rationale', *Economic Journal*, March 1986.

LETWIN, S., and LETWIN, W. (1986). *Every Adult a Share-owner: The Case for Universal Share Ownership*. Centre for Policy Studies.

MAYER, C., and MEADOWCROFT, S. (1986). 'Selling public assets: techniques and financial implications', *Fiscal Studies*, November 1986.

MINFORD, P., PEEL, M., and ASHTON, P. (1987). *The Housing Morass*. Institute of Economic Affairs.

MUELLBAUER, J. (1990). *The Great British Housing Disaster and Economic Policy*. Institute for Public Policy Research.

PRYKE, R. (1981). *The Nationalised Industries: Policies and Performance since 1968*. Martin Robertson.

REDWOOD, J. (1976). 'Government and the nationalized industries', *Lloyds Bank Review*, April 1976.
REDWOOD, J. (1986). *Equity for Everyman: New Ways to Widen Share Ownership*. Centre for Policy Studies.
SMITH, M. (1989). *Guide to Housing*. Housing Centre Trust.
TREASURY, HM (1977). 'Share ownership in Britain', *Economic Progress Report*, March–April 1987.
TREASURY, HM (1990). *The Government's Expenditure Plans 1990–91 to 1992–93*. Cm 1008, chapter 8, Environment, and Cm 1021, chapter 21, Supplementary Analyses and Index. HMSO.
TREASURY AND CIVIL SERVICE COMMITTEE (1981). *Financing of the Nationalised Industries*. Cm 348-I, II, III. HMSO.
UNITED RESEARCH (1990). *Privatisation: Implications for Cultural Change*. United Research.
VELJANOVSKI, C. (1987). *Selling the State*. Weidenfeld and Nicolson.
VELJANOVSKI, C. (ed.) (1989). *Privatisation and Competition*. Institute of Economic Affairs.
VICKERS, J., and YARROW, G. (1985). *Privatization and the Natural Monopolies*. Public Policy Centre.
VICKERS, J., and YARROW, G. (1988). *Privatization: An Economic Analysis*. MIT Press.
WOLMAR, C. (1990). 'Was it right to buy?', *Search*, November 1990. Joseph Rowntree Foundation.

6. Industrial performance: miracle or mirage?

BANK OF ENGLAND (1990). 'Company profitability and finance', *Bank of England Quarterly Bulletin*, August 1990.
BENZIE, R. S. (1988). 'The financial behaviour of industrial and commercial companies, 1970–86', *Bank of England Quarterly Bulletin*, February 1988.
BENZIE, R. S. (1989). 'Takeover activity in the 1980s', *Bank of England Quarterly Bulletin*, February 1989.
BORRIE, SIR G. (1987). 'Competition, mergers and pricing-fixing', *Lloyds Bank Review*, April 1987.
CALLEN, T., and CONVEY, A. (1988). 'Trends in real rates of return', *Bank of England Quarterly Bulletin*, August 1988.
DIRECTOR GENERAL OF FAIR TRADING (1990). *Annual Report of the Director General of Fair Trading 1989*. HC 502. HMSO.
DIXON, H. (1990). 'Telephone users overcharged by world cartel operation' and 'Reconnecting charges with costs', *Financial Times*, 3 April 1990; 'BT profit margin at 60 per cent for international calls', *Financial Times*, 23 April 1990.
EMMOTT, B. (1989). 'The end of the beginning: a survey of business in Britain', *Economist*, 20 May 1989.
FORD, R., and SUYKER, W. (1990). 'Industrial subsidies in the OECD economies', *OECD Economic Studies*, Autumn 1990.
HARRIS, R. (1985). *No, Minister*. Institute of Economic Affairs.
KING, M. (1986). *Takeover Activity in the UK*. London School of Economics.

LOMAX, J. (1990). *A Model of ICCs' Dividend Payments*. Bank of England.

MCWILLIAMS, D., and SENTANCE, A. (1990). *The United Kingdom's Inflation Performance*. Confederation of British Industry.

MILES, D. (1990). *Profitability and Investment in British Manufacturing*. Birkbeck College.

MONOPOLIES AND MERGERS COMMISSION (1989). *The Supply of Beer: A Report on the Supply of Beer for Retail Sale in the UK*. Cm 651. HMSO.

MONOPOLIES AND MERGERS COMMISSION (1990). *1989 Review*. Monopolies and Mergers Commission.

MONOPOLIES AND MERGERS COMMISSION (1990). *The Role of the Commission*. Monopolies and Mergers Commission.

NATIONAL ECONOMIC DEVELOPMENT OFFICE (1987). *British Industrial Performance*. National Economic Development Council.

OVERSEAS TRADE, SELECT COMMITTEE ON (1985). *Report from the Select Committee on Overseas Trade*. HL 238-I, II, and III. HMSO.

TRADE AND INDUSTRY, DEPARTMENT OF (1983). *Strategic Aims*. Department of Trade and Industry.

TRADE AND INDUSTRY, DEPARTMENT OF (1988). *DTI – the Department for Enterprise*. Cm 278. HMSO.

TRADE AND INDUSTRY, DEPARTMENT OF (1988). *Merger Policy*. HMSO.

TRADE AND INDUSTRY, DEPARTMENT OF (1988). *Releasing Enterprise*. Cm 512. HMSO.

TRADE AND INDUSTRY, DEPARTMENT OF (1988). *Review of Restrictive Trade Practices Policy: A Consultative Document*. Cm 331. HMSO.

TRADE AND INDUSTRY, DEPARTMENT OF (1989). *Opening Markets: New Policy on Restrictive Trade Practices*. Cm 727. HMSO.

TREASURY, HM (1982). *The Costs and Risks of Support for Capital Goods Exports*. A report prepared by an interdepartmental group of economists from the Treasury, the Departments of Trade and Industry and the Overseas Development Administration.

TREASURY, HM (1990). *The Government's Expenditure Plans 1990–91 to 1992–93: Chapter 4 – Trade and Industry*. Cm 1004. HMSO.

WALES, R. (1989). 'Trends in profit margins', *Bank of England Quarterly Bulletin*, May 1989.

7 Labour: the market that didn't work

Note: see figure 15 for Department of Employment White and Green Papers.

BLANCHFLOWER, D., and OSWALD, A. (1988). *The Economic Effects of Britain's Trade Unions*. Centre for Labour Economics.

BROWN, W., and WADWHANI, S. (1990). 'The economic effects of industrial relations legislation since 1979', *National Institute Economic Review*, February 1990.

CANTERBURY, ARCHBISHOP OF (1985). *Faith in the City*. The Report of the Archbishop of Canterbury's Commission on Urban Priority Areas. Church House Publishing.

CASSELS, J. (1990). *Britain's Real Skill Shortage*. Policy Studies Institute.

COE, D. (1985). 'Nominal wages, the NAIRU, and wage flexibility', *OECD Economic Studies*, Autumn 1985.

References

DICKS, M., and HATCH, N. (1989). *The Relationship between Employment and Unemployment*. Bank of England.

EMPLOYMENT AFFAIRS. *Passim*, quarterly. Confederation of British Industry.

EMPLOYMENT COMMITTEE, HOUSE OF COMMONS (1986). *Special Employment Measures and the Long-term Unemployed*. HC 199. HMSO.

EMPLOYMENT, DEPARTMENT OF (1986). 'Government response to Employment Select Committee Report on Special Employment Measures and the Long-term Unemployed'. Press notice 111/86.

EMPLOYMENT GAZETTE. *Passim*, monthly. Department of Employment.

EMPLOYMENT INSTITUTE ECONOMIC REPORT. *Passim*, monthly. Employment Institute.

FINANCIAL TIMES (1986). 'Work: an FT Special Report', *Financial Times*, 24 July 1986.

FOGARTY, M., with BROOKS, D. (1989). *Trade Unions and British Industrial Development* (second edition). Policy Studies Institute.

FORREST, D., with DENNISON, S. (1984). *Low Pay or No Pay?*. Institute of Economic Affairs.

GREGG, P. (1990). 'The evolution of special employment measures', *National Institute Economic Review*, August 1990.

HALLS, S., et al. (1987). 'The UK labour market: equilibrium or disequilibrium?', *Lloyds Bank Review*, July 1987.

HANSON, C., and MATHER, G., (1988). *Striking Out Strikes*. Institute of Economic Affairs.

HARRIS, R., et al. (1979). *Job 'Creation' or Destruction?* Institute of Economic Affairs.

HART, P. (1990) *Skill Shortages in the UK*. National Institute of Economic and Social Research.

HAYEK, F. (1980). *1980s Unemployment and the Unions*. Institute of Economic Affairs.

JOHNSON, P., and WEBB, S. (1990). *Poverty in Official Statistics: Two Reports*. Institute for Fiscal Studies.

JOSEPH, K. (1977). *Conditions for Fuller Employment*. Centre for Policy Studies.

LAYARD, R., and NICKELL, S. (1985). 'The causes of British unemployment', *National Institute Economic Review*, April 1985.

METCALF, D. (1990). *Trade Unions and Economic Performance: The British Evidence*. Centre for Labour Economics.

MINFORD, P., et al. (1983). *Causes of Unemployment in the UK*. Martin Robertson.

OECD (1986). 'The labour market', *UK Economic Survey 1985/86*.

OULTON, N. (1990). 'Labour productivity in UK manufacturing in the 1970s and in the 1980s', *National Institute Economic Review*, August 1990.

PHILPOTT, J. (ed.) (1990). *Trade Unions and the Economy: Into the 1990s*. Employment Institute.

ROBERTS, B. (1987). *Mr Hammond's Cherry Tree: The Morphology of Union Survival*. Institute of Economic Affairs.

ROBBINS, LORD, et al. (1978). *Trade Unions: Public Goods or Public Bads?* Institute of Economic Affairs.

ROBINSON, P. (1989). *Education and Training in Britain: Getting the Questions Right*. Campaign for Work Research Report, April 1989.

SOCIAL SECURITY, DEPARTMENT OF (1990). *Households Below Average Income: A Statistical Analysis 1981–87*. Government Statistical Service.

STARK, T. (1990). *Income and Wealth in the 1980s* (second edition). Fabian Society.

STEEDMAN, H. (1990). 'Improvements in workforce qualifications: Britain and France 1979–88', *National Institute Economic Review*, August 1990.

TREASURY, HM (1985). *The Relationship between Employment and Wages: Empirical Evidence for the UK*. Review by Treasury Officials.

TREASURY, HM (1986). 'A more flexible labour market', *Economic Progress Report*, Jan.–Feb. 1986.

TREASURY, HM (1987). 'Productivity and employment', *Economic Progress Report*, Jan.–Feb. 1987.

TREASURY, HM (1987). 'Trends in unemployment', *Economic Progress Report*, Oct. 1987.

TREASURY, HM (1989). 'Relative productivity levels', *Economic Progress Report*, April 1989.

TREASURY, HM (1990). *The Government's Expenditure Plans 1990–91 to 1992–93: Chapter 6 – Department of Employment*. Cm 1006. HMSO.

UNEMPLOYMENT, SELECT COMMITTEE OF THE HOUSE OF LORDS ON (1982). *Report*. HL 142. HMSO.

Further reading

BEAN, C., and SYMONS, J. (1989). *Ten Years of Mrs T*. Centre for Economic Policy Research.
BELESSIOTIS, T., and WILKINSON, R. (1990). *Country Studies: The United Kingdom*. Commission of the EC, Directorate-General for Economic and Financial Affairs.
BRUCE-GARDYNE, J. (1984). *Mrs Thatcher's First Administration: The Prophets Confounded*. Macmillan.
BUTT, R. (1986). *The Unfinished Task: The Conservative Record in Perspective*. Centre for Policy Studies.
CONSERVATIVE CENTRAL OFFICE (1976). *The Right Approach*. CCO.
CONSERVATIVE CENTRAL OFFICE (1979). *The Conservative Manifesto 1979*. CCO.
CONSERVATIVE CENTRAL OFFICE (1983). *The Conservative Manifesto 1983*. CCO.
CONSERVATIVE CENTRAL OFFICE (1987). *The Next Moves Forward. The Conservative Manifesto 1987*. CCO.
COOKE, A. (ed.) (1990). 'Eleven years' work'. *Politics Today*, 24 May 1990. Conservative Research Department.
DORNBUSCH, R., and LAYARD, R. (eds.) (1987). *The Performance of the British Economy*. Oxford University Press.
FINANCIAL TIMES (1987). *The Thatcher Years*. Financial Times.
HARRIS, K. (1988). *Thatcher*. Weidenfeld and Nicolson.
HESELTINE, M. (1987). *Where there's a Will*. Hutchinson.
JENKINS, P. (1987). *Mrs Thatcher's Revolution: The Ending of the Socialist Era*. Jonathan Cape.
JOHNSON, C. (1988). *Measuring the Economy*. Penguin/Macmillan.
KALDOR, LORD (1983). *The Economic Consequences of Mrs Thatcher*. Speeches in the House of Lords, 1979–1982. Duckworth.
KEEGAN, W. (1984). *Mrs Thatcher's Economic Experiment*. Allen Lane.
KEEGAN, W. (1989). *Mr Lawson's Gamble*. Hodder and Stoughton.
MAUDE, A. (ed.) (1977). *The Right Approach to the Economy*. Conservative Central Office.
MAYNARD, G. (1988). *The Economy under Mrs Thatcher*. Basil Blackwell.
OECD (various years). *Economic Survey: The United Kingdom*. OECD.
PRIOR, J. (1986). *A Balance of Power*. Hamish Hamilton.

PYM, F. (1984). *The Politics of Consent*. Hamish Hamilton.
RIDDELL, P. (1983). *The Thatcher Government*. Martin Robertson.
SKIDELSKY, R. (ed.) (1988). *Thatcherism*. Chatto and Windus.
TEBBIT, N. (1989). *Upwardly Mobile*. Futura.
THATCHER, M. (1977). *Let Our Children Grow Tall: Selected Speeches 1975–1977*. Centre for Policy Studies.
WALTERS, A. (1986). *Britain's Economic Renaissance: Margaret Thatcher's Reforms 1979–1984*. Oxford University Press.
WRIGHT, G. (ed.) (1989). *ABC of Thatcherism*. Fabian Society.
YOUNG, H. (1989). *One of Us*. Macmillan.
YOUNG, LORD (1990). *The Enterprise Years*. Headline.

Index

'accelerator' effect, 20
Advance Corporation Tax, 133
Aldington, Lord, 207
allocative efficiency, 167
Alternatives to Domestic Rates (Green Paper), 135
asset sales, 172–6
'automatic stabilizers', 78

Bacon, Robert, 78
Baker, Kenneth, 137, 138, 179, 180
balance of payments
  deficit, 22, 206–16
  external, 209
  successes and failures, 261–2
bank base rates, and mortgage rates, 71
bank deposits, 203
bank loans, 42, 203, 204
Bank of England, 39, 50
  monetary policy, 34
  role of, 28
bank reserve–asset ratio, 37
Banking Act (1987), 197
Barber, Anthony, 108, 114–15
'base drift', 87
Beckerman, Wilfred, 69
Beckett, Sir Terence, 215
Beesley, Michael, 159
Benn, Tony, 180
Bennett, Adam, 43
Beveridge Report, 242
Bishop, Matthew, 165
Blundell, Richard, 128, 129
Borrie, Gordon, 188, 190–91, 193

Bridgeman, Michael, 99–100
Britain's Economic Problem: Too Few Producers (Bacon & Eltis), 78
Britain's Economic Renaissance (Walters), 44
British Airports Authority, 162
British Airways, 166
British Coal, 166, 167
British Gas, 160
British Leyland, 86, 96, 162, 184
British Petroleum (BP), 158
British Rail, 163–4, 167
British Steel, 96, 166
British Telecom, 159–60, 167
  international calls profits, 192–3
Britoil, 158–9
Brittan, Leon, 181–2
Brittan, Samuel, 52, 195, 234
'broad money', 40, 56
  see also M3 aggregate
Brown, William, 234
Budgen, Nicholas, 58–9
Budgets
  1979, 6, 29, 30, 36, 38, 80, 110–12, 155
  1980, 7, 113
  1981, 7, 42, 45, 46, 69
  1982, 46, 47
  1983, 8, 205
  1984, 113–14, 132
  1985, 52, 53, 116, 124, 239
  1986, 56
  1987, 10, 57, 58
  1988, 60, 121

Budgets – *contd.*
 1989, 65, 118
 1990, 67
 fiscal and monetary stances, 272
Building Societies Act (1986), 197
Burton, John, 86
Business Expansion Schemes, 123, 185
business income, contributions to increase in, 303
business services
 balance, 213–14
 growth (1980–89), 18
Byatt, Ian, 186

C5 ratio, 191
Canterbury, Archbishop of, 240
capital
 fixed, *see* fixed capital
 productivity, 15, 16
capital gains tax, 122, 123
capital goods, surplus, 212
capital spending, 300
capital stock, 15, 16, 202
 public sector, 174
cash planning, 83–4
CBI *see* Confederation of British Industries
Central Policy Review Staff (CPRS), 85
Channon, Paul, 182
Chappell, Philip, 124
Charter for Jobs, 242
Civil Service, 19, 82, 98
 strike (1981), 227
Clarke, Kenneth, 182
Clegg Commission, 80, 102, 221
closed shop, 229
coal industry, 17, 163
coal strike (1984), 13, 53, 154–5, 228
Cockfield, Lord, 30, 131
Coe, David, 236
collective bargaining, free, 218
commodity prices, and inflation, 69
community charge, *see* poll tax
Community Programme, 241
companies
 1989 account, 305
 changes in assets, liabilities and ratios, 306
 statistics, 198–201
 UK acquisitions, 301
Competition Act (1980), 187
competitiveness, international comparisons, 310
'concerted action', 218
Conditions for Fuller Employment (Joseph), 219
Confederation of British Industry (CBI), 134, 205
Conservative Party
 1979 manifesto, 109, 220–21
 1987 manifesto, 138
 and restrictive–pricing agreements, 194–5
 and trade unions, 217
construction industry, 18
consumer goods, deficit, 212
consumption, private and public, 21
corporation tax, 131–4
'cost terms' planning, 84
council house sales, 146–8, 294
credit, 204
 growth of, 58
Criminal Justice Act (1990), 103
'crypto-incomes policy', 30, 85
'crypto-privatization', 106
Currie, Elizabeth, 152

D-mark, 'shadowing', 53, 59
de Gaulle, Général Charles, 254
debt interest, 96
defence, 81, 94
deficit, external, 307
demand, 8–9
 management, failure of, 24–6
Department of Trade and Industry (DTI), 177–83
 Blue Paper on mergers (1988), 190, 191
 deregulation, 195–8
 financial, 196–7
Director-General of Fair Trading, 187
dividends, 201
domestic saving, and domestic investment, 22
Dow, Christopher, 40
DTI, *see* Department of Trade and Industry

Index

DTI–The Department for Enterprise (White Paper), 182

earnings, real, 233
 rise in, 20
economic departments, ministerial changes, 179
economic growth, *see* growth, economic
Economic Trends (Treasury), 23
Edinburgh, Duke of, 149
education, 95
elderly, social security expenditure, 94
electricity industry, 161
Eltis, Walter, 78
Employee Share Ownership Plans, 169
employment
 creation, 247, 312
 income, non-energy, 19–20
 patterns, changing, 313
 programmes, 95–6
 public-sector share, 175
Employment Acts, 224–6
Employment for the 1990s (White Paper), 243
Employment Institute, 116, 240, 242
Employment Protection Act (1975), 225
Employment Training (ET), 241, 243, 244
EMS, *see* European Monetary System
energy balance, 211–12
energy sector, gross trading profits, 19–20
enterprise zones, 185, 196
Equity for Everyman (Redwood), 171
equity, value of, 202, 203
ERM, *See* exchange-rate mechanism
ET, *see* Employment Training
European Community, growth rates, 13–14
European Monetary System (EMS), 36
exchange controls, 37
 abolition, 197

exchange rate, 18, 38, 72
exchange-rate mechanism (ERM), 14, 36, 51, 53, 66, 67, 69, 74, 214–15
expenditure, control of, 98–102
Export Credit Guarantee Department, 186
exports, 22
 and domestic demand, 21
 trends, 307
external balances, 209

Faith in the City report, 240
Fforde, John, 43
Field, Frank, 240
financial assets, 202
financial deficit, 202
financial liabilities, 203
Financial Management Initiative (FMI), 82
financial services, growth (1980–89), 18
Financial Services Act (1986), 197
financial services balance, 213–14
Financial Statement and Budget Reports, *see* Red Books
Financial Times, 192
Financing of the Nationalized Industries (Treasury Committee), 156–7
fiscal privilege, 124
fiscal success, and monetary failure, 69–75
Fisher, Malcolm, 220
fixed capital
 gross domestic, 201, 304
 spending 189
fixed investment, 21–2
FMI, *see* Financial Management Initiative
Fogarty, Michael, 231
Fowler, Norman, 117, 226, 235
Franklin, Benjamin, 123
freeports, 185
Friedman, Milton, 41, 77–8

GDP, *see* Gross Domestic Product
general government expenditure (GGE), 87–9, 96–7
 and GDP, 89, 92, 104–5

GGE – *contd.*
  plans and outcomes, 283
  volume, 286
Goodhart, Charles, 40
Gregg, Paul, 244
Greve, John, 152
Grice, Joe, 43
Griffiths, Brian, 219
Gross Domestic Product (GDP)
  and GGE, 89, 92, 104–5
  and supply gap, 21
  deflator, 22, 23, 54, 61, 65, 73, 84
  growth, 12, 268–70
  measures, 14–15
  money, 9, 22–3, 24, 50, 52, 55, 56, 68, 271, 275
  projections, 9, 22–3
  public-sector share, 174–5
growth, economic, 5–26
  comparisons, 266
  labour and capital contributions, 267
  measurement of, 14–15
  policies, supply side, 24
  potential, medium-term, 10
  rates, 11, 12, 13
  successes and failures, 256–7
  trends, 265

Hanson, Charles, 219, 235
Hanson, Lord, 161
Harris, Ralph, 195
Hayek, Fritz von, 220
Heald, David, 104, 173
Healey, Denis, 29, 108, 177
health spending, 95
Heath, Edward, 30
Heath Government, 108, 217
  and monetarism, 27–8
  economic growth under, 13
Heseltine, Michael, 82, 135, 140–41, 149, 182, 183, 207–8
Hills, John, 99, 124
hire-purchase controls, 46–7
homelessness, 152–3
Hoskyns, John, 219
House of Commons, Employment Committee, 242
House of Lords, Select Committee on Overseas Trade, 207

Houses to Let (Bow Group), 147
housing
  policy, 146–8
  programme, 96
  tenure, changes in, 295
  see also council house sales
Housing Act (1988), 150
Housing and Building Control Act (1984), 150
Housing and Planning Act (1986), 150
Howard, Michael, 226
Howe, Sir Geoffrey, 6, 33–48, 74, 78, 197, 217–18
  1979 Budget, 6, 29, 30, 36, 38, 80, 110–12, 155
  1980 Budget, 7, 113
  1981 Budget, 7, 42
  1982 Autumn Statement, 48
  1982 Budget, 47
  1983 Budget, 8, 205
  and M0 statistics, 43
  and Mrs Thatcher, 251
  and PSBR, 44
  on rent control, 147
Howell, David, 78
Hundred Group of accountants, 167

IEA, *see* Institute of Economic Affairs
IMF, *see* International Monetary Fund
imports, 21, 22
  trends, 307
income inequality, rise in, 309
income tax
  and VAT, 6, 36
  basic rate, 114
  changes, gains from, 291
  cuts, 60, 109, 110–14
Income Taxation and the Equal Treatment of Men and Women (House of Lords), 120
incomes policy, 218
industrial performance, 177–216
Industrial Relations Act, 217
industrial training, 222
industry
  government expenditure, 299

Index

successes and failures, 261–2
inflation, 27–75
  accounting, 133
  and corporation tax, 131–4
  and money, transmission mechanism, 35
  and money supply, 45
  and MTFS, 48
  and unemployment, 237, 246–7
  and world commodity prices, 69
  CBI on, 205
  control policies, 25
  cures for, 27–33
  effects of, 30, 32
  indicators, 278
  international comparisons, 279
  Lawson on, 7
  means of control, 33–4
  successes and failures, 257–8
  UK average, 73
infrastructure, capital expenditure, 105–6
Institute for Fiscal Studies, 35, 113, 131
Institute of Economic Affairs, 32, 195, 206
interest rates, 72
  bank lending and, 42
interests, profits and dividends (IPD), 213–14
International Monetary Fund, 28
investment, fixed, 20
invisibles balance, 214

Jenkin, Patrick, 136, 137, 180
Jenkins, Peter, 18
Jenkins, Roy, 60–61, 108
Job 'Creation' or Destruction?– (Fisher), 220
job-creation measures, 239–45
Jobcentres, 240, 241
Johnson, Christopher, 100, 103
Johnson, Paul, 129
Jones, Colin, 147
Joseph, Sir Keith, 76, 77, 78, 81, 178, 180, 183–4, 217–18, 219

Kaldor, Nicholas, 113
Kay, John, 113, 115, 165

Keynesian economics, 9, 48, 52, 78, 100
King, John, 16
King, Tom, 225

labour, 217–49
labour costs, unit, 233–4
labour market, successes and failures, 262–4
labour productivity, 15, 203
'Laffer Curve', 110
Laing, Sir Hector, 215
Lawson, Nigel, 7–8, 45, 49–58, 74, 103, 124, 144, 158–9, 228
  1984 Budget, 113–14, 132
  1985 Budget, 52, 53, 116, 124
  1986 Autumn Statement, 88
  1986 Budget, 56, 114
  1987 Budget, 10, 58
  1987 Red Book, 9
  1988 Autumn Statement, 64
  1988 Budget, 60, 121
  1989 Budget, 65, 118
  and Mrs Thatcher, 251–2
  and policy unit, 252
  and shareholder democracy, 171
  Bow Group lecture (1980), 33, 34
  Mais Lecture (1984), 7–8, 9, 25, 33
  Mansion House speech (1985), 56
  monetary policy, 34
  on balance of payments, 206, 207
  on Bank of England, 28
  on ERM entry, 66
  on exchange rate, 54
  on inflation, 50
  on poll tax, 137
  on public expenditure, 87
  on taxation, 128, 143
  resignation, 65
Layard, Professor Richard, 116
Layfield Report, 135
Leigh-Pemberton, Robin, 50–51, 55–6, 59, 62
Liesner, Hans, 193
Lifting the Burden (White Paper), 196
Lilley, Peter, 183

liquidity measure, 46
  see also PSL2
Littlechild, Stephen, 159
Lloyds Bank Economic Bulletin, 207
Lloyds Bank Review, 154, 159
Lomax, J.W., 201
London Regional Transport, 163–4
Louvre Agreement (1987), 53, 59

M1 aggregate, 46, 50
M2 aggregate, 43
M3 aggregate, 35, 37, 39, 42, 47, 50, 52, 55
  and PSBR, 36
  see also 'broad money'
M4 aggregate, 72
MacGregor, Ian, 166
MacGregor, John, 98, 101, 252
Madrid summit (1989), 68
Major, John, 66, 68–9, 89, 141, 208
  1990 Budget, 67
Malone, Gerry, 139
Malpas, Robert, 161
Manpower Services Commission, 239, 240
  see also Training Commission
manufacturing
  and services, 14–19
  competitiveness, 214
  employment, 15–16
  labour productivity, 16
  share in economy, 17–18
Mason, Douglas, 136
Mather, Graham, 235
Meacher Report, 115, 118
Meade, Professor James, 52, 58, 113
Meade Report, 113, 125
Medium-Term Financial Strategy (MTFS), 7, 31–2, 56, 61, 65, 67–8, 74, 236
  see also Red Books
mergers, 186–91, 300
  1990 EC directive, 188
  DTI Blue Paper (1988), 190, 191
Metcalf, David, 219
Middleton, Peter, 35
Minford, Professor Patrick, 38, 128, 238
Minimum Lending Rate (MLR), 36, 44

MINIS management system, 82
ministerial changes, 179
MIR, see mortgage interest relief
'misery index', 246–7
MLR, see Minimum Lending Rate
MO aggregate, 43, 50, 52, 55, 72
monetarism, 38, 67, 77–8, 195
  'pink', 29
  and Heath Government, 27–8
  principles of, 34
  split in, 32
monetary base control, 34
monetary conditions, 57
Monetary Control (Green Paper), 34–5, 41
monetary control, and free financial markets, 33
monetary failure, and fiscal success, 69–75
monetary indicators, 277
Monetary Policy (Green Paper), 63
monetary policy
  relaxation in, 46
  schools of thought, 33–4
monetary targets, results, 273
money
  and inflation, 35, 45
  GDP, see under Gross Domestic Product
  quantity theory of, 34, 42
  successes and failures, 257–8
Money in Boom and Slump (Walters), 32–3
monopolies, 159
Monopolies and Mergers Commission, 187
Moore, John, 164, 166
mortgage interest relief (MIR), 66, 149
mortgage rates, 147, 148–50
  and bank base rates, 71
motor industry, 162
MTFS, see Medium-Term Financial Strategy

'narrow money', 39, 46
  see also M1 aggregate
National Council for Vocational Qualifications, 244
national curriculum, 243

Index

National Economic Development Council (NEDC), 232
National Freight Corporation, 169
National Insurance, Contributions, 114–18
 changes, gains from 291
National Insurance Fund, 125
National Insurance Surcharge, 46, 131, 239
National Power, 161
National Union of Mineworkers, 219
nationalized industries, 154–6
NEDC, *see* National Economic Development Council
'New Conservatism, The' (Lawson), 33, 34
New Training Initiative, A (White Paper), 242
News International strike, 228, 229
Next Ten Years, The (Green Paper), 86–7, 101
1980s Unemployment and the Unions (Hayek), 220
North Sea oil, 10, 15, 17, 18, 54, 131, 212

O'Brien, Sir Richard, 240
OECD, *see* Organization for Economic Co-operation and Development
Office of Fair Trading, 187
oil, North Sea, *see* North Sea oil
oil prices, 12, 13
Oliver Twist, 10
OPEC, *see* Organization of Petroleum Exporting Countries
Opening Markets: New Policy on Restrictive Trade Practices (White Paper), 194
Organization for Economic Co-operation and Development (OECD), 14
 Economic Surveys of UK, 17, 67–8, 164, 213, 230, 231, 236
Organization of Petroleum Exporting Countries (OPEC), 36
Oulton, Nicholas, 234
'overfunding', 47, 48
overseas investment, 300

owner-occupation, increase in, 151–4

Parkinson, Cecil, 181, 197
part-time employment, 248
Patten, Chris, 140
pay differentials, 231
pay increases, 232
Paying for Local Government (Green Paper), 137
pension plans, 124, 169
Personal Equity Plans (PEPs), 123
personal saving ratio, 20
personal sector, wealth, 172, 298
Petroleum Revenue Tax, 131
PEWP, 99, 100, 103
Phillips Curve, 237
Pickford, Stephen, 62
planning totals, 90
Plaza Agreement (1985), 53
Pliatzky, Sir Leo, 84–5
poll tax, 89, 134–41
 see also rates
Post Office, 167
poverty traps, 115, 117
PowerGen, 161
Price Commission, 30
price competition, 191–5
price fixing, 194
prices and incomes policy, 29
Prior, James, 78, 217–18, 222, 224
private sector
 borrowing, 63
 demand outruns supply, 20–3
 rents, 147
privatization, 144–76
 and public finances, 296
 effects of, 164–8
 main corporations privatized, 297
 motives for, 145
 successes and failures, 260–61
productivity, 233
 total factor, *see* total factor productivity (TFP)
profit margins, 192
profit performance, 198–201
Profit Related Pay, 123
profit share, 19–20
profitability, 199–200
profits, gross trading, 302

PSBR, *see* public-sector borrowing requirement
PSDR, *see* public-sector debt repayment
PSL2, 46, 47, 50
public-asset sales, 172–6
public corporations
  performance, 298
  privatization, *see* privatization
public expenditure, 76–106, 280
  accounting methods, 105
  changing priorities, 284
  cuts, 49
  objectives, 103
  percentages of GDP, 276
  plans and outcomes, 281, 282
  priorities in, 102–6
  real terms, 90–98
  relation to finance, 101
  successes and failures, 258–9
  White Paper, 80
public sector
  capital expenditure, 288
  demand, 21
  employment, 98
  housing sales, 294
  job cuts, 287
  pay, 19, 30
  percentage shares in economy, 299
public-sector borrowing requirement (PSBR), 37, 40, 41, 44, 46, 48, 52–3, 58, 69–70
  and M3 aggregate, 36
  and money creation, 62
  forecasts and outcomes, 274
  Lawson policy, 49–50
  percentages of GDP, 276
public-sector debt repayment (PSDR), 61, 65, 67
Pym, Francis, 238

R & D spending, 184
Radcliffe Report (1960), 35
Radice, Giles, 59
Rates (White Paper), 136
rates, *see also* poll tax
  domestic, 135–41
  non-domestic, 134
Rayner, Sir Derek, 82

RDGs, *see* Regional Development Grants
'real balance effect', 45
real national disposable income (RNDI), 21
'real-terms' planning, 84
recessions
  1980–81, 11, 16, 18, 25, 203, 256
  1990–91, 184, 203, 216
Red Books, 7, 8–9, 30–31, 61
Redwood, John, 154, 171, 190
regional development grants (RDGs), 184–5
regional selective assistance, 184
relative price effects (RPEs), 84, 93, 101–2
Releasing Enterprise (White Paper), 196
Removing the Barriers to Employment (Green Paper), 226
rented sector, 19, 147, 150–54
Restart interviews, 241
restrictive trade practices, 192, 193–4
retail deposits, *see* M2 aggregate
Retail Prices Index (RPI), 36, 72, 140
return
  on capital employed (ROCE), 167
  rates of, 200
Review of Restrictive Trade Practices (Green Paper), 193
Revising the Rating System (Mason), 136–7
Richardson, Sir Gordon, 39
Ridley, Nicholas, 138, 154, 164, 182–3, 219
Rifkind, Malcolm, 224
Right Approach to the Economy, The, 5, 28, 78–9, 81, 108, 155, 178, 217–18
RNDI, *see*, real national disposable income
Robbins, Lord, 79, 220
Robinson, Bill, 123
Rooke, Sir Denis, 160
'round-tripping', 39
Rowe, Andrew, 240
Rowlatt, Penelope, 69
RPEs, *see* relative price effects

RPI, *see* Retail Prices Index
Ryrie, William, 157–8

savings
  private-sector, 22
  tax on, 122–5
Scottish Hydro-Electric, 161
Scottish Power, 161
Securities and Investments Board, 197
self-employment, 15, 19, 20, 199, 247
Selling the State (Veljanovski), 164–5, 175
SEMs, *see* special employment measures
Serious Fraud Office, 197
SERPS, *see* State Earnings Related Pension Scheme
services
  and manufacturing, 14–19
  exports, 209, 210
  growth, 18
  imports, 209–10
Sex Discrimination Act (1986), 225
share ownership, 168–72
Small Firm Loan Guarantee Scheme, 185, 245
Small Firms Service, 245
Smith, Stephen, 139
Soames, Lord, 227
social security, 93, 94, 285
special employment measures (SEMs), 239, 240
'Star Chamber', 102
Stark, Graham, 129
State Earnings Related Pension Scheme (SERPS), 94, 124–5
'State of the Market, The' (Lawson), 206
statistics, official, 62
  deficiencies in, 22
  unemployment, 245–9
Steedman, Hilary, 244
steel strike (1980), 227
Stepping Stones (Hoskyns), 219
Sterling M3, *see* M3 aggregate
Stock Exchange
  1987 crash 58, 66, 158
  reform, 197

restrictive practices, 181
stock relief, 132
Stockton, Lord, 173
Strategic Aims (Jenkin), 180–81
strikes
  and pay rises, 226–35
  and trade-union membership, 308
  incidence, 226–35
Striking out Strikes (Hanson & Mather), 235
Structure of Personal Income Taxation and Income Support (Meacher), 115
subsidies, 183–5
Supplementary Petroleum Duty, 131
supply-side policies, 6–7, 10, 24
Sweeting, Adam, 250

takeovers, 186–91, 300
  argument against, 190
Taming of Government, The (IEA), 79
tangible assets, *see* capital stock
tax(ation), 107–43
  allowances, 114, 118–22, 290
  as percentage of total taxation, 293
  by income range, 292
  changing structure, 141–3
  complexity, 143
  corporate, 131–4, 142
  cuts, 24, 63, 70
  employer, 238
  family, 118–22
  incentives, 125–31
  income, *see* income tax
  independent, 118–22
  indirect, 141
  international comparisons, 289
  percentages of GDP, 276
  rates (1978–90), 112
  savings, 122–5
  strategy, 108
  substitution effect, 126
  successes and failures, 259–60
tax-credit scheme, 114–15
Tax-Exempt Special Savings Accounts (TESSAs), 123

'tax wedge', 239
Taxation of Husband and Wife, The (Green Paper), 118–20
Tebbit, Norman, 181, 185, 224–5
Technical and Vocational Education Initiative, 242
TECs, *see* Training and Enterprise Councils
Telecom, *see* British Telecom
Temporary Short-time Working Compensation Scheme, 241
TESSAs, *see* Tax-Exempt Special Savings Accounts
TFP, *see* total factor productivity
'Thatcher factor', 38
Thatcher Government, relationship with industry, 215
Thatcher, Margaret, 75, 124, 187, 217
  and 1988 Budget, 60
  and asset sales, 173
  and banks, 39
  and centralized control, 195
  and ERM entry, 68
  and Keynes, 48
  and policy unit, 252
  and poll tax, 134
  and trade unions, 218–19
  conviction politics, 222
  disagreements with colleagues, 254
  on inequality, 232
  on tax credits, 115
  relationships with Chancellors, 251–2
  style, 250–56
'Think Tank', *see* Central Policy Review Staff
total factor productivity (TFP), 15, 17, 167
trade
  balances, 211
  government expenditure, 299
Trade Union Immunities (Green Paper), 224
trade unions, 30, 218–19
  legislation 224–6
  membership, 227, 308
  reform, 222
  secret ballots, 225
  successes and failures, 262–4
Trade Unions and their Members (Green Paper), 226
Trade Unions: Public Goods or Public Bads? (IEA), 219
Training and Enterprise Councils (TECs), 243
Training Commission, 243
  see also Manpower Services Commission
Training for Employment (White Paper), 243
Training for Jobs (White Paper), 242
training programmes, 95–6
transport spending, 96
Treasury
  accounting methods, 105, 172, 173–4
  Economic Progress Report (1988), 24
  forecasting record, 22
  monetary policy, 35
Treasury Select Committee, 34–5, 40, 45, 99–100, 101, 156–7
  and Bank of England, 28–9
Truck Act (1831), 195
Tullock, Gordon, 79

ULC, *see* labour costs, unit
unemployment, 25, 49, 116, 221, 235–9, 239–40
  and inflation, 237, 246–7
  international comparisons, 311
  statistics, 245–9
unemployment benefit, 81, 93, 94
unemployment trap, 117
unions, *see* trade unions

VAT, 112, 142
  and income tax, 6, 36
Veljanovski, Cento, 164, 175
volume planning, 83

Wadwhani, Sushil, 234
wage bargaining, 229
Wages Act (1986), 225
wages, real, rigidity of, 236
Walker, Peter, 224
Walker, Richard, 128, 129

Walters, Professor Sir Alan, 11, 32-3, 39, 44, 53, 65, 103-4
water boards, 160-61
Westland affair, 182
Where There's a Will (Heseltine), 149
Why No Cuts? (Burton), 86
Williams, Shirley, 240
Wilson, Harold, 180
Wilson-Callaghan Governments, 13
Wilson Governments, 107, 108
Wolmar, Christian, 152
women employees, 248
Wren-Lewis, Simon, 42

Young, David (Lord Young), 162, 182, 190, 194, 195-6, 215, 225, 239, 241, 242, 244
Young, Hugo, 221
Youth Training Scheme, 242